Winning Together

Winning Together

The Natural Resource Negotiation Playbook

Bruno Verdini Trejo

The MIT Press
Cambridge, Massachusetts
London, England

This book was set in Stone Sans and Stone Serif by Toppan Best-set Premedia Limited. Printed and bound in the United States of America.

Library of Congress Cataloging-in-Publication Data

Names: Verdini Trejo, Bruno, author.
Title: Winning together : the natural resource negotiation playbook / Bruno Verdini Trejo.
Description: Cambridge, MA : The MIT Press, 2017. | Includes bibliographical references and index.
Identifiers: LCCN 2017011362| ISBN 9780262037136 (hardcover : alk. paper) | ISBN 9780262534376 (pbk. : alk. paper)
Subjects: LCSH: Diplomatic negotiations in international disputes. | North America. | Boundary disputes--United States. | Territorial waters--United States. | Territorial waters--Mexico. | Water resources development--Colorado River Watershed (Colo.-Mexico) | Riparian rights--Colorado River Watershed (Colo.-Mexico) | Energy development--Law and legislation--Mexico, Gulf of. | United States--Boundaries--Mexico. | Mexico--Boundaries--United States.
Classification: LCC KZ6047 .V47 2017 | DDC 346.04/679--dc23 LC record available at https://lccn.loc.gov/2017011362

10 9 8 7 6 5 4 3 2 1

Amalia, the melody of your beauty and intelligence underpinned this journey. There were so many memorable conversations, bouncing ideas about the research, walking around Cambridge while experiencing big blue morning skies or the stars and the silence of the night. And in those moments where it felt like climbing a steep mountain, searching for the right words, to know that I could look into your eyes to unpack any subject and recover a deep sense of peace, through your wisdom and loving embrace, was magical. There is so much light, happiness, and laughter every day at your side. I am honored to live my life with you.

Contents

Part I: Beyond Hard Bargaining

Examining Transboundary Negotiations

Have you ever found yourself negotiating against the backdrop of a history of mistrust, confrontation, and deadlock? How did you, your colleagues, leaders, and fellow citizens respond to the situation? We live in a world in which the answers to these questions have great impact. The principles we believe in, the strategies we rely upon, and the decisions we make to attempt to resolve our conflicts are crucial to the well-being of our communities.

My interest is in conflicts over the allocation of natural resources. I focus on long-term water, energy, and environmental disputes between the United States and Mexico. As a former Mexican governmental official, I have seen the difficulties that surround and impede these negotiations. My research at the Massachusetts Institute of Technology (MIT) aims at figuring out ways to handle these interactions more effectively.

This book explores two landmark negotiations between the United States and Mexico. The first involves a conflict over the management of the shared hydrocarbon reservoirs in the Gulf of Mexico. The second concerns a dispute over the management of the shared waters and environmental resources of the Colorado River. For over 70 years, pursuing unilateral development, the United States and Mexico alternated between confrontation and deadlock in both cases. However, the two countries were able to break out of this vicious cycle, reaching two significant agreements in 2012. As a result, the two sides have established a binational framework through which to codevelop and jointly manage these transboundary natural resources as partners.

This book tries to address how the negotiators shaped these agreements and in what ways they contributed to the resolution of these long-standing disputes. In this work, I attempt to explore whether the manner in which countries conduct natural resource management negotiations alters the prospects for finding agreement. Such factors include:

- How they frame the dispute.
- Who they send as representatives.
- What preparatory work they do.
- What principles they use to structure the negotiation process.
- How they define their interests and assess those of the other side.
- What ground rules they establish and follow at the table.
- How they respond to unpredictable circumstances.
- Which criteria they use to create and distribute value.
- How they insulate the agreement against spoilers.
- How they structure follow-through.

The two case studies in this book examine to what extent the two countries reinterpreted the broader political and economic circumstances surrounding the shared water, environmental, and energy resources, as well as how they may have been influenced in part by drastic disruptions, including an earthquake and severe drought in the Colorado River and plummeting productivity and declining energy revenues in the Gulf of Mexico. The cases explore the questions of how and to what degree the countries' alternatives changed, if stakeholders were drawn to the negotiations with revised mandates, whether new back-table coalitions evolved, and if this led to a reframing of beneficial trades that may not have been obvious earlier. Changes in political leadership, especially with regard to the interpretations of and responses to transboundary challenges, may have served as additional enabling factors that made new outcomes possible.

To present the most complete picture of each case, this book pieces together detailed accounts, through the eyes of the negotiators on both sides, of how both agreements were negotiated. After extensive research on the geographic and economic background, as well as the political, environmental, and legal context underpinning the two cases (presented in detail in appendices A and B), the first phase of inquiry into assessing the players involved in the negotiations consisted of compiling a list of the parties through researching publicly available sources. After I reached out to this initial list, the people with whom I spoke provided me with additional contacts. With each successive round of interviews, the list of stakeholders grew. This allowed me to piece together the web of negotiators with increasing clarity.

In all, I conducted four successive rounds of stakeholder assessments between the fall of 2013 and spring of 2015. Throughout that process, I have been fortunate to interview every one of the chief negotiators who had decision-making authority at the negotiating table, as well as more than 90 percent of the people directly involved in negotiating each of the 2012 bilateral agreements. More than 70 leaders in the United States and Mexico, from the public, private, and nongovernmental sectors and at the federal, state, and local levels, have generously shared their insights and experiences. A full list of the negotiators I interviewed can be found in appendix C; it includes presidents, ambassadors, secretaries, and deputy secretaries, as well as the chief industry, technical, scientific, and nongovernmental experts.

While the conversations that I had with the interviewees flowed according to the topics in which they were most involved, I made sure to touch upon a series of consistent themes related to dispute resolution, leadership, collaborative decision-making, and political communication. I did this by structuring the interviews around a core set of 25 conversation points. The list of sample questions is provided in appendix D. The one-on-one interviews lasted an average of over 60 minutes each and were conducted with negotiators working around the Gulf of Mexico, in the southwestern United States, northwestern Mexico, Washington, D.C., and Mexico City.

An analysis of these two case studies may present a number of ideas regarding better ways to handle transboundary resource management disputes between the United States and Mexico. By focusing on the negotiation process and the tension between creating and claiming value in offshore energy development, water management, and environmental restoration, the book attempts to draw prescriptive negotiation and leadership advice that may be useful in other international resource management disputes, particularly between developing and developed countries. The work examines whether and how stakeholders might be able to get beyond hard-bargaining tactics and avoid the ultimatums that accompany the presumptions that there are not enough resources to go around and that one side must win and the other must inevitably lose.

Embracing an Interdisciplinary Approach

In this research, I explore whether and how the willingness, effort, and strategies by both countries to rethink how to take into account the core interests on the other side contributed to the success of the negotiations. Other factors, such as the broader political and economic context, the leadership decisions, and internal pressures from important constituencies, were also in play. With a particular focus on how the negotiation processes and the negotiation outcomes may be affected by a shift from defining conflicts in terms of who should make sacrifices to figuring out instead how to allocate benefits, the research enlists insights from four areas of scholarship:

- Dispute resolution.[1]
- Adaptive leadership.[2]
- Collaborative decision-making.[3]
- Political communication.[4]

By drawing concurrently upon the scholarship related to dispute resolution, adaptive leadership, collaborative decision-making, and political communication, the book seeks to explore a set of insights about how to build and reach more robust agreements between political, industry, and civic stakeholders. The aim is to discover if it is possible to lay out some critical interdisciplinary steps with which to aid effective problem-solving, leading to more satisfying agreements—those that work in the interest of all stakeholders while fostering learning and adaptation. Can agreements be reached more efficiently, optimizing the use of time and resources and improving the ways in which value is created and distributed? Can they be completed in an amicable manner, strengthening relationships of trust, promoting long-term commitments, and making future interactions easier?

Discussions in the media and in the public arena about natural resource management disputes often rely on static assumptions about the stakeholders' aspirations, interests, relationships, power, knowledge, and alternatives. These assumptions provide a general overview of the features that are critical to conflict resolution, but they do not fully capture the highly dynamic and interactive nature that defines these features in practice. In light of this gap, this book asks whether, given the large degree of uncertainty and complexity that characterizes transboundary water, energy, and environmental resources, stakeholders can enhance their management decisions by considering the ways in which their negotiation strategies may need to evolve in adaptive response to ever-changing contexts.[5]

In this sense, the two case studies can be used to reflect on three insights presented in the Water Diplomacy Framework (WDF), which while focusing on contingent approaches to managing complex water problems, may also apply to energy and environmental conflicts. Proponents of this framework suggest that resource management decisions are often shaped by complex interactions among multiple stakeholders with conflicting interests and values. Decisions about the allocation of natural resources tend to occur within interconnected domains (i.e., natural, social, and political), as well as at multiple scales (i.e., spatial, temporal, disciplinary, jurisdictional, and institutional). These features presumably determine the ultimate quantity, quality, and use of natural resources. According to the WDF, these interconnected domains and scales must be taken into account whenever resource management decisions are negotiated and made, in order to address the ambiguity, nonlinearity, and feedback loops involved.[6]

This perspective suggests that decision-makers with resource management responsibilities could better handle these interconnections by taking three steps. First, they must envision water, energy, and environmental systems as open. This means that they should expect and prepare for persistent boundary crossing between domains and scales. Second, they ought to conceive of complex resource management problems as highly sensitive to small disturbances. This requires working with alternative scenarios that capture fluid and unpredictable effects. Third, they should consider the possibility that the same actions in a particular place and time will not have the same results in another context. The WDF argues that emphasizing these three features of resource management can enable decision-makers to better diagnose and identify intervention points.[7]

If natural resource negotiations require flexibility and a great deal of improvisation, stakeholders stand to benefit from strategies that enhance their capacity to manage evolving and interconnected challenges, as well as to better discern, evaluate, and act upon their interests. As such, it may be worth exploring whether reconsidering transboundary water, energy, and environmental conflicts on the basis of the mutual gains approach to negotiation, as opposed to the common zero-sum bargaining that floods the airwaves, can provide a more robust framework to seek improved outcomes in the public arena.

Dispute Resolution

The conventional notion of negotiation—the kind portrayed on the news—is of a zero-sum, win-lose interaction. It frames negotiation as the process of arguing and bargaining to induce the other side to do what you want, when you want, and the way you want by imposing your will through the use of threats, bluffs, delays, manipulation, disruption, deceit, belligerence, and even force. These actions often breed opposition, instability, and retaliation, thus undermining trust and credibility between the parties and with the public at large.

Some would argue that this is not surprising, as stakeholders can rarely be convinced to support agreements that are not in their best interest and about which they feel overpowered, resentful, contemptuous, regretful, or desperate. Although these counterproductive negotiation tactics may regularly lead to wasteful and suboptimal outcomes, they remain the standard practice in a wide range of political conflicts, including transboundary disputes. This may explain why many public disputes persist in a hopeless deadlock, even when there might be a wide number of solutions available that would benefit all the parties involved.[8]

The mutual gains approach to negotiation, also known as *principled negotiation* and *integrative bargaining,* is built on an entirely different premise. Concerned with the rate of public disputes that lead to sustained confrontation and backlash, it fundamentally questions the assumption that to achieve one's own interests in a negotiation, the other side must get little or nothing of what they want. Based on experimental findings and real-world cases from around the globe, the mutual gains approach holds that the best strategy to satisfy one's interests in a negotiation is to find an effective way to meet the core interests of the other side. The purpose of this approach is to transform supposedly zero-sum problems into opportunities for mutual gains by fostering a negotiation process through which the stakeholders can better frame, understand, anticipate, and respond to each other's core needs, working together to resolve their dispute.[9]

The process of mutual gains negotiation involves bringing together the stakeholders concerned and affected by the potential outcome of the conflict, so that they can develop a better understanding of the problems they face. This is accomplished by engaging in joint fact-finding and drawing upon tactics and tools that enable the parties to make their way into the trading zone, a space in which they can explore how their interests genuinely differ in terms of their aspirations, values, and alternatives. Once in the trading zone, by actively suspending criticism and inventing options without committing, the stakeholders can test whether they can work collaboratively to increase the total value available to everyone, examining "what if?" scenarios, discussing trade-offs, and evaluating tentative solutions for mutual benefit.[10]

This approach to negotiation holds that after crafting and examining multiple packages that simultaneously try to meet their core interests and optimize the value at stake, the stakeholders can return to their back tables to propose and test their response to concrete solutions, evaluating and determining how to better advance their constituencies' concerns and needs. In turn, without compromise or concession, by flexibly managing the tensions between cooperating to create value and competing to distribute value, each side can claim more value than would have been the case in the absence of a negotiated agreement.[11]

The mutual gains approach is said to foster fairer interactions by providing opportunities for an array of stakeholders, not only to voice concerns and priorities, but also to shape together the implementation of actions to address them. Likewise, proponents claim that the mutual gains approach creates wiser decisions that withstand technical scrutiny and independent analysis, by producing reasonable insights responsive to the available information. Such style of negotiation also is argued to yield more stable agreements through realistic engagements, including provisions for renegotiation in light of changing circumstances, fostering relationships of reciprocity. This is said to enable more efficient results by enhancing side-by-side problem-solving, addressing underlying interests, and conveying a sense of ownership by the stakeholders over the collaboratively chosen solutions.[12]

Neither the zero-sum nor the mutual gains approach to dispute resolution dismisses the disparities in relative power that inevitably exist between the stakeholders, nor the diverse spatial, temporal, disciplinary, jurisdictional, and institutional scales in play. However, they strongly differ in the response to such imbalances. The zero-sum approach to conflict tends to suggest that quick and sharp battle lines must be drawn, that confrontation ought to be continued in the media, the streets, and the courts, and in the case of transboundary disputes, through unilateral moves and diplomatic sanctions, in order to balance the scales. On the other hand, the mutual gains approach argues instead that the parties in a dispute can constructively shape several factors critical to conflict resolution, in spite of the disparities between the stakeholders, by actively focusing on their communications, interests, options, legitimacy, relationships, coalitions, commitments, and alternatives.[13]

Stakeholders can improve how they prepare for, perform, and adapt before, during, and after the negotiations. This could potentially begin by reshaping how they manage their *communications*—by choosing open, authentic, and precise deliberations rather than limited, secretive, and adversarial exchanges. Another area for improvement could lie in how parties impart their *interests*; rather than clinging to extreme demands, ignoring the needs of the other side, and conceding stubbornly, they might have more success by listening and learning from one another, outlining the reasons behind their core concerns, and speaking with reference to principles, precedents, and standards.[14]

Stakeholders may also find value in assessing a wider array of *options* by being receptive to new evidence and interpretations that increase the value available to everyone, as opposed to a fixed-pie mentality in which mutual gains are impossible. In tandem, by fostering fairness and a sense of trust through criteria selected by and persuasive to all the actors involved, rather than fighting to define who is right and who is wrong, the negotiators might also build greater *legitimacy*.[15]

Relationships could be enhanced by creating partnerships that foster joint fact-finding and effective cooperation, rather than undermined through tense interactions filled with distrust and ruled by deferring to partisan experts. Building *coalitions* across the table by effectively sequencing and linking trades may in turn enable better outcomes than jumping into negotiations that disregard careful disclosure, inquiry, and rapport.[16]

Negotiators also might be served well by handling *commitments* with well-drafted and realistic trades that are responsive to monitoring and feedback instead of unclear, unworkable, and regrettable concessions. Finally, a wide set of *alternatives* might be thoughtfully considered, such that the parties agree to the terms only when all sides have been guaranteed better results than if they had walked away, rather than accepting a deal whose outcome is worse than no deal at all.[17]

Under this lens, conflict, present in virtually all interactions in the public arena, might be used as the springboard to create value, not only through reaching an agreement, but also precisely through the process that leads to the terms of the agreement. Non-zero-sum deals, which could in turn facilitate more robust partnerships among political, business, scientific, civic, and nonprofit stakeholders, may then be more stable and scalable than conventional wisdom suggests. By seeking mutually advantageous trades rather than overpowering, accommodating, or compromising, the mutual gains approach to negotiation suggests that stakeholders in transboundary water, energy, and environmental disputes could step back, be mindful of the stakes, and work toward durable and agile solutions that respect identities, further interests, and reconcile values.

Adaptive Leadership

The conventional notion, widespread in the media and in our political debate, is that leadership is about crafting a vision, establishing incentives, defining punishments, and getting a majority to follow. This approach to leadership is less concerned with the specific substance of the problems that stakeholders face than it is with the exercise of authority and influence. As such, it illuminates how individuals in positions of leadership secure and retain power, often through a hierarchical, leader-follower dynamic, given specific behavioral and institutional constraints.[18]

This notion of leadership, however, is of limited use when applied as a tool for conflict resolution. It does not focus on problem-solving strategies and has little to say about whether and how leaders can provide timely answers and thoughtful solutions for the communities that they serve and the specific public disputes that affect them. The adaptive leadership framework, which focuses on the potential for individuals to foster constructive change in a wide variety of settings, might offer a more nuanced discussion about the role and practice of leadership to enhance problem-solving.[19]

This lens might suggest that resource management problems in transboundary disputes will be far more difficult to resolve when individuals in positions of authority do not empower stakeholders to carefully question their ideas, concerns, and relationships. Although it may seem counterintuitive to many parties caught in the heat of a high-profile dispute, accustomed to consider their own side's goals, behaviors, and practices as justified, the willingness and ability to seriously critique, rank, and revise them effectively might be crucial to negotiate and devise feasible solutions—particularly over complex water, energy, and environmental systems.

For example, as citizens and stakeholders, we often suffer through a series of hurdles, viewing them as inherent to the practice of leadership in the public arena, though in retrospect, these obstacles tend to be hardly accidental or unavoidable. These leadership shortcomings include:

• The inability to contribute on a consistent basis to a common goal.
• The failure to use readily available information to gauge events and their consequences properly.
• The refusal to seek new evidence and adapt to it.
• The absence of independent thought and reflective learning.
• The lack of scrutiny to put the responsibility on those who need to make the change.
• The incapacity to remain engaged while simultaneously stepping back to get perspective.
• The scarcity of the required skill to turn a conflict into an opportunity to improve and innovate.[20]

Not surprisingly, the fact that these hurdles tend to go unquestioned in the exercise of leadership further infuses stakeholder interactions with an added degree of anger, mistrust, and hostility. This tends to hamper the possibilities of resolving conflict, for without engaging with competing frames of reference, the parties to a dispute are unlikely to scrutinize the features of their environment, remaining at the mercy of their blind spots, unprepared for what they do not know and unable to address the deficiencies in their judgment.[21]

Poor public dispute leadership in both process and outcome, therefore, is to a great extent the result of relying on the wrong interpretations, strategies, and procedures. It is not uncommon for parties to be risk-averse, overestimating the likelihood of losses, underestimating the potential for gains, resisting any substantial change, and pushing back as their known references are disturbed. Such distress and resistance are said to partly explain the propensity to avoid serious action, reject valuable feedback, place the burden on the other side, and wait to be rescued.[22]

The practice of adaptive leadership would presume that none of these tendencies support the effective resolution of transboundary resource management disputes. In this sense, the exercise of adaptive leadership would call on stakeholders to engage with new ideas that challenge their conventional mindset and modus operandi in order to face changing circumstances and respond effectively to the uncertainty that characterizes the ebb and flow of natural resources. The aim would be not only to dislodge aversions, but also to encourage mindfulness about common biases in the stakeholders' judgment. These biases might include the following:

• Plunging into a challenge without thinking about what information to gather first and how to do so.
• Making insufficient adjustments from past references, even after these references are proven false or no longer relevant.
• Focusing disproportionately on data that confirm one's assumptions without seeking evidence to the contrary.
• Giving more weight to short-term considerations than medium- and long-term concerns.
• Evaluating solutions on the basis of past results without acknowledging new circumstances.
• Making decisions that account for one potential outcome instead of preparing for multiple scenarios.[23]

Proponents of adaptive leadership would thus encourage stakeholders to review their long-standing goals and behaviors, all the while outlining how they can be more attentive to the hurdles and biases that undermine their efforts. By being actively spurred to question their interpretations and strategies, stakeholders involved in resource management disputes could better engage with meaningful feedback and develop a more accurate picture of the problems they face. They could constitute and redefine the exercise of leadership to foster conflict resolution, enhancing a shared sense of purpose in the allocation and management of natural resources. Such leadership steps may offer a foundation from which to build more effective transboundary partnerships.

Collaborative Decision-Making

According to best practices in the field of collaborative decision-making, partnerships ought to be understood not as an end, but as a means to build capacity, broaden influence, and strengthen measurable progress toward mutually agreed-upon goals.[24] In this vein, the purpose of enhancing collaboration in transboundary resource disputes would be to foster interpersonal and institutional linkages, with relevant stakeholders informing and having increased ownership over the conflict resolution process. To foster and sustain better decision-making in such disputes, government officials may be better served by advancing negotiation processes that actively empower a wider set of stakeholders to embrace trial-and-error, confidence building, and benefit sharing.

This would require government officials to overcome two conventional assumptions (at the very least). The first holds that business, scientific, civic, and nonprofit stakeholders have little to no official role in devising and implementing solutions and instead should be restricted to voting at the polls, lobbying agency decisions, adhering to regulations, and challenging policies in court.[25] The second assumption is that government officials ought to take the relative power between the stakeholders as they find it, at most seeking compromise in response to outside pressure.[26]

Instead, effective collaborative decision-making in transboundary disputes would actively seek a stronger interaction between government accountability, industry expertise, and civic participation, in order to leverage the skills of diverse stakeholders to resolve their disputes. Mutual understanding, shared problem frames, agreed-upon baselines, and technically informed scenarios would in turn contribute to foster higher-quality outputs in the form of more flexible studies, guidelines, standards, and policies.[27]

Robust stakeholder engagement, mindful of the relationship between expert insights and issues of stakeholder representation, transparency, and legitimacy, also could work against the widespread practice of pitting experts on either side, each accusing the other of misinterpreting the facts. Such disagreements tend to severely undermine any negotiation, dominate the news cycle, and frustrate the public at large. This is particularly counterproductive in conflicts that require robust technical solutions, such as natural resource management disputes. Instead, a collaborative practice of learning and acting together, emphasizing joint fact-finding, could provide a better structure through which to overcome deadlock.[28]

Fostering effective partnerships with clear lines of responsibility could entail a wider and more transparent sharing of data, allowing the parties to identify points of contention, draw upon a larger set of linkages, and work through multiple scenarios. A skillful combination of cooperation and adaptation might empower stakeholders to review their options, seek a wider range of solutions, build more stable agreements, and move toward implementable actions.[29]

This type of collaboration could be better suited to producing legitimate, creative, and resilient decisions that are in turn more responsive to the contingency, ambiguity, and variability that characterize open water, energy, and environmental systems. In turn, by drawing upon an enhanced level of stakeholder coordination and exchange, government officials working in transboundary resource management disputes might be able to work with insights that more effectively anticipate and respond to the needs of the communities they serve. By relying on expert and local knowledge through joint research and fact-finding, the stakeholders may be able to reconcile a wider array of values, legal interpretations, scientific insights, and political priorities.

Political Communication

In the process of examining transboundary negotiations, it is also important to be mindful of how people are wired to understand, make sense of, and communicate events. The conventional notion, derived from the Enlightenment, that solely through reason do we find progress, truth, and justice is deep and enduring. It is frequently accompanied by the assumption that emotions degrade reason, distorting it through impulse and desire. Brain and cognitive science finds, however, that reason works under the initiative and guidance of emotions, which in turn help to shape decision-making.[30]

Our emotions gather far more sensory information than could ever be managed by any other conscious mental process. Emotions store and convey significant information about the state of the world and the state of our own resources than is ever available by reason alone. This means that emotions know more and know faster. They influence what we focus on and what we remember, thus underlying our imagination, reflection, and judgment.[31]

Emotions, therefore, lie at the center of our stories. Every single one of the narratives that we tell and hear is filtered by two pathways in our limbic system: the dopamine circuit for positive emotions (happiness, satisfaction), and the norepinephrine circuit for negative emotions (anxiety, anger). Our brains bind emotions to particular markers in every story, with consequences in our behavior relative to them. We approach ideas, people, and situations that trigger positive emotions and avoid those that do the opposite.[32]

This is why it is critical to question, discuss, and be aware of the stories that underpin the ways in which people approach a dispute, as they may contribute to shaping their attempts to understand the situations at stake. Fairly regularly, the narrative in a resource management conflict, whether from the stakeholders themselves or reported in the media, emphasizes the rift between the parties by highlighting perceived grievances and injustices, rather than examples to the contrary. This further exacerbates the chasm between the sides and a sense of animosity, compounding the conflict and narrowing the stakeholders' maneuvering room. Instead, communicating more balanced public stories may serve to provide a better sense of solidarity and efficacy about where the parties are coming from, the reasoning behind their actions, and what they can achieve by moving forward together.[33]

To recognize the power of public narratives requires being mindful of language and terminology. Stakeholders are said to be psychologically and politically wired to reject burden sharing; they are more likely to interpret it as having purely negative impacts on their prospects.[34] When natural resource management disputes emphasize the sacrifices rather than the opportunities at stake—solely the costs instead of the benefits—the stakeholders might reject the message and prolong their behavior, however risky or counterproductive it may be even for themselves.

Instead, the narratives communicated in public disputes might focus not on how the stakeholders can ever get along, but rather on how they can thrive in collaboration with each other, acknowledging the mistakes of the past and figuring out, together, how to move ahead effectively.[35] Simple, short, and memorable stories could be more discerning about the intensity with which the parties relate to different values and more insightful about the ways they experience different situations. Such narratives could foster more flexible strategies, enhancing the stakeholders' opportunities to redefine how they allocate rights, responsibilities, and benefits.[36]

These insights suggest that the parties ought to look at the narratives surrounding water, energy, and environmental disputes and ask, "What place is there for us in this language, in this legal text, in this political space, in this story? What voices does it allow to be heard? What relationships does it establish between us?" To review resource management disputes in this way can direct attention to the ways in which our public stories may limit how we can negotiate with each other.

Stakeholders could work against those limitations and broaden their scope of action by empowering new interpretations, embracing new sources of resilience, and creating new meaning. They can benefit by setting out to shape compelling stories that resonate and enable them to resolve their disputes proactively. Such stories would focus on empowering the parties to work together to seize the gains that could clearly leave them better off. This may be a critical step to facilitate reconciliation, foster creativity, and enhance problem solving in resource management disputes.

In sum, to further explore the aforementioned themes, in the following chapters, I examine two landmark transboundary negotiation cases between the United States and Mexico. Part 2 focuses on the Gulf of Mexico negotiations; part 3 centers on the Colorado River negotiations; and in part 4, I explore how the experiences and outcomes of these negotiations relate to the scholarship and practical underpinnings discussed in this introduction. Following the lessons learned from the cross-comparative case analysis, and with the aim of assisting future transboundary water, energy, and environmental resource negotiations, I offer prescriptive advice about what the United States and Mexico, as well as other developed and developing countries, could do moving forward in order to build and strengthen negotiation and dispute resolution capacity.

Part II: Gulf of Mexico Negotiations

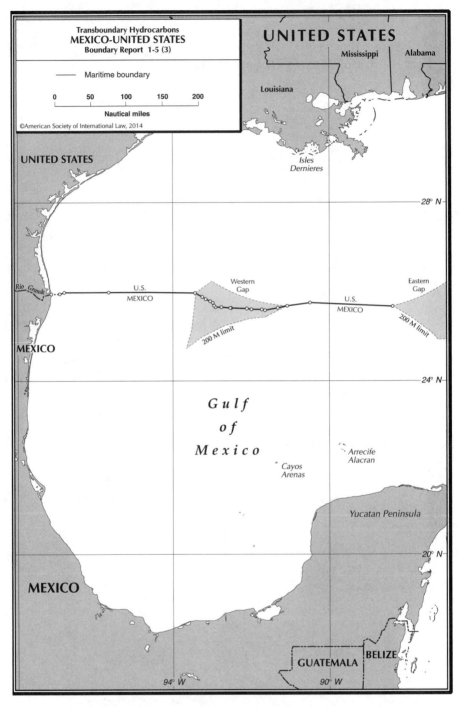

Maritime boundary between the U.S. and Mexico in the Gulf of Mexico.
Source: U.S. Department of State.

1 Introduction to the Gulf of Mexico Negotiations

The high-stakes negotiations that led to the landmark 2012 Transboundary Hydrocarbons Agreement between the United States and Mexico present a significant opportunity through which to explore various strategies related to negotiation, leadership, collaborative decision-making, and political communication. The diverse obstacles, breakthroughs, and decisions that shaped the negotiation process, examined through the eyes of the key actors on both sides, offer insights by which stakeholders in developed and developing countries can resolve energy resource management disputes, enhance coordination between publicly traded and state owned companies, improve transition and planning, and re-define the scope and impact of diplomatic partnerships.

Overview

This section provides a thematic outline of the upcoming four chapters covering the Gulf of Mexico negotiations, followed by a brief discussion summarizing and outlining the scope of the binational agreement.[1] In chapter 2, *Setting the Stage*, the section "Getting the Other Side to the Table" explores how Mexico was able to convince the United States to start negotiations. After decades of deadlock, in response to changing political and resource-availability contexts on both sides of the border, and through the strategic engagement of government and industry stakeholders, Mexico was able to finally persuade the United States of the need to create a framework through which to comanage the transboundary hydrocarbon reservoirs. Next, "Getting Your Own Side to the Table," examines how U.S. federal agencies, through the thoughtful leadership of key individuals, were able to resolve a set of internal political and logistical hurdles, get past preconceptions about Mexico, and bring the necessary stakeholders to the binational negotiations. This crucial step involved creative adaptations of both formal and informal processes at the highest levels of the executive branch.

Chapter 3, *Changing the Mindset*, explores how and why the negotiators took a series of steps outside the typical protocol. The section "Building Trust by Sharing Information" outlines the innovative ways that the two sides relied upon to share sensitive geological information without giving up confidential components, which in turn empowered the two countries to get their technical and political experts on the same page. The next section, "Analyzing Precedents to Define a Road Map," illustrates how Mexican officials prepared for the negotiations by evaluating international examples of transboundary hydrocarbon reservoir agreements, which in turn allowed them to devise a new set of alternatives for consideration and soften internal opposition. Then "Switching from an Adversarial to a Mutual-Gains Approach" explores the genesis and impacts of the transformative suggestion by the lead U.S. negotiator to set up binational working-group sessions from the start, discarding the typical draft-counterdraft strategy that characterized prior diplomatic negotiations.

With a collaborative structure in place, chapter 4, *Exceeding Zero-Sum*, studies the ways in which the negotiators were able to foster new vantage points, engage with different stakeholders, and move past the proverbial fixed-pie concept. The section "Finding the Zone of Possible Agreement" recounts how a binational joint fact-finding effort between federal agencies, along with Mexico's consultation with a U.S.-based law firm, aided stakeholders on both sides to uncover mutually beneficial trades. Next, "Overcoming Preconceptions by Defining a New Narrative" explains how Mexico, through the strategic management of communications with the public, was able to overcome the long-held narrative that the United States could not be trusted and would inevitably seek to undermine Mexican interests in the energy sector. "Involving Concerned Stakeholders Preemptively" tells the story of how the U.S. negotiators were able to bring nongovernmental organizations (NGOs) on board, especially in light of the catastrophic 2010 Macondo oil spill, also known as Deepwater Horizon. This underscored that shaping the binational agreement, instead of opposing it, was preferable to the status quo of unilateral development, as a binational framework would entail fewer wells and help improve environmental protection standards on both sides of the border.

Chapter 5, *Exercising Leadership*, begins with the section "Building in Incentives Rather than Requirements," which describes the crucial involvement of the U.S. oil industry in the binational negotiations. With private-sector input, the two countries were able to re-think seemingly irreconcilable operational, political, and commercial issues and instead devise an incentive mechanism, unlike any other in the world, to manage potential conflicts between state-owned and private companies while encouraging the codevelopment of the reservoirs. The next section, "Creating Better Outcomes through Relationships of Trust," concludes by illustrating the ways in which the counterintuitive thinking fostered at the working-group meetings and the principles underpinning the formal and informal interactions between the stakeholders enabled the ultimate success of the Gulf of Mexico negotiations.

Summary and Scope of Agreement

The two countries signed the United States–Mexico Transboundary Hydrocarbons Agreement on February 20, 2012, at the G-20 Summit held in Los Cabos, Baja California.[2] The landmark agreement marks the first significant offshore energy partnership in the history of relations between the two countries. As the first such agreement for either government regarding the management of transboundary hydrocarbons anywhere in the world, it redefines the norms and practices that had shaped energy investment, exploration, and production between the two countries for the past 70 years. The deal resolves a 40-year dispute over maritime claims and removes a 10-year moratorium on oil and gas drilling 1.4 miles within a section of their maritime boundary in the Gulf of Mexico called the Western Gap.

The binational agreement is structured to incentivize U.S. international oil companies (IOCs) and Petróleos Mexicanos (PEMEX), Mexico's national oil company (NOC), to jointly explore, discover, and produce from offshore transboundary hydrocarbon reservoirs straddling the two countries' 550-nautical-mile-long maritime boundary in the Gulf of Mexico. The agreement encompasses the statutory 3 nautical miles on each side, establishing a 6-nautical-mile-wide band along the entire maritime boundary that separates the two countries. This is equal to an area of 3 million acres (i.e., more than twice the size of Delaware), that the U.S. Department of the Interior (DOI) estimates contains over 170 million barrels of oil and over 300 billion cubic feet of natural gas.[3] In addition, the agreement quintuples the scope of the area, extending to parts of the territorial sea and continental shelf, by creating the legal and market framework to form partnerships within 15 nautical miles on either side, establishing a 30-nautical-mile-wide zone that stretches the length of the maritime boundary. This area is equal in size to three times the state of Massachusetts.

Through the Transboundary Hydrocarbons Agreement, the United States recognizes Mexico's ownership of the oil and gas resources on its side of the continental shelf, a right originally vested to Mexico through the United Nations Convention on the Law of the Sea, to which the United States is not a party. Simultaneously, through the agreement, Mexico overhauls 70 years of practice in its oil and gas sector, dating from the government's nationalization of the oil industry in 1938. The agreement creates a binational framework that, for the first time, provides IOCs with the right to bid for and develop hydrocarbon reservoirs in partnership with PEMEX. Prior to this deal, the NOC had been the sole entity with the right to conduct these activities on Mexico's side.

The agreement sets up a multistep, market-oriented process to encourage private parties to jointly explore, identify, and produce from transboundary offshore energy reserves through voluntary unitization. In the case of hydrocarbon reservoirs owned by two or more separate interests, unitization implies a commitment to codevelop the energy resources in order to do the following:

• Minimize the number of wells drilled and infrastructure built (i.e., platforms, pipelines, etc.).
• Allocate costs and risks between multiple parties, rendering projects more feasible from an economic standpoint.
• Promote strategic partnerships where proprietary data and technology are shared.
• Maximize the recovery rates and reduce physical, financial, and environmental waste.

Having such commercial relationship opportunities built into the agreement is unprecedented for the U.S. and Mexican energy sectors. In stark contrast to the approach of the previous 70 years, the agreement further examines a broad agenda of interlocking issues regarding collaboration in the exploration, discovery, and development of ocean-based energy resources. This includes joint scientific and geological consultations, the notification of exploration and discovery data, and the potential sharing of facilities and infrastructure, such as drilling vessels, floating production systems, storage units, seafloor well heads, platforms, pipelines, as well as logging, repair, and intervention equipment.

By including this degree of cooperation, the agreement aims to decrease costs by avoiding duplication and to allow the stakeholders in the two countries to do more with less at each step of the energy production cycle. In a departure from any other transboundary hydrocarbon agreement in the world, it empowers titleholders (i.e., the IOCs and NOC) to form partnerships before a transboundary reservoir is even identified. From exploration to production, the titleholders are enabled to appoint a single operator to optimize discovery and extraction. To ensure equitable development, single continuous deposits of hydrocarbons, trapped by a structural feature extending across the delimitation line in the maritime boundary, are identified as transboundary only once pressure registered on wells on both sides of the maritime boundary is linked. Since deepwater wells in the Gulf of Mexico cost between $100–$200 million, political interference based on pure speculation is ruled out.

By means of a bidding process, where multiple entities can compete to offer the most compelling development plan, a single operator is selected. The parties to the unit agreement can then submit for joint governmental approval by U.S. and Mexican authorities. Safeguarding the two countries' sovereign natural resource interests, the unit agreement must allocate rights, liabilities, and responsibilities between the private parties. Once royalties and taxes are determined according to the each government's regulatory directives, the parties can begin exploration, extraction, commercialization, and revenue-sharing.

The Transboundary Hydrocarbons Agreement further establishes dispute resolution mechanisms that go from consultation, to referred mediation, to expert determination. Under the agreement, a permanent joint commission composed of a representative from each country, in coordination with their respective executive agencies, is tasked with fostering joint working groups to directly address issues of contention that may arise regarding each unitization agreement. The purpose is to ensure that the energy stakeholders take cooperative measures and strive for consensus in the interpretation and implementation of their partnerships.

In terms of a brief timeline of the negotiations that led to the signing of the Transboundary Hydrocarbons Agreement, the diplomatic talks began in earnest during the first two years of Barack Obama's first term. By May 2010, through a Joint Statement at the White House at the conclusion of a state visit, U.S. president Obama and Mexican president Felipe Calderón recognized the "close link between economic development and competitiveness in the region" and underscored the need to increase the "reliability of the countries' energy infrastructure."[4] On the heels of the Macondo oil spill, they expressed their commitment to seek "a safer, more efficient, and more equitable bilateral energy framework," which in turn ensures a "higher degree of safety and environmental oversight" in the exploration, extraction, and production of oil and gas through offshore facilities.[5]

A month after this Joint Statement, the two countries announced their intention to negotiate an agreement to govern the disposition and regulation of hydrocarbon reservoirs crossing their maritime boundaries in the shallow and deep waters of the Gulf of Mexico. As highlighted in "Appendix A: The Gulf of Mexico Case Background," offshore energy issues had been a source of contention for decades, with each country trying to unilaterally shape its claim regarding the oil and gas resources in the shared ocean basin. The formal negotiations were launched in the winter of 2010–2011, with a focus during the spring on conducting binational work-group sessions on various thematic areas related to offshore energy development.

On the Mexican side, the Foreign Ministry led the negotiations, given that the issue at stake was national natural resources. This leadership was conducted in close partnership with the Office for Hydrocarbons and the Office for International Affairs at the Ministry of Energy. The negotiators received strong advisory support from PEMEX's Legal Affairs, Exploration and Production, and Upstream business units, as well as the National Hydrocarbons Commission. On the U.S. side, the Department of State (DOS) led the negotiations, with support from the DOI's Minerals Management Service (MMS), which during the course of the negotiations was reorganized into the Bureau of Ocean Energy Management and the Bureau of Safety and Environmental Enforcement, among other entities.

The two countries' negotiators started to work in earnest on a text agreement during the second half of 2011. The negotiators reached an agreement in less than six months, by the end of that year, which was a fairly quick resolution by binational negotiation standards. In February 2012, U.S. Secretary of State Hillary Clinton and U.S. Secretary of the Interior Ken Salazar joined Calderón and Mexican Minister of Foreign Affairs Patricia Espinoza to sign the agreement in Los Cabos, Baja California, at the G-20 Summit.

At the signing ceremony, Secretary Clinton remarked that it was a "great pleasure to sign this groundbreaking agreement," following through on the leadership of President Obama and President Calderón "to improve energy security for both countries" and "shift to more environmentally appropriate means of extracting fossil fuels."[6] Secretary Clinton underscored that by promoting the "safe, efficient, and equitable exploration and production of transboundary reservoirs," the two countries were actively establishing a cooperative framework to "prevent and resolve disputes," creating new opportunities that, for the first time, allowed "American energy companies to collaborate with their Mexican counterparts."[7] Calling "this agreement a win-win that benefits the U.S. and Mexico alike," Secretary Clinton highlighted that the agreement was "further proof of how Mexico and the United States come together to solve shared challenges."[8]

Both countries soon after enacted the agreement. The Mexican Congress ratified the Transboundary Hydrocarbons Agreement in April 2012 and implemented a series of related constitutional reforms in December 2013. For its part, the U.S. Congress introduced legislation to auction leases and enhance oil and gas pipeline infrastructure in the Gulf of Mexico beginning in June 2012 and then ratified the agreement in December 2013 through the Bipartisan Budget Act.

2 Setting the Stage

Getting the Other Side to the Table

In the year 2000, through the Treaty for the Delimitation of the Western Gap, the United States and Mexico established a 10-year moratorium on the exploration of, and production from, potential hydrocarbon reservoirs in the Western Gap, a zone near the continental-shelf maritime boundary.[1] The moratorium's aim was to provide the two countries with the time to reach an agreement about the most effective, efficient, and fair mechanism to manage those potential reservoirs. This was no small task, given that their oil and gas industry frameworks were on opposite ends of the spectrum, with a market-based lease system for exploration and production by private companies on the U.S. side, and a state-owned national oil company (NOC) with monopoly control over the resources on the Mexican side.

During the first five years of the moratorium, in binational discussions and meetings at the United Nations where both countries had to engage in periodic consultations about the rules that should govern the extended continental shelf, it became clear that the United States had little interest in discussing the topic of the Western Gap, and even less in potential transboundary reservoirs straddling the maritime boundary along the Gulf of Mexico, between the two countries.[2] Multiple U.S. agencies argued that since it was not evident that any transboundary reservoirs existed, there was no point in defining a legal framework regarding how to manage them. Mexico, on the other hand, maintained that the two countries needed to define such a framework beforehand, as a preventive measure.[3]

While the two countries remained at odds over if and how to proceed on transboundary reservoirs, Mexico was being affected by a stark downturn in its domestic oil production. For decades, the country had relied heavily on the Cantarell oil field, off the coast of Campeche, in the Yucatán Peninsula. This was a massive structure—by far the largest in the nation and one of the largest in the world—which reached a peak production of 2.1 million barrels per day in the early 2000s. This oil field, which carried a very low production cost, accounted for more than half of Mexico's total crude output. However, production had been declining substantially since 2004, increasing Mexico's need to develop new fields. By 2008, Cantarell was producing half a million barrels per day fewer than in the early 2000s, a roughly 25 percent decrease, which was extremely worrying for the Mexican government.[4]

When it slowly became evident that the decline was irreversible, Mexico needed to find new sources of oil and gas, as a third of the revenue that finances all public spending in the country comes from taxes on the NOC, Petróleos Mexicanos (PEMEX).[5] Would PEMEX have the capability to explore the whole country, both offshore and onshore, by itself? Would it have the experience and resources to try to move forward with the more technically challenging exploration, appraisal, and development of deepwater resources in the Gulf all on its own? The answers to those questions pointed to the need to create a new framework, both at PEMEX and in the overall domestic energy sector, so that the NOC could build the sort of international partnerships that had been out of the question for decades.

As the Barack Obama administration began its first term (2008–2012), Mexico's president, Felipe Calderón (2006–2012), who had been Mexico's Energy secretary in the early 2000s, decided to raise the topic of transboundary reservoirs with the White House. He already had before, at the twilight of the George W. Bush administration, but was met with a tepid response. Calderón was mindful of the changing circumstances in Mexico's oil production and of the fact that no regulatory framework governed the exploration and development of potential transboundary reservoirs, and he was concerned about the conflicts that could ensue.[6]

Meanwhile, Chevron was drilling 10 miles from the maritime boundary in the Trident and Hammerhead fields, and along with Royal Dutch Shell, in the neighboring Great White, Tobago, and Silver Tip fields. At the same time, PEMEX had estimated that the Perdido Fold Belt formation on the Mexican side of the maritime boundary, near the alluvial of the Rio Grande in the Gulf of Mexico, 25 miles south of U.S. waters, held 350 million barrels of oil in proven, probable, and possible reserves. Perdido's geology heavily influences the western part of the southern Alaminos Canyon area, where international oil companies (IOCs) had already made investments on the U.S. side.[7] In light of these points, President Calderón summarized the challenge at hand as follows:

Because the energy resources at stake are substantial, both countries needed to look at how to address two interrelated elements. First, the political aspect, the concern that the country that begins extraction unilaterally on one side may end up draining resources from the other side due to the unexpected vagaries of reservoir pressure. Second, and more important, that in order to efficiently exploit these oil fields, you need to inject natural gas and carbon dioxide at different locations, and we cannot do that working just on one side of the border.[8]

When President Obama and Secretary of State Hillary Clinton took office, they were receptive to Calderón's arguments and demonstrated an increased commitment to discuss this issue. For many years previous to this, however, the conditions, and thus the impetus, to move forward with binational negotiations had been lacking on the U.S. side. First, the seismic data that the U.S. agencies relied on had not been sufficient to presume the existence of any transboundary reservoir. Second, U.S. officials were uninterested in pursuing an agreement, as they were worried that engaging in negotiations with Mexico would set a negative precedent that could affect disputed areas in other parts of the world.[9]

This started to change, however, as the IOCs' leasing and drilling activity got closer to the maritime boundary in the Gulf. The United States began to recognize that private industry was hesitant about acting directly along the border because of the potential dispute that it would cause with Mexico. Renee Orr, chief at the Office of Strategic Resources at the U.S. Bureau of Ocean Energy Management (BOEM), describes this shift being based on "a glimmer of hope of partnerships down the road with Mexico. It did not make sense to muddy the waters. The near-term unilateral gain was not meaningful enough as compared to the potential shared long-term gain."[10] The newly appointed U.S. ambassador to Mexico, Carlos Pascual, was entrusted to further explore this issue. As he described it:

The first time I began to think about the topic was on my first flight to Mexico coming here as Ambassador in August 2009. I was flying in Air Force One with President Barack Obama and Assistant Secretary of State James Steinberg. Jim asked me to take a look at this issue of a transboundary agreement that had come up in discussions before. We wanted to look at it carefully again. That weekend was the North American Leaders' Summit in Guadalajara, Mexico, and a number of meetings took place. I met there with Mexico's energy secretary, Georgina Kessel, where we briefly discussed this topic. I then met with her again three weeks later in Mexico City. One of the things she conveyed was that Mexico was looking to implement reforms that would allow international participation in the energy sector. One area that could offer promise to both sides, in terms of political acceptability, was to engage in negotiations about transboundary reservoirs. The core component was to provide an opening for cooperation on hydrocarbons that had not been possible in the past.[11]

Ambassador Pascual reported these insights to Steinberg, who concurred that this was an interesting opportunity. Steinberg conveyed the message that he would talk with his colleagues in Washington, D.C., to see what could be done to advance the process. Soon thereafter, Pascual visited Washington to speak with colleagues at the U.S. Department of State (DOS) and further explain what he thought were the important factors in pursuing the issue.

In turn, the U.S. Embassy personnel in Mexico City conducted a wide stakeholder consultation with Mexican officials and IOCs. The aim was to better understand the interests and concerns that could shape the potential binational negotiation process. These consultations, on many occasions hosted at the U.S. ambassador's house in Mexico City, were open-ended, small, informal dinners, in which an array of IOC and NOC representatives from across the globe described industry priorities and practices. The purpose of this outreach was to gain a better understanding of what the negotiations would entail.[12]

Throughout all of 2010, Ambassador Pascual remained engaged with the political players on the Mexican side, including key members of the Senate and the Lower House, reporting back to his colleagues in Washington that the political context in Mexico remained favorable for a binational effort. Mexican officials noticed this increased interest on the part of the U.S. authorities and understood it as a political gesture to (1) define the rules of the maritime boundary; (2) enhance hydrocarbon exploration and production; and (3) support Mexico's domestic energy reform efforts.[13] Luis Macías, the manager for new business ventures for exploration and production at PEMEX, recounts this shift:

Prior to the Obama Administration, we often encountered U.S. officials who suggested that Mexico did not have the will or the capacity to address the issue of transboundary hydrocarbon reservoirs. When the Obama Administration came to office, we noticed a change and the willingness to shape mutual gains by working together.[14]

Simultaneously, on the domestic side, the United States had become increasingly concerned about strengthening its energy security by relying less on specific oil-rich countries with whom diplomatic relationships were geopolitically complex.[15] This context encouraged the United States to strengthen its energy relations with Mexico. As Guillermo Zúñiga, director for petroleum operations at Mexico's Ministry of Energy recalls, the Mexican officials realized that the window of opportunity to move forward that they had been waiting for was right in front of them:

Between government agencies, we had discussed what kind of binational agreement we should seek. One option was to reach a merely declarative agreement, highlighting principles and leaving real negotiations for the future. However, as circumstances evolved, we realized we needed this agreement to be a critical part of our efforts to turn around the country's declining oil production. In the face of this window of opportunity with increased receptivity from the U.S., we thought it was the moment to go all in and try to reach a comprehensive agreement.[16]

PEMEX wanted better and more solid instruments with which to engage third parties in the private sector, particularly mechanisms that go beyond service contracts. The Mexican Constitution, however, had ruled out production and profit-sharing instruments in the 1930s, and the political context seven decades later indicated that a constitutional reform was still not feasible. Mexico had, however, enacted a set of regulatory reforms in 2008 that opened the door for the participation of the private sector in the Mexican oil industry for the first time.[17]

The 2008 Mexican legislation stated that the production from transboundary reservoirs could be subject to the mandates established in an international treaty. These reforms created an opportunity to bridge the gap between two very different domestic legal frameworks.[18] As deputy secretary for hydrocarbons at Mexico's Ministry of Energy Mario Budebo points out, it was imperative for the country to find a way to substantially increase deepwater exploration and production. "We needed to do that through international partnerships. This meant going well beyond what had ever been legally and logistically in place on our side of the border."[19]

However, when the Mexican Ministry of Energy contacted the U.S. Department of the Interior (DOI) Minerals Management Service (MMS) to kick-start the process on a technical level, the response from U.S. officials once more was that they did not see any need to reach an agreement of any kind.[20] They conveyed to Mexico that they had no data suggesting that any transboundary reservoirs existed, at least not at the time, and that therefore, there was no urgency to begin negotiations that they imagined would be very complex and demand employee resources that they did not have available.[21]

As a consequence of this response, Mexico's Energy Ministry decided, as a first step and in coordination with PEMEX, to gather all Mexican seismic data on the maritime boundary and get the publicly available seismic data about the areas near the maritime boundary on the U.S. side. Once they had that, they cross-referenced it in order to highlight continuous formations where the probability of transboundary reservoirs was considerable. Aldo Flores, director-general for international affairs at Mexico's Ministry of Energy, summarizes Mexico's perspective at that time thus:

The strategic vision was to first argue, "We have a problem here; the other side may not think we do, but we do. Let's acknowledge it is there. Once we agree there is a problem, let's sit to discuss what each side thinks would be useful to solve the problem. Once we have a broad understanding, let's home in on the steps we should take together and solve it."[22]

As part of these efforts, Mexico researched, reviewed, and analyzed publicly available official U.S. documents in which the MMS outlined the principles and strategies that it was pursuing to ensure the effective stewardship and sustainable management of U.S. natural resources in the Gulf of Mexico. When Mexico contacted the MMS again, having gathered such knowledge, they highlighted the fact that the more the countries worked together to devise a framework to jointly manage shared natural resources, the more efficient and optimal the MMS sustainability efforts would become. Leonardo Beltrán, deputy secretary for energy transition and planning at Mexico's Ministry of Energy, and at the time the director for international negotiations, led this tactic. As he explains:

We used their own official arguments to make the case that it was not effective to work separately, when instead Mexico and the U.S. could develop medium- and long-term strategies to sustainably manage our shared natural resources. Building a flexible binational framework would enable working jointly towards this common sustainable management goal.[23]

Mexico's second step was to consult with the companies conducting exploration and production activities on the U.S. side of the Gulf of Mexico to see if they saw the need and would be interested in a binational agreement. If so, Mexico hoped, they would be willing to lobby the U.S. Congress in favor of such an agreement.[24] Exxon, Chevron, BP, and Shell, among others, have offices in Mexico City and are in close contact with PEMEX and the Ministry of Energy as a result of the fact they own gas stations, produce industrial lubricants, and have technological partnerships in the country. The companies expressed to Mexican officials that technological advances in drilling were facilitating their ability to work in deep water, and that their only concern regarding working near the maritime boundary was the possibility of having a dispute with Mexico. The IOCs explained that this uncertainty was limiting investment flows.[25]

The IOCs saw the discrete possibility that the binational negotiations would affect the relationships between industry and government, as well as between energy companies. Hence, they sought to ensure that those interactions could be determined primarily by the stakeholders themselves, removing the threat of confrontation between the countries but allowing the companies to define the particulars of each transboundary reservoir joint venture.[26]

In turn, after those two steps, with the data gathered by PEMEX and the information gathered from the IOCs, the Mexican officials met again with U.S. representatives. As Budebo explains:

We met to discuss Mexico's seismic insights and highlight that on the heels of the domestic energy reform, PEMEX would ramp up the efforts to conduct oil activities in deep waters. In turn, the U.S. became more intrigued, understanding that we were committed to moving forward and that unilateral moves on our side of the maritime boundary were not necessarily in their best interest either.[27]

Soon thereafter, discussions intensified, until eventually on May 19, 2010, in a White House summit between presidents Obama and Calderón, the issue of transboundary reservoirs in the Gulf of Mexico was officially announced as a priority in the bilateral agenda.[28] In a joint statement that summarized the presidents' discussions about finding new ways to enhance mutual economic development, cooperate against transnational organized crime, protect vulnerable communities, and meet future energy needs, they expressed their commitment "to ensure energy security in North America and to the safe, efficient, and equitable exploitation of transboundary reservoirs with the highest degree of safety and environmental standards."[29]

This was a significant announcement for the binational energy sector. It was further solidified a month later, on June 23, 2010, when the DOS issued a joint statement by the United States and Mexico outlining a mutual intention to negotiate an agreement governing the disposition and regulation of hydrocarbon reservoirs that cross their international maritime border in the Gulf of Mexico. In the joint statement, the two countries said that "although no entity had yet discovered a transboundary reservoir, they deemed it important to have a bilateral regulatory regime in place should such a discovery be made in the future."[30] This echoed Mexico's original argument and signaled that the mandate on the U.S. side had been redefined.

In the interim, both governments agreed to extend the moratorium on drilling and exploitation in the Western Gap. The moratorium, which was set to expire in January 2011, as per the 2000 Western Gap Treaty, was extended until January 2014 without prejudice to any further extension. In the announcement, the two countries indicated that any agreement resulting from their transboundary reservoir negotiations would include the Western Gap and take precedence over their joint decision to extend the moratorium in that area.

These developments underscored a level of intent to reach a mutually beneficial agreement that had never been present before.[31] Michael Taylor, the desk officer in charge of Mexican affairs at the DOS, summarizes the impact of this political mandate, coming from the leaders of the two countries:

When our two presidents issued a very public statement indicating that they wanted this agreement, it really helped to defuse much of the potentially serious opposition that either side could bring to the table. Had it not been the case, maybe we would have had more difficult discussions. In this instance, where the political leadership had established the goal and it was our job to live up to that goal, that really put people in the same kind of cooperative mindset. We knew we had to produce something that worked for both sides.[32]

Soon thereafter, as part of the efforts to foster a broad political consensus, Secretary of the Interior Ken Salazar and the special envoy for international energy affairs at the DOS, David L. Goldwyn, visited Mexican officials in the fall of 2010. In January 2011, Secretary Clinton came to visit Mexico as well. One of her meetings with the Mexican minister of Foreign Affairs, Patricia Espinoza, was specifically on transboundary reservoirs.[33] By then, a strong political agreement to conduct the negotiations was set.

Getting Your Own Side to the Table

For years, from the perspective of U.S. officials, the Mexican government had requested an agreement to unitize transboundary reservoirs and comanage energy development for two main reasons. First, Mexico believed that there were transboundary oil reservoirs in the Gulf of Mexico, and they wanted to take advantage of these available resources. Second, they wanted to address their concern that U.S. operators with wells close to the maritime border could drain reservoirs on the Mexican side.

The United States, for its part, had not been interested in having these negotiations for three reasons. First, the DOI did not believe that there were any transboundary reservoirs, so there was no sense of urgency. Second, Interior had long adhered to the rule of capture, which was essentially first-come, first-served, so long as the location of the well itself was within the jurisdictional boundary. So, from the DOI's bureaucratic point of view, which was to maximize the value of U.S. acreage for the U.S. Treasury, there was no motivation to have a transboundary agreement. Third, Interior's perspective was that the "drainage" argument was unfounded because the nature of the geology in the Gulf of Mexico, at least on the U.S. side of the Gulf, is such that the reservoirs tend to be narrow and quite deep, and the formations do not allow much lateral oil movement. Therefore, the DOI did not think that there was any communication between oil fields on the U.S. side, that they had already licensed, and oil fields on the Mexican side, should Mexico choose to operate them.

The push to engage in binational negotiations from the U.S. side, thus, would not come from the DOI. Instead, it would emerge from the DOS through the initiative of Goldwyn, the highest-ranking official on energy issues at the DOS, reporting directly to Secretary Clinton. As he explains, "when I got to the State Department in 2009, the topic of transboundary reservoirs looked to me to be one of two or three issues which could dramatically improve U.S. energy security."[34] At the time, the U.S. belief was that the United States would continue to be dependent on energy imports, so ensuring both a Canadian supplier and Mexican supplier would give the United States physical security as well as market security. As Goldwyn describes, the aim was to encourage Mexico's reform efforts to open up their energy sector to foreign investment:

The way to do that was to help the Mexicans help themselves to build the public confidence that this could happen for their own benefit. From my point of view, it did not matter a great deal whether there was or there was not a transboundary reservoir. By supporting an agreement and negotiating it, hoping frankly that maybe someone would find a transboundary reservoir, the possibility for joint development would emerge. This would show the Mexican population that you could introduce foreign technology and capital and that the Mexican government and their citizens would profit.[35]

Typically, in this kind of a negotiation, the DOI would have taken the lead because 90 percent of the substance at stake is firmly within its purview and jurisdiction, such as identifying acreage, determining the notice to leaseholders, the unitization of fields, and the regulations that would apply. However, in this case, Interior did not have the bandwidth. Michael Bromwich, a former assistant U.S. attorney, appointed by President Obama to oversee the reorganization of the MMS, and simultaneously head the BOEM, explains that at the time, the DOI people who were responsible for the Gulf of Mexico office had their hands full with this organizational change.[36]

The MMS became three different entities: the BOEM, responsible for managing the development of offshore resources; the Office of Natural Resources Revenue (ONRR), in charge of collecting royalties; and the Bureau of Safety and Environmental Enforcement (BSEE), to enforce safety and environmental regulations. In general terms, what the U.S. government was trying to do was to completely separate the money collection from the day-to-day facility inspection.[37]

As a result of the MMS reorganization, the transboundary negotiation process had to be driven instead by the DOS, though not without significant hurdles. The trepidation to start lengthy and involved negotiations that were thought to likely lead nowhere was a sentiment shared at various U.S. agencies. State's Legal Adviser's Office was initially tepid on engaging in negotiations because Mexico had attempted to engage the United States on the issue of transboundary reservoirs a number of times before, but each time, attention on the topic would die down, with no concrete results. Moreover, the late 1990s negotiations with Mexico to delimitate the Western Gap had been very challenging, and it seemed like a substantial amount of work to undertake while focusing on global climate negotiations. As Goldwyn recalls, "this was not something top of the agenda; too many were asking, 'Do we really need this?'"[38]

These sentiments are summarized by Kevin Karl, later senior adviser to the regional director of the Gulf of Mexico Outer Continental Shelf Region at the BSEE, and previously regional supervisor at the Office of Production and Development in the Gulf of Mexico region for the MMS. He explains, "the first time I went to Mexico to discuss a transboundary reservoir was in 2004. There would be a push, and then it would die off. There would be another push, and then it would die down again. And the years would pass by."[39]

In this context, having an energy-security advocate at the DOS would prove critical to get people to move from their entrenched positions and build a consensus about the benefits of launching binational negotiations. In order to sustain this new approach, Goldwyn led efforts on two fronts, one informal and the other formal. First, he made sure that he had Secretary Clinton's support:

When I first came in on the job, I used the many opportunities in the Department to focus on this, to express my priorities to Secretary Clinton, to convey it was one of my top three of issues, as a way of communicating and getting buy-in. In my first month in the job, I had a presentation with the Secretary's staff describing basically, "This is how I see my job, this is where I think the key drivers of the energy world are, and these are the issues." Then every so often you have reviews, where you outline what are the priorities for the next six months. At the same time, I worked with colleagues, Carlos Pascual, U.S. ambassador to Mexico, Arturo Valenzuela, assistant secretary for Western Hemisphere at the State Department, DOI's Deputy Assistant Secretary Ned Farquar, and Dan Restrepo, the senior director for Western Hemisphere Affairs at the White House, all of whom understood the critical role the energy sector plays in financing Mexico's development. I would just talk to them and explain, "I am going to try to do this, this is important, can I have your support."[40]

The formal process involves Circular 175 Authority, which requires that in order to enter into formal negotiations with another country, the secretary of state must approve an official memo. It also involves getting clearance from all the other agencies concerned. Ultimately, Circular 175 Authority is what allows the parties involved to move forward. The groundwork to get this approval requires several steps: educating multiple partners, having ongoing conversations, persuading people who are uncertain to at least hear what you are proposing, explaining the history and what is at stake, and then finally asking for a formal meeting. As Goldwyn explains, Secretary Clinton was extremely supportive in understanding the issue, being willing to weigh in to push it forward, and providing the space and resources to advocate for it:

The White House was also very receptive; so I got them to call the meeting. We were going to need an Assistant Secretary level meeting to do this. Once the meeting date is set, you talk to the parties that are coming to the meeting about which position you are going to take. You explain what it is that you are going to try to accomplish through the meeting, so that they can lubricate the process and make sure that the outcome is approved. Then you take that outcome and you say, "We got agreement to go forward, now let's move the memorandum and advance the process." So, it is a lot of informal communication and listening to the others about what they are worried about, so that you present a package that they can approve.[41]

In this way, the DOS took the strategic lead on both the informal and formal steps, bringing the BOEM and the BSEE along somewhat begrudgingly, though cooperatively and effectively under Bromwich's leadership. A person of high credibility, Bromwich had been an inspector general at the Department of Justice, was a renown corporate lawyer, and as an experienced political appointee, he conceived of the broader strategic benefit of a negotiation with Mexico over transboundary reservoirs. Bromwich foresaw that "if Mexico were to open its oil and gas sector to outside private enterprise, the U.S. private industry would be in a favorable position to reap the gains from offering the kind of commercial experience and technical expertise that Mexico had yet to develop, given its limited offshore exploration and nearly nonexistent deepwater production."[42] In the same vein, as Taylor further explains:

The U.S.'s underlying interest was to ultimately gain better access to the Mexican energy sector. That is a very sensitive sector in Mexico. It had been for decades after the nationalization in the 1930s. However, there had been signals from the Mexican government, certainly when President Calderón came into office, that Mexico realized that PEMEX needed an infusion of fresh capital from overseas, because a lot of their primary reserves, particularly Cantarell, were near the end of their production cycle. If Mexico was to continue generating the source of revenue it had been generating from energy sources, it had to do things differently. So, the door they wanted to open first, as a test, was how do you manage the reservoirs straddling the maritime boundary. "Let's see how it goes," I think that was their attitude. If it went well, I think both sides knew, or hoped, that it would lead to further activities in the future.[43]

With the proper political motivations in place, the White House was planning to announce, as part of the joint statement from the binational summit between President Obama and President Calderón in May 2010, the mutual desire to pursue transboundary hydrocarbons negotiations in the Gulf of Mexico. Public mention was postponed for a few weeks, however, as in April, the catastrophic Macondo oil spill occurred. Remarkably, rather than unraveling the desire to conduct negotiations, the countries were able to postpone official statements for a while, holding off on sharing the latest developments with the public until things settled down.

After Macondo, during the summer and fall, the two countries took another look and continued to agree that the motives to pursue a transboundary agreement remained. On the U.S. side, there was a foreign policy reason to help Mexico shore up its declining oil revenues, as this would enable greater economic stability and hence have critical effects on border security, immigration, and trade.[44] Environmental safety was another impetus, as a binational agreement represented an opportunity for any future development in the transboundary space to adhere to clearly defined safety standards.[45] The United States had an energy security objective as well, because in the event that the countries did find a transboundary reservoir, this would add a geopolitically stable source of oil.

3   Changing the Mindset

Building Trust by Sharing Information

The subject matter of the negotiations—the exploration and exploitation of transboundary hydrocarbon reservoirs—involved a high degree of technical intricacy. Throughout the process, the sequence in which seismic data would be shared among the parties was critical. From Mexico's perspective, Petróleos Mexicanos (PEMEX) first had to convey a level of certainty about the plausibility of transboundary reservoirs to the Mexican government agencies.[1] Then it was necessary to forge a partnership with the U.S. energy industry to confirm whether the international oil companies (IOCs) believed the existence of transboundary reservoirs to be conceivable, as well as whether it would be in their commercial interest to explore and produce from them.[2]

After that, in a coalition, Mexico and the IOCs could approach the U.S. government about defining a binational framework. Without the U.S. energy industry lobbying the U.S. Congress, arguing that it was in the commercial interest of both sides to launch negotiations, Mexican authorities did not believe that the two countries could reach an agreement.[3] From PEMEX's point of view, the best counter to the decades-old argument by U.S. officials that PEMEX was not willing and able to explore and produce in deep water was to have U.S. energy companies lobbying Congress with information to the contrary, highlighting the business opportunities at stake.[4]

Mexico's first challenge, therefore, was to persuade U.S. officials that the management of transboundary reservoirs was an issue that needed to be addressed, and that it was in their best interest to sit at the negotiating table as soon as possible. In this endeavor, the work of PEMEX's technical team was instrumental. PEMEX needed to convey that along with the political and economic reasons to pursue offshore energy development, there was a geological basis for pursuing the issue—and they had the seismic data to prove it.

However, given Mexico's Constitutional framework and the historic sensitivity of public opinion regarding oil resources, Mexican officials also needed to deal with U.S. concerns about their political commitment and ability to see this process through.[5] The cost of engaging in such a process, only to have it be curtailed suddenly by the vagaries of the Mexican domestic political landscape, was enough to make the U.S. officials reluctant to enter into the negotiations. As Aldo Flores, director-general for international affairs at Mexico's Ministry of Energy, explains, Mexico needed to make a compelling case about its credible commitment:

The U.S. could argue that it has not interfered with the Mexican oil industry for decades. And in turn, ask, "You are inviting us to be a part of this new process, and we want to know if you actually mean it, if you have the mandate, political clout, and credibility to see this through, because if it fails, we are going to be accused of intervening in Mexico."[6]

This implicit doubt hovered over the process. Hence, Mexico needed to persuade the U.S. officials that the context of the Mexican oil industry was changing and that the political mandate was for that process to continue. As described by Ambassador Arturo Dager, chief legal adviser for the Ministry of Foreign Affairs and head of the Mexican negotiating team:

One of our critical tasks was to explain to the U.S. officials that what we were working on together was absolutely new for Mexico, had never been tried before, and that to take such a step was not easy at all, but that we were completely committed to forging a new path. Perhaps, had our delegation been led by people with a traditional sense of Mexican history, the results would have been different. But we were convinced that we could protect and enhance Constitutional principles while substantively innovating.[7]

To convince several U.S. officials of this was no easy task because it made no sense for them to negotiate about something that, in their view, did not exist. Furthermore, they were wary about setting an international precedent that did not reflect the rule of capture (i.e., the status quo).[8] The United States believed that there was no geological proof of transboundary reservoirs, and if they ever turned out to exist, negotiating still would not be necessary, as under the rule of capture, unless you drill a well, no resource can be claimed.

Another challenge for Mexico, then, was to make the case that because potentially shared natural resources were at stake, Mexican law, not only U.S. law, must be considered. The Mexican argument was that Mexico's legislation did not have any provision recognizing the rule of capture, and that if each side chose to follow its own legislation unilaterally, they would be heading into a political conflict that they could clearly avoid. Flores summarizes the situation:

Our argument was that the moment the two countries found a transboundary reservoir, if they did not have a solid framework in place, then the likelihood of a very serious conflict would increase exponentially. We did not want to find ourselves in the same sort of bind that had historically, several decades ago, in the 1930s, led to the revocation of private property rights and the establishment of Mexico's Constitutional principles, indicating oil belonged solely to the Nation. We needed to define a transboundary framework beforehand. Mexico wanted to proactively prevent a crisis. We needed to have a binational framework in place in accordance with the Mexican Constitution and supported by public opinion to uphold the principles of the Constitution.[9]

One significant hurdle to achieve this was the degree of mistrust between the two countries, given that each side had different information as to the physical characteristics on the other side of the maritime boundary. On the Mexican side, PEMEX held the geological data and nobody else had access to them, whereas on the U.S. side, the data were dispersed between myriad private companies. In both countries, the information was proprietary and confidential, which meant that an asymmetry was inevitable. When PEMEX met with U.S. Department of the Interior (DOI) officials, they were told that the U.S. government had neither the access to nor the authority to share the IOCs' seismic data.[10] PEMEX officials believed that it was unfair under these circumstances for the U.S. government to ask for Mexican data when Mexico would not receive information from the U.S. government in return.

In light of these circumstances, as Leydi Barceló, deputy director for international negotiations at Mexico's Ministry of Energy, explains, figuring out how to reach an agreement about the amount of information to share "when there were so many different degrees of information, with several critical details at stake, was an extremely nuanced task."[11]

In order to decide how to share some of the information that the two countries had and what to exchange, in a way that would protect the natural resources at stake, while discussing what Mexico believed were transboundary fields to move the process along, both sides needed to step back and rethink their circumstances. They needed to realize that they were not negotiating a precise exploration and production agreement, but instead defining the framework by which the operators would then try to identify and manage such reservoirs. According to Leonardo Beltrán, the director for international negotiations at Mexico's Ministry of Energy, it was necessary to foster a more flexible and constructive mindset:

The critical challenge was to reach a common understanding about the sequence at stake: that both countries needed to first define the space where the partnerships between the IOCs and PEMEX would be conducted, and then do the exploration to assess the split of resources, not the other way around.[12]

Therefore, since the two countries wanted to negotiate an agreement that ensured best practices and efficient development of the energy resources, figuring out an effective way to share meaningful information was a necessary step.[13] To this end, the international team at the Ministry of Energy had spent several years reiterating this critical need in side-talks and informal conversations whenever they visited Washington, D.C., or met with U.S. officials in multilateral events, building the relationships and the confidence to push the process forward.

Eventually, the breakthrough came when Mexico suggested that each country share meaningful seismic information in a presentation format, though without sharing detailed documents that could be taken away from the venue. In this way, the other side could get a general sense of the information that formed the basis for the hosting country's assumptions without any confidential information leaking out.[14]

Mexico took the first step in this direction, holding a meeting in a state-of-the-art, three-dimensional visualization center owned by PEMEX in Villahermosa, Tabasco. The U.S. officials had never before been invited to see Mexican seismic data to this degree and in such a setting. As Sigrid Emrich, deputy economic counselor at the U.S. Embassy, recalls:

It was transformative because it was the first time the Mexicans were presenting seismic data to which we had never had access before. It showed us how serious Mexico was about moving forward with this process. Our interactions with PEMEX had never been as open as what happened in that meeting; it put our relationship on a whole other level. We could relate quite well with the Ministry of Energy officials, but for us, interactions with PEMEX, as an NOC, were always in a uniquely different category. It was extremely helpful to get to know our colleagues in PEMEX in a different way and have such an open conversation. Our impression was that the Mexican government was trying to signal the beginning of a new era with concrete actions.[15]

Thus, the presentation was significant, beyond its substantive considerations, in terms of building trust between the two countries. As David Madero, director-general for exploration and production of hydrocarbons at Mexico's Ministry of Energy, explains, "being transparent about our intentions and presenting the seismic data we had, especially as the latter is not common in the oil industry, helped trigger an enhanced sense of commitment and receptiveness from the U.S."[16] This was indeed the case, as David L. Goldwyn, special envoy for international energy affairs at the U.S. State Department corroborates: "[T]hat was a great move on Mexico's part, as a confidence-building measure. It is unclear whether the Department of Interior folks were persuaded of the existence of transboundary reservoirs, but at least they could see there was a rationale to Mexico's request."[17]

The United States then reciprocated by hosting Mexican officials for presentations in New Orleans, Louisiana.[18] Kevin Karl, regional supervisor for the Office of Production and Development of the Gulf of Mexico region at the U.S. Minerals Management Service (MMS) of the DOI, recalls that this visit further allowed the two countries to clarify the outcome they were looking for:

The Mexican officials came, and for two days, we presented in depth how the unitization process works on our side in the Gulf of Mexico. We explained how we do it and why we do it. That process of information-sharing then became the foundation of the agreement. The Mexicans liked what we proposed. There was a lot of back and forth, but our interests were the same. We wanted to protect our rights as governments and we wanted to ensure the efficient exploration and development and production of the resource. That was the basic premise of what we were doing and we all agreed.[19]

Following the information-sharing presentations, officials at the DOI started to signal that they were more willing to go along with the political mandate to see this binational agreement through.[20] They began to argue that while the original impetus behind the negotiations was to continue to foster positive relations between Mexico and the United States, the situation also presented an opportunity to potentially enhance U.S. energy security and bury once and for all the "drainage" argument that had been used for so long to muddle the binational interactions.[21]

Analyzing Precedents to Define a Roadmap

Although U.S. government officials at the highest levels were eager to engage in constructive talks, some hesitance from working-level officials remained. In light of this, the Mexican authorities decided to write a draft proposal agreement, with the aim of triggering a more concrete response from the United States. To write the draft, in accordance with the Constitution, Mexico created a working group led by the Ministry of Energy and the Ministry of Foreign Affairs. Following instructions from President Felipe Calderón, the group discussed some of the key issues that should underpin the potential agreement. These topics included the structure of the fiscal regime, whether there would be a binational body to oversee activities, and if the two countries should harmonize legal and environmental standards.[22]

Through this work group process, the Energy Ministry consulted with the Mexican Senate, where leading senators Francisco Labastida and Rosario Green of the Institutional Revolutionary Party (PRI) and Rubén Camarillo of the National Action Party (PAN) were instrumental in joining forces between the different political parties. The cooperation between PAN, which controlled the executive branch, and PRI, which controlled Congress, remained steady throughout the process and was instrumental in building domestic support.[23]

Meanwhile, representatives on the left of the political spectrum, who normally would have been against this kind of interaction with the United States, particularly as it pertains to the oil industry, proved instead to support launching binational negotiations. Their agreement was in part based on a concern about the potential drainage of Mexican oil resources by U.S. companies working near the maritime boundary, which elicited a sense of nationalism and the belief that Mexican reservoirs should be protected by the establishment of a binational framework, under international law.[24]

The executive branch, however, did not share the full draft agreement proposal with the Mexican Senate. Officials at the Ministry of Energy were advised that such a move would trigger a never-ending discussion. Key senators recommended this approach; Mario Budebo, deputy secretary for hydrocarbons at the Ministry of Energy, recounts that they expressed to him, "'Describe the major items and the principles underpinning the draft, but do not go into the details; you drive the negotiations, we are here to support and comment; let the Executive lead the charge.'"[25] This flexible mandate was critical and instrumental in facilitating the efforts of the Mexican negotiators.

In the process of preparing the draft, Mexican officials reviewed more than 15 transboundary hydrocarbon agreements from across the globe to assess the best practices. According to Elizabeth Ceballos and Fernando Rosenzweig, legal counsels at PEMEX's International Legal Affairs Office, the treaties reviewed included the 1965 United Kingdom–Norway Agreement, the 1965 United Kingdom–Netherlands Framework Agreement, the 1971 United Kingdom–Denmark Delimitation Treaty, the 2002 Timor Sea Treaty between East Timor and Australia, the 2007 Trinidad and Tobago–Venezuela Framework Agreement, and the 2011 Russia-Norway Delimitation Treaty.[26] The people who analyzed these agreements concluded that unitization partnerships would be the best way to move forward.[27]

In their research, Mexican authorities met with experts from several countries to discuss and learn how to adapt their insights to the circumstances in the Gulf of Mexico.[28] This process gave the Mexican authorities a sense that in spite of the inevitable asymmetry between the United States and Mexico, they could build an effective binational framework. As Guillermo Zúñiga, the legal director for petroleum operations at the Ministry of Energy, explains, "if East Timor could reach a workable hydrocarbons agreement with Australia, securing a fair share of the benefits, there was no reason for Mexico not to achieve the same with the U.S."[29]

However, the challenge was to strike a balance in framing the negotiations through the draft between the opening signaled by the 2008 domestic energy reform and the inevitably restrictive Constitutional framework which tied oil to nationalism in Mexico.[30] As Manuel Uribe Aviña, minister for legal affairs at the Mexican Embassy in Washington, D.C., summarizes, the domestic political context in Mexico regarding oil "had a dual effect: it made apparent to both countries the space in which we could try to find a sweet spot, but equally limited our flexibility."[31]

Mexico's task was to propose a framework for transboundary hydrocarbon reservoirs that would simultaneously protect and develop the natural resources near the maritime border, prevent unilateral development on the U.S. side, spur reform for the domestic energy sector, and provide PEMEX with a legal, financial, and technological template through which to collaborate effectively with IOCs in the Gulf of Mexico.[32] Beltrán describes the country's overarching aim:

This was part of a conscious effort to reshape the narrative around the Mexican energy sector by taking a first step to announce to an international audience that a new era of investment and collaboration with international stakeholders was about to begin. This was important on a substantive level and from a strategic perspective.[33]

Once ready, the Mexican officials presented the draft to President Calderón, highlighted a dozen key items, and outlined what they thought would be the best outcome and what they imagined the U.S. response was likely to be.[34] With the president's approval, Mexico sent the draft to the United States. The U.S. government received the draft and analyzed it for several months without issuing a response. When they finally did respond, in late 2010, they put the draft aside and proposed instead that before the two countries reviewed the document, they engage in a series of binational workshops to develop a deeper understanding of how each country operated in the Gulf of Mexico.[35]

Switching from an Adversarial to a Mutual-Gains Approach

For many years, one of the reasons that the United States and Mexico had not pursued a comprehensive negotiation was their stark difference of opinion regarding the legal principles that should regulate transboundary reservoirs. The United States had long argued that the underlying international law should be based on the rule of capture, and that should not be compromised in any agreement.[36] Mexico, on the other hand, which does not have the same level of technology and capital investment for pursuing wells in deep water, where most of the likely transboundary prospects lie, had always insisted on cooperative development, wherein one side cannot develop unilaterally and mutual decisions are required to develop oil resources.[37] The latter is the basis for most transboundary agreements around the world.

As previously stated, the United States developed its energy business according to the rule of capture, an old English legal concept dictating that if a wild herd of animals comes onto one's property, the landowner has the right to take them; since they belong to no one, whoever happens to capture them on his land becomes their owner. In the late 1800s, the United

States equated oil to a wild herd of animals, and the rule of capture stuck.[38] For example, in the United States, with a reservoir crossing nine parcels, each parcel owner who drills down owns the oil extracted, even if it comes from a reservoir connected to a contiguous parcel that they do not own.

However, in practice, both onshore and offshore, if the same owner has all nine parcels, drilling on each of the parcels simultaneously will likely prove counterproductive, leaving oil underground given how the geology works. In addition, having nine wells is far more expensive than having one or two strategically placed ones. If it makes more sense for one owner to carefully select where to drill, this same strategy also makes more sense in the case of multiple owners. Hence, the emergence of the industry practice of unitization, which enables any number of parcel owners to jointly manage a reservoir and divide the extracted resources among themselves, sharing the upfront costs and risks.[39] However, the practice of unitization is voluntary in the United States, not mandated by any government authority, as is the case in other places around the world.[40]

Given the differing positions regarding the rule of capture and cooperative development, and the previous failed attempts to overcome this divide, how could the countries break this long-lasting deadlock? As confirmed by the negotiators from both countries, a critical factor proved to be the decision to take a completely new approach to the negotiation process.[41] David Sullivan, the lawyer leading the negotiations for the United States, was responsible for proposing a transformational move, facilitating a switch in the negotiators' mindsets from adversarial to cooperative and allowing them to create value before engaging in value distribution.

To understand how Sullivan was able to accomplish this switch, it helps to understand his background. A mechanical engineer, he began his career in the oil industry after graduating from college, working for a couple of years at Schlumberger. There, he generated well logs, the well data that determine where the oil is, in developing countries, including India. He therefore had firsthand experience determining the properties of geological formations, evaluating whether oil could be extracted, and generating mapping systems in order to figure out how to manage a reservoir as a whole.[42]

Sullivan then got a master's degree in public policy, followed by a law degree. After that, he began a career with the U.S. government, where he earned a reputation as an astute attorney and became involved in multiple international negotiations. His background, covering many areas of expertise, was uniquely suited to this case, and as Goldwyn stresses, "once assigned to this mission, he took it upon himself to encourage each side to collaboratively frame the negotiations and render them mutually benefi-cial."[43] Sullivan explains how he first became involved with the negotiation process:

I came in to the State Department after working at the National Security Council at the White House, and assumed control of the Office of Oceans, International Environmental and Scientific Affairs. Mexico had recently approached the Obama Administration. President Calderón had spoken to President Barack Obama, and re-iterated the desire to negotiate on this issue. I talked to my former colleagues at the White House, and the notion there was that we needed something positive in the bilateral agenda. "There is a lot that we ask of Mexico, here is something in fact we could pursue that is a big plus for Mexico." In international relations, you try to sat-isfy each other's requests to be able to satisfy your own. I knew there were long-term skeptics in the legal offices in multiple U.S. government agencies, convinced "there is no point in doing this," but I very much pushed to argue we should give it a try.[44]

In turn, U.S. officials had a meeting at the White House, where the State Department (DOS), the DOI, and the Department of Energy came together to decide whether to pursue Mexico's request to begin negotiations. After the DOS, represented by Goldwyn on the policy side and Sullivan on the legal side, pushed very hard to move forward, the group agreed. Hence, the State Department was assigned to lead the negotiations.[45]

Mexico had sent in a draft text agreement that was based on multiple transboundary hydrocarbon international treaties. Insights from these agreements had been adapted for the Gulf of Mexico context, according to Mexico's interests.[46] During the spring of 2010, the New Orleans office of the DOI conducted an in-depth analysis of the Mexican draft, producing a 100-page report outlining the various objections, paragraph by paragraph. Although structurally sound, the Mexican draft was not a feasible blueprint from the U.S. perspective.[47]

The draft did not work for many reasons, including the fact that it pro-posed a government-consent-based structure to green-light production—a prospect for which, as a political matter, the United States would not sign up. The United States also considered the draft problematic from an eco-nomic development perspective, as under the terms, it would have to compel private companies to enter into partnership arrangements that the companies may not want to enter for commercial reasons.[48]

The U.S. government authorities feared that this would result in shutting down the market. As Mark Hanan, chief of the Development and Unitization Office for the Gulf of Mexico Region at the U.S. Bureau of Safety and Environmental Enforcement, explains, "this would limit the possibility of development along the boundary and essentially freeze hydrocarbon development on both sides."[49] Sullivan further describes the dilemma:

Our conclusion was, "Okay, we need to be very realistic. If we follow this draft, and it becomes the framework, it will not work because the U.S. government does not drill; we only put conditions on the lease, and allow companies to go do it. So, if these conditions are such that companies deem them not workable as a business matter, we could sign up to an agreement with Mexico, but all it will do is freeze up the possibility of any development along the maritime boundary." So the draft to us was a nonstarter. We did not share that first draft with the U.S. industry, because had we done so, they would have come to Capitol Hill and to the White House to shut down negotiations before they even began.[50]

As the United States was analyzing the Mexican draft and determining that it would require fundamental alterations, the Macondo oil spill occurred in April 2010. The catastrophic event eliminated the political feasibility of announcing the mutual desire to pursue binational negotiations, which had been scheduled for a presidential summit between presidents Barack Obama and Felipe Calderón at the White House in May. It also halted a significant number of the technical preparations on the U.S. side. Government officials from the DOI and the DOS had to focus most of their efforts on a whole host of issues related to the oil spill response, in the midst of the reorganization of the MMS into three agencies.[51]

Mexico, however, remained politically engaged at the highest executive levels, and it contacted the United States again in November 2010. Within two weeks, a full Mexican team arrived at the Mexican Embassy in Washington, D.C., for the official launch of the negotiations. Goldwyn and Carlos Pascual, the U.S. ambassador to Mexico, among others, agreed to this start because the political will was there, though it was well ahead of the substantive preparations. Sullivan explains the bind in which he and his team found themselves:

I was charged with going to the first binational negotiating session, and there was no way we could work off the Mexican draft. The night before, I sat with the DOI colleagues, and we explored our options. I could look at Mexico's draft and know the problems it would trigger with the BOEM and the IOCs. "We don't have any way to walk them off of the draft, but we can't start a negotiation from the draft because we are going to tear it apart. And what we really need to do is to avoid what we have done for the past 20 years, which is to be at odds with these guys."[52]

The U.S. negotiators understood that domestic conditions in Mexico had changed as a result of the energy reform that took place in 2008, indicating that an international treaty establishing joint investment in hydrocarbon reservoirs straddling the maritime boundary was a real possibility.[53] The United States knew that through these negotiations, the two countries could lift the moratorium and open more acreage for deepwater development.[54] There was a strong incentive to reach an agreement, but it still required talking to a wide array of stakeholders—government, industry, environment, law, and policy experts—in order to research the problem in depth, figure out what had to be done and what spaces had to be filled in, and come up with a solution to meet industry and environmental concerns. As Sullivan highlights, the United States had not done the requisite preparatory work:

If the business side did not kill the draft, the environmental [nongovernmental organizations (NGOs)] would. So we had our needle to thread on our side. We had not conducted any discussions with industry. We had not discussed with NGOs. We had not surveyed other actors in U.S. agencies to see what their views were. We had not had time to do enough homework and had no draft of what we would do. Normally in negotiations, we would have opened with a counterdraft, or comments on the current draft, to describe our starting points and goalposts. We had done none of that. So, in order to buy us time and to build a more collaborative environment, I proposed on the fly: "Let's not negotiate from the text, let's have working group sessions so that we can all get very smart about this technical challenge. Let's divide the substance of the agreement on thematic areas, and let's meet every month and talk about these thematic areas, so that we do this in a collaborative way among good colleagues and friends rather than through hard-bargaining, fighting over an apple on the table."[55]

The Mexican counterparts were surprised by the U.S. proposal to hold these workshops. They knew that their political mandate was to reach an agreement before the Calderón administration finished its term in office. With just a few months left, how could the two countries devote time to working groups meetings? Was the United States relying on a delay tactic? Shouldn't they begin negotiations as soon as possible? Mexican officials hesitated, but they accepted the U.S. invitation to visit Washington, D.C. Subsequently, the negotiators met monthly, for two to three days at a time, over the next five months, at sessions during which everybody could share his or her own expertise on myriad issues.[56]

The thinking on the U.S. side was that Mexico was probably going to have to trade certain things in a binational agreement that would be very hard for them to do as a domestic political matter and get Senate ratification, and the only way for Mexico to do that is if they had a good understanding of the constraints on the U.S. side.[57] The same applied to the United States, given the challenges of going through Congress, with all the stakeholders that this would involve, and the conundrums of approving any international agreement proposed by President Obama. As Sullivan describes:

Each of us had tremendously difficult domestic problems to solve. However, if we could work together and have a common understanding of that before we began negotiations, then not to be explicit about it, but instead of fighting for items, we could start trading away, and say, "I understand now how you approach this problem, how your domestic constituency thinks about this problem, and I understand on this particular provision why you can't agree to what we propose on our side. I can give you this, and it will help you get approval, because I am keeping my eye on the long-term prize, which is to have an agreement that gets ratified by both domestic sides and gets done."[58]

By starting formal binational interactions in the workshops, the negotiation process had been fundamentally altered; the two sides did not need to focus right away on the Mexican draft, article by article, as would have originally been the case. Rather, they collaboratively explored the energy-sector models with which they came to the table.[59] Issue by issue, they began to develop a deeper understanding about the market, environmental, and worker-safety provisions at stake, as well as how these were intertwined.[60] As Michael Taylor, the desk officer for Mexico at the Department of State, explains:

The simple mechanics of sitting together were very important. Mexico was looking at managing energy resources in a different way. There was a lot of information that the U.S. needed to provide as it pertains to a strictly commercial perspective, as opposed to a more sovereign, state-centered approach of mobilizing energy resources. Everything we discussed centered on principles, information sharing, questions, and answers. We spent a lot of time in that phase before addressing the text of the agreement.[61]

This improvised and unplanned stage of the negotiations was very useful because it allowed each side to explain how it did things and where it wanted to go without competing with one another. Such trust building and knowledge sharing was necessary. Renee Orr, chief of the Office of Strategic

Resources at the U.S. Bureau of Ocean Energy Management (BOEM), summarizes the impact of the working groups:

The most important reason we were able to negotiate an agreement as quickly and as
comprehensive as we did was that we started with quite a bit of informal discussions
before we began the negotiations. We had a number of meetings and exchanges
where we just talked about how we do things in each country and why, so that the
two parties could fully understand what the programs, laws, restrictions, regulations,
and political realities were. Afterwards, when we did sit down to begin formal negotiations, there was a full understanding of where we could go and where we could
not go. In turn, we did not spend any time chasing after or going in a direction that
the other was not going to be able to follow. We were able to think about how to
make the agreement work on all different levels and for the different constituencies
involved.[62]

For example, in Mexico's originally proposed draft, if the countries were
not entirely certain about the existence of a transboundary reservoir, they
had to either agree or not agree, and if one did not agree, they would go to
arbitration. From the perspective of the U.S. negotiators and the U.S. industry, this would hinder investment and development. As Taylor explains:

The two countries had a slightly different organizing concept at the beginning of the
negotiations. We wanted to unlock the resources, whereas Mexico, perhaps wary of
U.S. unilateral action, wanted to make sure it could block the unequal development
of the resources. On the U.S. side, we had to gradually show that we were going to
put the processes in place so that the two sides effectively come together, that they
co-develop, and that the question is how. Some Mexican officials started out thinking, "We have to make sure that there is no development that we cannot veto."
We moved off from that position once Mexico became more comfortable with our
approach.[63]

The U.S. negotiators proposed instead that the two countries would
either agree or not that that a reservoir is transboundary, and if not, then it
would go to expert determination rather than arbitration. This mechanism
would not undermine Mexico's overarching aim of codevelopment, but it
would actually meet the interests of the U.S. stakeholders better than arbitration. As Sullivan explains:

The key was that, in order to bring something into the binational agreement, there
needed to be an economic reason to do so. You could not assert, based on specula-
tive data, "We just think this reservoir is transboundary," and then you freeze it.
We proposed a significant change, that there be well data from the U.S. side and
from the Mexican side, in order to go to the experts to discuss whether something
is transboundary. Each side needs to drill a well. In deep water, a well costs between

$100–200 million. So, this provision does not allow for speculative assertions that something is transboundary; it requires real investment, a well drilled on your side to be able to say, "I think this is a transboundary reservoir." So, if Mexico drills a well on their side, and the U.S. argues, "We think that reservoir is transboundary," Mexico can say, "Yes we agree with you," or "No, we do not agree with you, not from our data, we think it is not transboundary, if you think it is, go drill a well."[64]

Essentially, the two countries set up a price tag to go to expert determination because a well would be needed on both sides in order to be able to go to a dispute resolution mechanism to determine if the reservoir in question is transboundary. Only reservoirs for which the two countries are willing to make a financial investment go into the binational agreement; neither side can use the agreement for political reasons or as a defensive measure to freeze out the other side. Michael Stewart, desk officer for International Energy and Commodity Policy at the DOS, summarizes, "What we wanted to avoid, contrary to all the other agreements in the world that mandate that both sides have to unitize before they can exploit the reservoir, is to make sure that no side could hold up exploitation on the other side on the basis of speculation."[65]

Hence, there are two layers to the solution that the two countries devised. The first is that the two countries expect that economic logic will reign—that oil companies will negotiate with each other and form unitization partnerships whenever they find a transboundary reservoir, thus optimizing efficiency and profit. This is what IOCs already do in the Gulf of Mexico away from the maritime boundary, without a regulatory mandate, because it makes financial sense. In the rare case in which these incentives are not enough for the energy companies, then both countries can protect their oil by drilling wells and then going to expert determination. The agreement, therefore, encourages the parties toward unitization agreements (Mexico's objective) without the danger of political considerations hindering the industry's decision-making (the U.S. concern).[66] As Hanan explains, "The big issue was how to protect every drop of oil under Mexico's sovereign rights in the context of the U.S. rule of capture. In order to do so, we needed to rely on voluntary unitization. We had to create a system of incentives that would significantly encourage voluntary unitization. It was a breakthrough neither side could envision right at the beginning."[67]

This is a critical provision in the binational agreement which differs significantly from the original draft, as well as from any other transboundary agreement in the world. It effectively finds a way to meet the strategic interests of Mexico and the United States, bridging the divide between contrasting market and legal perspectives. It does so through a mechanism that neither team of negotiators could imagine before the working-group collaboration.

Through that process, the negotiators were able to better understand the other side's interests, move away from positions, and create more value. By rethinking their initial approach to the challenge of identifying and producing from transboundary reservoirs, they found a way to mutually satisfy their fundamental aims and reach agreement.

4   Exceeding Zero-Sum

Finding the Zone of Possible Agreement

After five months of monthly work-group meetings during the first half of 2011, the negotiators were able to explore options and test trades that would have been very hard to figure out beforehand. Following the work-group sessions, the negotiators on both sides had a better understanding about the key legal directives, fiscal instruments, technical aspects, and commercial incentives that shape industry performance and investment on either side of the maritime boundary.

Across the negotiating table, there were two clear reference points: there was no conflict about the maritime boundary, which had been determined in previous negotiations, and neither side had yet identified a transboundary reservoir.[1] The fact that the two countries were discussing how to deal with transboundary reservoirs in the abstract, without any explicit reservoir at stake to tilt the outcome in one direction or the other, made the negotiation process easier. Neither side could try to take advantage of the other, given that any clause would be applied mutually. This helped to balance some of the inevitable political and economic asymmetries between the United States and Mexico. As summarized jovially by Luis Macías, manager for new exploration and production ventures at Petróleos Mexicanos (PEMEX), "If you are dividing a cake, it's your birthday, and they tell you, 'you cut the pieces, but your sister chooses first,' you'll carefully make sure to cut two pieces of the same size!"[2]

Prior to the formal negotiations, PEMEX had already held workshops with industry stakeholders in the Gulf of Mexico, including Exxon, Chevron, Shell, and BP, in which the parties simulated the potential partnership process between operators, should they discover transboundary reservoirs.[3]

As explained in the section "Building Trust by Sharing Information," in chapter 3, PEMEX had also hosted technical sessions for U.S. officials without industry representatives in attendance. There, PEMEX's exploration and production staff presented their interpretation of the most recent geological information about potential structures on Mexico's side of the maritime border, and they also became better acquainted with U.S. industry standards and practices regarding issues such as financing, contracting, and accounting. Xavier Antonio de la Garza, general manager for international legal affairs at PEMEX, explains that from Mexico's standpoint, developing a plan for the exploration and production of transboundary reservoirs "hinged first on assessing international best practices, then finding a way to fit those practices into the domestic legal framework, which still forbid risk, incentive, and production-sharing contracts."[4]

In an effort to find the right fit and better understand the boundaries of the space where an agreement could be reached, the Mexican negotiators hired a U.S. law firm for consulting purposes. They did so following the advice of Leonardo Beltrán, the director for international negotiations at the Mexican Ministry of Energy, who in previous international travels for other engagements had built a relationship with U.S. attorneys, whose expertise Mexico could trust to better understand an array of industry directives according to U.S. law.[5]

Strategically, this move was extremely useful. From the law firm, the Mexican negotiators had an expert opinion from a neutral third party with whom to consider options, when U.S. officials explained to Mexico that certain avenues could not be pursued under U.S. law. The firm would analyze each scenario and explain which ideas that had been rejected by the United States in fact could not be explored from a legal standpoint; and, on the other hand, for which ideas little was known, but nonetheless viable legal precedents suggested that they were worth pursuing. Moreover, the consulting attorneys confirmed that the binational agreement would serve to cement unfamiliar legal strategies with further legal standing.[6]

Having a deeper sense of what was feasible according to U.S. law provided guidance to some of Mexico's counterproposals and enhanced the negotiators' flexibility. For example, one of the challenges was deciding whether the two countries should pursue a treaty or an agreement. The

Mexican Senate initially requested a treaty so it could have Constitutional bearing in Mexico.[7] However, it later became clear that a congressional-executive agreement on the U.S. side, between the executive and the two houses of Congress, would have the same legal effects in terms of Mexico's domestic legislation. This congressional-executive agreement option, in turn, would enable skipping critical hurdles in the United States, requiring 50 percent of the votes in both houses instead of Senate ratification by two-thirds of the vote. The latter would have threatened to put the agreement in limbo, as is the case with many international treaties in the United States.[8]

Another issue for Mexican negotiators concerned the leases that had already been issued by the United States to international oil companies (IOCs) for production near the maritime boundary. Mexico was not particularly apprehensive of leases where production was already taking place since it was fairly sure that such reservoirs were not transboundary. The negotiators focused their attention instead on seven identifiable leases that had yet to start production, which Mexico estimated could plausibly include a transboundary reservoir.[9] The United States conveyed to Mexican officials that such leases could not be included within the binational framework that the two countries would negotiate until their terms were up for renewal on the U.S. side, many years down the line. The two countries were at odds on this issue until the United States offered, creatively, to have the U.S. Department of the Interior (DOI) and the Bureau of Ocean Energy Management (BOEM) sit with the private companies to encourage them to adhere to the binational framework voluntarily.[10] This tactic was ultimately successful and served the interests of all involved.

One other topic of negotiation was related to the fact that Mexico had originally argued that the agreement should apply to the entire maritime boundary in the Gulf of Mexico. However, some waters in the Gulf of Mexico are under the jurisdiction of the state of Texas, not U.S. federal authorities. It became apparent that addressing the Texas waters would considerably delay the negotiations, as would including the Eastern Gap, where jurisdiction is shared with Cuba.[11] Mexico and the United States resolved to leave those waters out of the agreement for the time being, while including a line indicating that when discussion with other Gulf of Mexico stakeholders becomes feasible in the future, the current binational agreement will serve as the template.[12]

Overcoming Preconceptions by Defining a New Narrative

Behind the scenes, with their back table (i.e., the constituents to whom negotiators answer), the Mexican negotiators faced the critical task of working against the preconceptions that stood in the way of reaching agreement, not the least of which was the traditional narrative of mistrust of the United States.[13] The negotiators faced the perennial domestic perception that American interests would inevitably trump Mexico. As Aldo Flores, director-general for international affairs at the Ministry of Energy explains, it was not considered a matter of *if* Mexico would come up short, but instead, "the only mystery was how much of Mexico's natural resources were going to be lost in the process."[14]

Ambassador Arturo Dager, chief legal adviser at Mexico's Ministry of Foreign Affairs and the head of the Mexican negotiating team, further explains the challenge:

Given the binational history in the Mexican energy sector, if you were told that you had to negotiate a hydrocarbon agreement with the U.S., it was natural to think it was mission impossible. This was a heavy burden. We needed to remain undeterred by what was said by colleagues outside of the negotiations, who scoffed at the chances of ever reaching a fair agreement. Their argument was that a beneficial deal could not happen between two completely different legal, fiscal, and energy frameworks, and between two countries with such different degrees of social and economic development. Simply put, however, that was not our mindset, nor the mindset from the President's Office.[15]

To fight this skepticism about negotiating with the United States, the Mexican negotiators had to first make a compelling case that, though it might be technically possible that the country that begins extraction unilaterally on one side may end up draining resources from the other side, the decades-old fear about the "drainage effect" was extremely unlikely to be realized. The negotiators had to convince domestic constituents that from a geological standpoint, due to the narrow and deep formations of the Gulf of Mexico, it was a remote possibility. Further, from a commercial standpoint, it would not be in the interest of any IOC to jeopardize its reputation, especially where such large investments required in deepwater energy production are concerned, if the possibility existed of triggering a conflict with Mexico by draining Mexican natural resources.[16] As Flores points out, "no board of directors of any company would risk such litigation and such a dispute."[17] David Sullivan, assistant legal adviser for oceans, international environmental, and scientific affairs at the U.S. State Department (DOS), confirms this assessment:

No IOC wanted to be the one to go drill into a transboundary reservoir, and drain Mexican oil, because if you are Shell, and you do that, you will never work in Mexico again. The IOCs did not establish offices in Mexico City for many years for nothing. They wanted a framework where industry would be unlocked and have the possibility to develop together.[18]

The Mexican negotiators also had to be careful about dealing with public opinion. The aim was to minimize the opportunities for people, guided by political interests, to accuse the officials of betraying their country, whatever the circumstance. This explains why the two countries agreed to keep joint declarations to a minimum. In the rare occasions when press releases were developed, they were only released once both sides agreed to their content.[19]

Simultaneously, PEMEX conducted a media campaign that, without mentioning the binational negotiations, did stress that it was necessary for the national oil company (NOC) to find adequate mechanisms to associate with other energy companies in order to better undertake the risks that deepwater offshore exploration entails. The message was simple: PEMEX stood to gain substantially if it was able to rely on better infrastructure, foreign investment, and international partnerships.[20]

Slowly, the negotiators laid the foundation for a new narrative regarding the energy sector. This narrative hinged upon a choice—to continue living in the strict memory of the 1930s and the fears of the 1970s, or to proactively figure out how to meet the country's current challenges head-on. The latter option better fit the circumstances and strategic opportunities that the country needed to seize, and eventually, it won out.

Involving Concerned Stakeholders Preemptively

The U.S. negotiators had a mandate from the White House and the Obama administration to create a framework that would produce offshore energy from the transboundary region, in a safe and efficient way. If the negotiators came up with an agreement that was not actionable, and counterproductively served to freeze development in the whole maritime boundary, it would be a waste since the energy industry would not support it. Development would need to be mindful, however, of the key interests of all the stakeholder groups; environmental organizations would need to be considered, along with the energy companies.[21]

The assumption on the U.S. side was that everyone in the environmental community would be hostile to the notion of a binational agreement on transboundary hydrocarbon reservoirs. As Sullivan explains, however, the alternative of unilateral deep-water exploration by Mexico was less appealing:

We had just had the Macondo oil spill. There were massive environmental objections that you would assume ensue after the largest oil spill in U.S. history, an uncontrolled well blowing oil for two months in the Gulf of Mexico, causing catastrophic environmental damage. And the U.S. federal government response is "we are going to open up substantial new acreage for drilling in deep-water with Mexico that does not have a deep-water capacity yet." How do you sell that? How do you have that accepted by the U.S. Congress, with a Senate majority by the Democratic Party? So, our notion, and I spent a lot of time talking to the U.S. environmental [nongovernmental] organizations, we all did, was basically to convey the facts. First, "It is going to happen, Mexico is going to move into deep water." Second, "Mexico does not have the capacities we do, if we do this collaboratively with Mexico, all the better."[22]

In order to discuss with the environmental stakeholders how to shape an agreement they could live with, the U.S. negotiators conducted extensive and preemptive outreach. The DOI and the DOS developed a fact sheet on the negotiations, which they then sent to as many different nongovernmental organizations (NGOs) as could possibly have an interest in the subject. As Michael Stewart, desk officer for international energy and commodity policy at the DOS, summarizes:

It was an open invitation to all the environmental NGOs. We invited anyone who wanted to come and sit in, and we would just describe where we are in the negotiations. They could ask questions and raise concerns. There was not a lot of contentious exchange. It was instead about keeping each other in the loop from the get-go.[23]

The consultations, very technical in nature, were helpful. The briefings allowed U.S. negotiators to build an understanding with the NGOs and work against potential spoilers looking to derail the process. Michael Taylor, the desk officer in charge of Mexican affairs at the DOS, highlights why:

There was the concern of whether, by engaging in information sharing, we were somehow arming someone with the information to mount their opposition, but that turned out not to be the case. The point was to make sure that we were moving in the right direction, and the way we achieve that is by checking in with the stakeholders. If they know what we are doing and like what we are doing, then we will not have any spoiler problems.[24]

One of the critical arguments that the U.S. negotiating team relied on to bring the environmental NGOs on board was to highlight the lower risks of codevelopment through unitization, as compared to the alternative. The binational agreement would reduce the number of wells built. If and when the two countries find a transboundary reservoir, would it be preferable that they drill 10 wells or 2 wells? If one deepwater well is $1x$ in terms of risk factor, why would anyone risk $10x$, when they can have instead a binational framework where the two countries are encouraged to unitize, lowering the number of wells and thus risk?

The first two steps related with the environmental NGOs were to make the case for enhanced expertise in deepwater exploration and production, coupled with the lowered risks involved in drilling through binational collaboration. Then, after highlighting those two benefits instead of the costs, the U.S. officials crafted a third benefit. With their domestic constituencies in mind, such as the Sierra Club and the Natural Defense Resource Council, they designed a unique joint inspection regime. The regime indicates that Mexican inspectors can come with U.S. inspectors to oversee any activity on the U.S. side of the maritime boundary, and vice versa. To protect the sovereignty of each party, neither country gets to control what happens on the other side of the maritime border. Mexican inspectors cannot tell the United States, "You need to do this, this, and that," nor can U.S. inspectors tell Mexico what to do. There is no joint supranational legal structure. Each side keeps control of their inspection laws and is able to enforce them.[25]

However, as a matter of an international legal obligation, if a Mexican inspector is on the U.S. side and the U.S. inspector is not enforcing the directives in the U.S. law, and the Mexican inspector sees that there is a significant safety threat to health, life, or the environment, he or she can compel the U.S. inspector to shut down operations on the rig to safeguard against that risk. As Sullivan describes:

This has never been done anywhere else in the world. The Mexican inspectors are not enforcing any law they have control over, but they are exercising an international obligation under which the U.S. has to respect their view to enforce our own U.S. law to shut down risky activity if Mexico determines, while under our jurisdiction, that we are not properly carrying out. This gets reported right away to what is called the Executive Agency, composed by the Department of Interior in Washington and the Ministry of Energy in Mexico City. There is a four-hour period where they can uphold or overturn that order.[26]

Therefore, just in case there is too close a collaboration between inspectors and companies, the two countries established a safeguard against the inspectors choosing to turn a blind eye. They devised an alert system wherein anything that gets flagged immediately goes back to the capitals, which then talk to each other and figure out what to do on a case-by-case basis. Thus, the inspection regime is done in such a way as to not compromise national law, yet enforce international law.[27] In this way, the two countries circumvent any issues of sovereignty while providing an additional safety check to avert risks to life, serious personal injury, or damage to the environment.

In turn, even though the two countries open more acreage for oil and gas in the Gulf of Mexico, which is logically not a positive development according to the environmental community, this binational agreement is better than allowing development to take place (as it inevitably would) without such an agreement in place. Compared to unilateral development, which would occur under the rule of capture, the binational agreement lowers risk by enhancing the technology in place, incentivizing the development of fewer but strategically placed wells through unitization, and improving safety enforcement through the joint inspection regime. As Sullivan explains:

We asked the NGOs, "Do you still want to oppose the binational agreement, or do you want to take these environmental benefits and come along with it?" The environmental organizations conveyed, "We see the point, it sounds good, we obviously cannot advocate for passage of this agreement, particularly post-Macondo, but we are not going to stand in the way either."[28]

Therefore, some of the key concerns of an important stakeholder group that could have stood in staunch opposition to the agreement were met, not by forcing an outcome upon them, but instead by involving them in shaping the substance of the provisions that most concerned them. As a result, as Michael Bromwich, the director of the BOEM, recalls, "the environmental organizations, which were very active in the wake of the Macondo oil spill, were not visible and did not advocate against the binational negotiations."[29]

5   Exercising Leadership

Building in Incentives Rather than Requirements

The absence of a transboundary framework agreement on exploration and production along the maritime boundary had created uncertainty over the previous two decades—not only for the two governments, but also for the U.S. private sector. Even under the U.S.-based rule of capture, Mexico could threaten international oil companies (IOCs) with litigation in an international court if Mexican oil resources were deemed to be in danger of being drained by drilling conducted on the U.S. side of a transboundary reservoir. Unlike their predecessors in the 1980s and early 1990s, who were hesitant about discussing any binational solution that did not hinge on the rule of capture, the U.S. private sector was more supportive of exploring a binational agreement this time. As Renee Orr, chief at the Office of Strategic Resources at the U.S. Bureau of Ocean Energy Management (BOEM), explains:

The conversations around rule of capture were difficult. The rule of capture was the fundamental tenet of U.S. authority to develop the resources in the near term. It was our walk-away point. However, it was not at all Mexico's view about how activity should be undertaken along the maritime boundary. Evidently, that was why we were at the table. Furthermore, from an ultimate resource development perspective, the rule of capture did not make sense to us either. You need more certainty to undertake the significant financial investments to develop the resources. You need that certainty on both sides.[1]

In particular, the IOCs would be supportive if the agreement removed the possibility of a binational confrontation, as they were hoping and preparing for the day in which Mexico's entire offshore domestic energy sector would be open to foreign investment. As David L. Goldwyn, the special envoy for international energy affairs at the U.S. State Department (DOS), summarizes, the IOCs "took a long-term view of the relations with Mexico, and one potential transboundary field was not worth spoiling what they hoped someday would be a future relationship."[2]

As discussions about launching transboundary negotiations gained steam, from the perspective of the U.S. government, a critical task became keeping representatives of the U.S. oil and gas industry informed about the parameters underpinning the binational negotiations. Aiming to ensure that any agreement would be economically and commercially beneficial, the United States invited industry representatives to several workshops where they could outline their needs and concerns to U.S. officials. As Michael Taylor, the desk officer in charge of Mexican affairs at the DOS, describes the situation:

There are other topics where you do not need as much commercial input as we needed in this case. We needed to be confident that the agreement we produced would unlock the resources, but it was also important to get a sense from industry about the stakes. We really wanted to hear from the private sector, "If we accomplish this, on a scale from 1 to 10, how happy are you going to be?" And the answer was pretty high, because they had an interest in getting to the Mexican energy sector, and if this was a step toward achieving that goal, then they were very enthusiastic. Furthermore, they had a lot of the technical expertise. The U.S. government could bring the legal and regulatory expertise, but "how do you prove a reservoir, what sort of well structure do you need to have," that had to come from the private sector, because that is their business. So we had to make sure that as the text came together, their practice fit in that legal structure.[3]

In these consultations, the oil and gas industry expressed its support for the negotiations but did not want an agreement obliging it to work with any party on Mexico's side. Rather, it wanted the freedom to conduct business with whomever it chose and wanted partnerships to be determined between market participants, not the two governments. As Goldwyn highlights, "It was clear we were going to need a permissive agreement rather than a mandatory agreement when that came to play."[4] This meant, for example, that the U.S. oil and gas industry saw that there could be an advantage to making the U.S. subsea energy infrastructure available to Mexico so that oil produced on the Mexican side could be put into a pipeline to refineries in the United States. However, it did not want to be obliged to do anything; instead it wanted the ability to decide on a case-by-case basis, operator to operator.

As the binational process evolved, the United States made a suggestion to Mexico's Foreign Ministry to actually have an observer from the U.S. oil and gas industry sitting in on the latter part of the negotiations. Rather than simply consulting outside of the negotiations, the industry representative could act as an advisor, answering questions from both countries as to how various topics would be addressed by international oil companies.[5] This would be equivalent to the participation of Petróleos Mexicanos (PEMEX), Mexico's national oil company (NOC), which had been present at the negotiating table from the start in an advisory role. Mexico agreed to this request. As Michael Bromwich, the director of the BOEM, summarizes, "If the agreement did not make offshore exploration in the region attractive to the private sector, then we were all wasting our time."[6]

The Department of the Interior (DOI), through the directorate of the BOEM, reached out to a committee in the United States called the Outer Continental Shelf (OCS) Advisory Board. This group, consisting of 25 different companies active in the Gulf of Mexico, is the most important consortium of outer-continental-shelf operators, supermajors (i.e., the world's leading oil and gas companies), and small investment banks, representing a thorough cross section of the energy industry. Through these conversations, U.S. officials learned that "there was consensus by the largest publicly traded oil and gas companies in the world as to Keith Couvillion as the person they agreed was the most knowledgeable about the relevant issues, and whom they trusted to represent their views fairly and completely."[7]

Keith Couvillion, the deepwater land manager for Chevron, was formerly chairman of the OCS board. He was recommended by the board, selected by the DOS, and agreed to by the Mexican Foreign Ministry. With more than 35 years of experience working offshore in the northern part of the Gulf of Mexico, in all the facets of the upstream portion of the business (exploration, appraisal, and production operations), he was asked to share industry views on the features of the offshore regulatory framework, the operating procedures that companies pursue through joint ventures, and the structure of third-party investments. Couvillion recalls one of his first impressions as he came into the binational negotiation process:

As an outsider looking in, being the only nongovernment employee in the room on either side, it was very interesting to see the concerns of the countries. There was a reluctance to agree too quickly on all aspects of the discussion. On one side, the U.S. arguing, "We think this is a good thing, the President of the United States has directed us to work with the Mexicans, it has been a concern for a long time." On the other side, the Mexicans arguing, "We need to reach an agreement, we understand we have little experience, and we do not want to be taken advantage of."[8]

Couvillion was well acquainted with government officials and understood the stakes on both sides. As Kevin Karl, senior adviser to the regional director for the Gulf of Mexico Outer Continental Shelf region at the U.S. Bureau of Safety and Environmental Enforcement (BSEE), explains, "We know Keith pretty well down here in Louisiana, he is very good at what he does, and understands the politics. Having him as an industry observer helped us get the feedback we needed to shape something that would work."[9]

In addition to his prominent role in the U.S. offshore energy industry, Couvillion had spent significant time in Mexico City over the preceding decade. As part of Mexico's efforts to build and develop a regulatory structure to manage offshore development in consultation with industry, he had been working with the Mexican government at various levels, discussing what Chevron does in deep water, how the company operates around the world, and the regulations that they subscribe to in the United States. As he summarizes:

The U.S. has spent more than 60 years developing a code of regulations. There is more oil and gas offshore activity that has happened in the northern part of the Gulf of Mexico than any place on the planet. The last time I checked, over 55 percent of all offshore activity in the world is still in the northern part of the Gulf of Mexico. Most of the offshore oil and gas activities started here. The Chevrons, BPs, and Exxons of the world, we took what we learned in the Gulf of Mexico and took it to the North Sea, Australia, West Africa, Brazil. So the message to Mexico has been: leverage what has happened on the U.S. side. This includes the Environmental Protection Agency, the Clean Water Act, and the Coast Guard. Learn from these entities, adapt and create your own version that works for you.[10]

In addition to the regulatory insights that Couvillion could offer, Mexico's government, through PEMEX, was also interested in the investment, commercial, and technological aspects of the partnerships that could ensue with the major oil and gas companies operating in the Gulf of Mexico. To the extent that the IOCs and the Mexican NOC could share the costs and risks involved in deepwater exploration, it became more likely that Mexico would succeed with discoveries and production, meaning greater tax earnings and increased public spending.

Couvillion's technical and commercial expertise was highly regarded. This helped the two governments to bridge certain divides, as he effectively conveyed, "You are both sovereign governments, you do what you want, but this is how industry will react to this."[11] The PEMEX representatives could understand where he was coming from, particularly Luis Macías, the manager for new business ventures in exploration and production, who had previously worked for Exxon and understood very well the dynamics on both sides. Couvillion described what he would do as the Gulf manager for Chevron and explained that there probably would not be much difference between him and his industry counterparts in the Gulf of Mexico.

For example, one of the instances in which the involvement of industry representatives proved very useful to both countries related to how parties should share sensitive information once an agreement was in place. Ambassador Richard Morningstar, one of the leaders of the U.S. delegation, and special envoy for Eurasian energy affairs at the DOS, describes the challenge:

An issue Mexico felt very strongly about at the beginning of the negotiations was the mutual release of confidential information. On the U.S. side, we felt we could not force companies to release confidential information. In this sense, Mr. Couvillion was very helpful because he explained that even though the companies could not release absolutely everything, they did understand that if they wanted to have a definition of a transboundary reservoir, they would have to release seismic information, and since the definition of a reservoir has to be done country to country, inevitably that information would have to be shared, for the benefit of everyone's certainty.[12]

Hence, by working with PEMEX and the U.S. companies, a more nuanced understanding developed between the two countries about how to share information effectively in order to identify transboundary reservoirs. There were, however, some concerns on the U.S. side about whether these partnerships could really happen and how they would unfold. As Bromwich describes:

I think there was a legitimate fear because PEMEX, as a state-owned company that at the time had a monopoly on Mexico's oil and gas for seven decades, that they may want rules incompatible with the kind of incentives the private companies would need. Particularly to want to devote the resources to drilling in the area that was the subject of the transboundary negotiations.[13]

At the crux of this concern was how both sides would reach an agreement on dividing the benefits from codeveloping the reservoirs. Deepwater activities are high-risk and high-reward. Until drilling occurs, the parties cannot be certain about the amount of oil that can be extracted. IOCs spend significant sums of money, factoring in the challenges of engineering, worker safety, and environmental considerations, but on occasions there is nothing to show for their efforts. For offshore activities to ensue, private investors seek the most profitable ratios between risk and reward. If the risk is too high and the reward too low, the IOCs will not bid for a lease. Therefore, one of the major issues that had to be discussed between the two countries was that split between risk and reward, as well as whether it should be defined within the binational agreement or determined on a case-by-case basis between the IOCs and PEMEX. The twist, as Couvillion describes, was that industry on both sides of the border did not necessarily come to the table with the same view:

I would have informal conversations with people at PEMEX, and ask, "Are you guys negotiating for PEMEX or negotiating for the government?" Because PEMEX's view should be very similar to Chevron's view. We needed to make sure we were aligned, and tell the government negotiators in our countries: "Hey, you have to remember, you are protecting the interest of the country, we are talking about our ability to work between each other, share capital, risks and benefits, and meet our contract obligations." Understanding these differing interests was extremely important and not crystal clear from the beginning. PEMEX, they want to be independent, but they can't, they are a national oil company.[14]

This issue is further related to tax rates. On the U.S. side, if an IOC is going to sign a lease for an offshore property because it estimates that there is some oil and gas potential on that property, it pays the U.S. government for the exclusive right to assume the risk of exploration and development. When the IOC effectively makes a discovery and begins producing commercial hydrocarbons, on average, the oil company receives around 75 percent of the revenue from the hydrocarbons produced from that field, whereas the U.S. government gets about 25 percent of the revenue. In exchange for taking on 100 percent of the risk of exploration, the oil company receives the overwhelming majority of the benefit. The precise taxation rates can vary widely, depending on the terms of each contract.[15]

In this sense, the consideration of the risk and reward ratios that would be established in licenses, production sharing, and profit-sharing contracts between stakeholders highlighted a starkly different picture on the Mexican side. At the time of the negotiations, the rate at which PEMEX was taxed ranked the highest of any oil company in the world, amounting to 60 percent of the NOC's revenue. This was significantly higher than other oil companies with high tax rates, such as Norway's Statoil (50 percent), France's Total (45 percent), and Royal Dutch Shell (37 percent); and it was more than double what Chevron and Exxon had been charged by the U.S. government (28 percent) in the same period.[16]

The regulations for drilling added another layer of uncertainty for the potential partnerships along the maritime boundary. Once obtained, a lease on the U.S. side gives a company the exclusive right to request permission to drill in a geographic area. However, the U.S. government must still grant this authorization. Over the last 60 years, the United States has constructed a regulatory framework that basically indicates to the industry, as highlighted by Couvillion, that "with some certainty, if you submit the paperwork, along with additional requirements, you'll be granted permission to drill, develop, and commercialize with the lease we just sold you." As further explained by Couvillion, Mexico was then, and still is, in the midst of creating this regulatory framework, so it could not offer that level of predictability to the IOCs:

Here is where the rubber hits the road. You will not see this in the agreement because it is not there. You will see it ultimately when a transboundary resource is identified and a unitization partnership is formed. What happened was, and this was a suggestion I had made to both parties, but Mexico ultimately rejected it, the U.S. kind of supported it. The argument was that if there is a transboundary unit agreement, with a geographic area with acreage on both sides, with different licenses by different entities, I had suggested that within the unit, adopt the regulatory framework of either one of the two countries, I don't care which one, just adopt one, so that the rules within the boundaries of the unit will be the same. But the Mexicans rejected that concept. They said that their regulatory framework was just being developed, that they did not know what it was going to look like at the time, but that they would in future, so they could not agree on one or the other.[17]

Thus, the framework that resulted from the negotiations is such that when operators request approval for unitization in the future, both countries have the ability to review the proposal and request any changes or additions prior to granting their approval. This is where the risk and reward ratios, and the specifics of the regulatory framework, will be determined. The United States and Mexico found a way to foster a framework that pushes the operators on both sides to combine acreage so that the companies minimize the number of wells and enhance recovery rates, which encourages the coexploration and codevelopment of resources straddling the maritime boundary. The way in which certain costs and benefits will be allocated between the stakeholders, however, needs to be negotiated by the operators on a case-by-case basis.

The negotiators also had to decide how to include a certain degree of flexibility and reassessment in the agreement in order to cope with the vastly different legal and market conditions from which they come. One of these thematic areas was redetermination. When the parties discover a reservoir, they have limited knowledge of how much oil there is, what the reservoir properties are, and how much can be extracted. As production begins, the developer may in fact find that there is much more or much less recoverable oil than originally thought. This can create several conundrums.

For example, suppose that there is a joint venture in a geographical area with a reservoir 15,000 feet under the sea floor, straddling the maritime boundary. Some percentage of that reservoir is under U.S. jurisdiction, and some is on the Mexican side. So what is the breakdown? Is it 60/40, 50/50, or 90/10? Until drilling begins, no one can know for sure. Exxon on the U.S. side and PEMEX on the Mexican side could agree that the most likely split is 45/55 and sign a contract where they will share the costs of drilling and developing together 45/55. Once they begin to drill, however, it may turn out that 40 percent of the resources are on the U.S. side and 60 percent on the Mexican side. What should they do then?

In that circumstance, for the Mexican government, it was important not to be locked into the initial 45/55 split. Rather, Mexico wanted the ability to conduct periodic redeterminations to ensure that the resource allocation remained correct over time.[18] The IOCs countered that a redetermination process with potentially frequent recurrence would not be commercially feasible because of multiple factors: (1) the actual split of the reservoir, (2) the split of the investment cost, and (3) the split of the revenue.[19]

The IOCs asked, "If the parties were to do a redetermination, to which factors would it apply, and how would that happen? Is it assessed retroactively, going back to first production? Or is it prospective, from the redetermination date forward? Is there a cost-equalization?" The same question applies to equity. If the parties have worked for five years with a 45/55 split and now, after a redetermination in the sixth year, the correct split is determined to be 40/60, are the companies to go back to year 1 and do an equalization of cost, or start instead from year 6 onward?

Adding another layer of complexity is the fact that even in the face of the same data, the operators can easily have different interpretations about the technically correct split. From Couvillion's perspective, "the reality of drilling and extraction is that very often only when production has finished would it be possible to have a precise breakdown of ownership, be it 48/52 or 35/65."[20]

Given these complex variables, any redetermination process would cause considerable tension between the parties, but if redetermination were to take place every two years, as Mexico had suggested, the IOCs indicated that this would severely hinder investment prospects, as the original split is what they rely on to get funding from capital markets. Mark Hanan, the chief of the development and unitization section for the Gulf of Mexico region at the BSEE, explains the dilemma:

> Industry is looking for an environment, political and regulatory, that gives them some certainty that if they follow a protocol, they will be able to make a set of economic decisions. If they feel they cannot make a decision because there is not enough certainty, they will not put their profitability at risk. I think the negotiators on both sides understood that. We are dealing with an industry that is very conscious about not having retroactive conditions that hinder their profits. Now, the industry also wanted to be able to book reserves on Mexico's side. That was a concern of theirs, but not a deal-breaker for us. We have seen what the companies have done in other parts of the world, where they cannot book reserves and they are still able to come out with agreements where operators make a profit. So, we had to balance these dynamics. We are not industry's best friends, we are very cautious about what they are going to say, and Mexico was the same way. Fortunately, we had Mr. Couvillion, who is a straight shooter.[21]

Therefore, the negotiators had to work together to imagine a framework that simultaneously worked for the energy and government stakeholders without tilting the balance to one side. In turn, the negotiators decided that redetermination would occur as it pertains to each transboundary reservoir, but that the private parties will determine the frequency in their partnership agreement.

Aside from the risk-reward split and the frequency of redetermination, the two countries also had to plan for instances to resolve their disputes regarding the existence of transboundary reservoirs, the allocation of production, and the redetermination of voluntary and compulsory allocations.

Mexico wanted to utilize international binding arbitration to settle potential disputes. This was not something that would be supported by the U.S. Congress or U.S. industry; their preference is not to use binding arbitration as a first option. Meanwhile, the IOCs prefer to settle out of court and lock down their equities, and the Mexican Congress would not support the absence of a binding mechanism to hold U.S. interests accountable.[22] The solution to this challenge was to build a three-tiered dispute resolution process, closely mirroring several joint operating contracts in the U.S. portion of the Gulf of Mexico, but with an added twist to satisfy government priorities.

The three-tiered process works in the following way: in a contract between two or more operators, if a conflict arises and no solution can be found among the parties, they escalate the matter to the senior management level. The first step is to see if the vice presidents can work out the dispute. If they fail to do so, the second step is mediation, where the parties sit down and attempt to resolve their differences with the help of a neutral third party. If a resolution cannot be reached at step two, the process moves on to arbitration, where each side selects an arbitrator and these two arbitrators jointly select another neutral professional to be the third arbitrator. Then, as in a trial, each side presents evidence and witnesses, and the three arbitrators make a decision. The ruling is not binding, but nonetheless, the binational agreement gives each country the authority to halt production if it does not approve of a company's operations in light of an unresolved dispute.[23]

This process allows the two governments to maintain oversight over any disputes without resorting to binding arbitration. The dynamic creates a significant financial incentive for the IOCs and the NOC to resolve their conflicts in one of the three stages of the dispute-resolution process. Otherwise, if they do not reach an agreement, either of the two governments can step in to stop production. The financial losses resulting from being required to halt production, when hundreds of millions of dollars are at stake, are significant. This is the incentive that should drive the parties to reach an agreement, even without binding arbitration.

By defining the split between risk and reward on a case-by-case basis, allowing operators to define the number of redeterminations, and relying on a multitiered resolution process, the two countries found the room to satisfy their underlying interests and move beyond their seemingly irreconcilable positions. The negotiators were able to create value by finding a way to incentivize desired outcomes without requiring them. As Morningstar, who led the U.S. negotiating team and reported directly to Secretary of State Hilary Clinton, explains, "Within the constraints each side had, we tried to go as far as we could. It is a pretty unique agreement. There is simply nowhere else in the world with anything quite like this one."[24]

Creating Better Outcomes through Relationships of Trust

Through the working-group sessions, and then through the negotiating sessions, the participants built critical capacity. Initially, some U.S. technical officials did not fully understand the strategic and political components of the bilateral relationship.[25] On Mexico's side, the Ministry of Energy had domestic reform on their minds, whereas the Ministry of Foreign Affairs knew the international law, but neither could be as savvy about the intricacies of reservoir management as PEMEX, and none of them could conceive of every incentive driving the considerations of the IOCs.[26]

As confirmed by every single official whom I interviewed in both countries, by working together, the negotiating teams were able to reach a degree of understanding and appreciation for one another, and for the interests that they were representing, that had a powerful effect on the final outcome. Hanan says that these interactions allowed the negotiators "to develop a good kind of camaraderie where you truly get to respect the other side. That atmosphere was very important. The Mexican representatives, they knew what they were doing, they were hard workers, and it showed."[27] This sentiment is echoed by José Luis Herrera, deputy general manager for international legal affairs at PEMEX, who similarly states that Mexico "deeply valued the efforts of the U.S. negotiators, who created a real space where we could discuss at length and in good faith."[28]

This mutual-gains approach to the negotiations was not a given from the outset. Before the working-group sessions, some had to fight those who argued that it was better to kill the negotiations from the beginning, due to the prevailing assumption that the process would be very time consuming and probably ineffective.[29] Others had to make a case against those proposing that the two sides should just get away with composing a couple of pages of principles without needing to agree to anything substantive in practice.[30] Neither side could envision the impact of the structure of the negotiation process itself. David Sullivan, assistant legal adviser for oceans, international environmental, and scientific affairs at the DOS, recounts the transformative effect of the mutual-gains approach:

At the end of the negotiations, the Mexican counterparts told me, "When you first proposed the work-group sessions, we thought it was crazy and awful, and it would be a disaster because we only had a year to do this, and if we did not start negotiating right away, we would not have enough time. But we were remarkably surprised that it made the negotiations so much easier because we did not need to fight over words or fight over concepts. In fact, we went to school together for five months, educating each other about our common problems, we had lunches together, we hung out, got to joke with each other, to get to know each other's personalities, realize what made us tick, and by the time we came down to talk about how to divide up these difficult issues, we were colleagues, not adversaries."[31]

Working in a more collaborative, noncontentious environment, structured by the insights of an array of policy, industry, legal, and geological experts, allowed the negotiators to move more quickly and effectively.[32] The two sides could emphasize direct communication, suspend criticism, brainstorm without committing, and think through the implications of multiple solutions.[33] Ambassador Arturo Dager, chief legal adviser at Mexico's Ministry of Foreign Affairs and head of the Mexican delegation, explains that this allowed them "to be proactive and build a more complete narrative about the challenge at hand and about what we could do together to solve it."[34] With that mindset came the ability to find mutual gains. As Sullivan, the lawyer leading the negotiations for the U.S., notes:

I would say that this negotiation, more than any other I have ever participated in, benefited from collegiality. There is the hard-bargaining guy that will bang the table to force the other side to reevaluate its position and whether it is willing to throw everything under the bus and walk away from a negotiation. You find many negotiators that do that as a standard course. It is never effective. I have found in my time negotiating international agreements that the most productive way to get to a good solution is to be able to have your opposite side understand that you are coming at it as a common problem. You are not there representing a national interest, trying to take away as much as you can in a zero-sum game.[35]

This enhanced level of trust was on display, for example, in one of the key hurdles to reaching an agreement: how to enhance voluntary unitization without a binding mandate.[36] The solution required significant flexibility, as well as counterintuitive thinking. The binational agreement indicates that if, after all the incentives to the contrary, the energy companies still refuse to unitize, they can go ahead and unilaterally produce from a transboundary reservoir. The companies can do so based on the estimated percentage of oil resources on their side of the maritime boundary, according to the seismic data available. At first glance, such a provision seems controversial, to say the least. Both sides know that the accuracy of seismic estimates before drilling is not infallible. To produce unilaterally is likely to ruin optimal extraction from the reservoir, while the side that begins production first inevitably damages the interests of the nonproducing party. This is the worst possible outcome from a geological, business, and political standpoint. It has binational conflict written all over it. There is a surprising logic to it, however, as Sullivan explains:

Anybody who looks at the agreement in a vacuum would say, "Why would they do this? This is unlike any other transboundary agreement in the world. Every other transboundary resource agreement in the world prevents this either by requiring that all parties consent to the development of a resource or take the case to binding arbitration. The U.S. and Mexico do neither. This is crazy." And yet, we structured the ability to resort to unilateral production with a clear purpose in mind, to get through the political conundrums we faced on both sides.[37]

The process is as follows. The energy companies can bank on the minimum percentage that they will get if they decide to go after a reservoir on their own.[38] They can estimate the percentage on their side of the maritime boundary, monetize it, and take it to the financial markets. Therefore, they can invest, drill, produce, and move ahead on their own. In the U.S. Congress, when the legislators read the agreement, they can argue that it sets no precedent against the rule of capture. This is politically crucial and explains their support. Meanwhile, as a practical matter, the companies know that they will form voluntary units because when they engage in binational efforts, they will reach a significantly more profitable outcome from a business standpoint.[39]

Mexico needed to have the security that not a single drop of Mexican oil would go to the United States. If the companies do not unitize, someone's oil could go to the other side. This is the conflict (and the ensuing litigation) that no IOC will risk, on top of the fact that unilateral production from one side of the maritime boundary minimizes recovery rates and is less profitable. Hence, the two countries achieve unitization, which is what Mexico required, yet with no binding mandate, which is what the United States needed. In turn, both sides have an agreement that is politically feasible and implementable so that the two energy industries can code-velop transboundary reservoirs.[40]

This solution hinges on the ability of the negotiators to think through the implications of their provisions from multiple angles, derived in part from a large degree of trust in one another. As Sullivan notes:

There is a lot of this in the agreement, as it relates to balancing the practical effects of the words on paper that does not really align with how the agreement is described as a political matter. These solutions, that encourage the stakeholders to invest and to produce in the maritime boundary region, we were able to find them, even though they are hard to devise, because across the table we were very cooperative. Nobody on our side or on Mexico's side believed that there was anything other than an honest approach to the problem. We informed all our discussions on the basis of "How are we going to get this through our domestic political process?" This allowed us to do things contrary to arm-wrestling the other side, and instead focus on trying to achieve a workable result.[41]

The people leading the negotiations were also adept at dealing with negative practices by outliers on their negotiating teams. As Leonardo Beltrán, director for international negotiations at Mexico's Ministry of Energy, explains, speaking of Ambassadors Hernández and Dager, "We had people helming the negotiations with a very keen sense of balance in terms of advancing the national interest and not being held back by unproductive preconceptions."[42] At tense moments, they were ready to call for a break, take their representatives aside, make the case that this negotiation process was following a different approach from traditional posturing, and protect the collaborative negotiation process.[43] The mindfulness to prevent posturing from undermining the process was crucial for both countries, as Sullivan describes:

There were some on our side who wanted to pound on the table, people on the Mexican side too, very much with that negative attitude. And when those people would show up in the negotiations, we sat there, let them pound, let them vent, let them go with the traditional posturing approach. Then we would break, go to side-talks, and the people on both sides would explain, "We will get through this, we have built a very good dynamic here, this is not part of what we are doing, that person is speaking in such a tone because he is very close to that political official, that is why he is here: it does not matter though, no need to cave on anything, just divert the river, satisfy his ego to make him feel that he accomplished his mission, and then move on, we will deal with this domestically and make sure this does not wreck future sessions." Now, who does that? In no negotiation I have ever been a part of, the two sides build the kind of relationship that they are willing to take aside some of their key political persons for the sake of achieving a common objective. That is what we achieved as a group. It was unique. Had it not been for the personality and choices of the people we worked with, we would not have been able to go beyond these hurdles.[44]

The negotiators also knew how to use humor to deal with unpredictable circumstances, defusing tensions. As Dager recounts:

We were at the State Department, negotiating, and both sides were tired and stubborn, so we called for a break. During the break, I began to walk through the hallways, calling on my cell phone, and without noticing I crossed a floor line where if you do not have your name tag, what happens, as it did to me since I left it in the negotiating room, is that a policeman kindly walks you to the exit. The U.S. delegation immediately tried to convince the policeman that we were working together, but the policeman was having none of that, I had broken the name-tag rules! So I waited for a while as I registered at the front desk again, and then was allowed to come back in. When both sides sat again together, you could hear a pin drop. I then told Ambassador Morningstar, "You do not have to arrest me, we can find an agreement," and we had a great laugh. I promised too, that next month, in Mexico, if someone were to be arrested, I would not be behind it![45]

As such, the relationships built through the binational work-group sessions and the formal negotiation process allowed the negotiators to build upon the expertise on the other side without hesitation, analyze the issues from different angles without suspicion, and test alternatives without pressure, focusing their efforts and ideas on figuring out what was feasible. This rapport facilitated the creation of value, as Sullivan summarizes:

The nature of the negotiation changed from "How can I get out of this with the biggest piece of the pie?" to rather, "How can we both together, collaboratively, work to figure out exactly that sweet spot?" So that the agreement is in just the right spot so that when Mexico takes it home, people will look at it and say "You have achieved something great here, the Americans gave you all of these items, which is fantastic, and we only had to give away this small piece, that is good." And on the U.S. we could say, "Look how the Mexicans agreed to all of these items, and we only gave up this much in return, we came out ahead." Then each of us has a good story to tell when we take the agreement home.[46]

This combination of effective ground rules, shared expertise, and balanced temperaments, with representatives engaged in a constructive interaction, formed a critical component of the negotiation's success.

Part III: Colorado River Negotiations

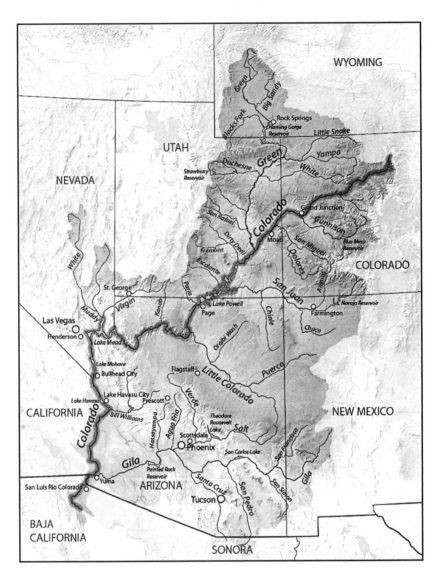

The Colorado River Basin.
Source: U.S. Bureau of Reclamation.

6   Introduction to the Colorado River Negotiations

Much like the Colorado River waters themselves, the story of the negotiations that led to the 2012 binational agreement has many twists and turns. The diverse hurdles, strategies, and decisions that shaped the negotiation process offer a valuable case through which to explore various elements and strategies related to transboundary negotiation, leadership, collaboration, and communication between government, industry, and nongovernmental actors. The negotiations, examined through the eyes of both sides, offer insights by which resource management practitioners focusing on water can effectively increase river-basin supply, rethink the possibilities of irrigation and storage infrastructure, and restore ecosystems and habitats.

Overview

This section provides a brief overview of the chapters to come, followed by a discussion summarizing and outlining the scope of the binational agreement.[1] The story of the negotiations begins in chapter 7, *Back to the Drawing Board*, by exploring how, in the context of drought, the parties were able to move "From Litigation to Cooperation." After a serious diplomatic confrontation and ensuing lawsuit in which both parties ended up worse off than before, leaders on both sides of the border set out to frame a new mandate. With this new approach, the two countries sought to redefine their relations on the Colorado River and begin negotiations from a constructive, mutual-gains mindset. The second section, "Turning Crisis into Opportunity," examines the ways in which the two sides seized a critical window of opportunity to move the negotiations forward following the devastating 2010 earthquake in Mexico's Mexicali Valley, which weakened the alternatives of several domestic constituencies in Mexico that were opposed to a cooperative process with the United States. The next section, "No Negotiation without Representation," studies another crucial component of setting the negotiation stage, which entailed breaking the traditional U.S. diplomatic protocol to allow the seven U.S. states that own the rights to Colorado River water to be represented appropriately at the negotiating table. Involved for the first time as cosovereigns with the U.S. and Mexican federal authorities, the contributions of the Basin states were critical to shaping an implementable agreement.

Chapter 8, *Broadening Perspectives*, explores a set of transformative steps toward changing the mindset of the players. The first section, "Seeing Is Believing," illustrates how, to overcome a long-held pattern of mistrust, the United States invited the Mexican negotiators to tour the water infrastructure in the United States. The visits along the Colorado River Basin led to a new, collaborative understanding of the parties' motivations and concerns. Section two, "Sharing Tools for Better Understanding," outlines how, by establishing a working group to jointly share data, learn, and test modeling tools, the United States and Mexico built a common reference framework, never seen before, that enabled Mexican technical experts to better evaluate the forecasts and scenarios that underpin operations on the U.S. side of the river. This in turn allowed both countries to start exploring mutually beneficial proposals that otherwise would not have been considered. The next section, "Putting Yourself in Their Shoes," recounts how, as the U.S. negotiators developed an increasingly better grasp of Mexico's back-table context, and vice versa; each side was able to actively help the other craft a more robust agreement that would represent a win for its constituents back home.

The focus, in chapter 9, *Tearing Down Walls*, turns to the strategies and contributions of the environmental nongovernmental organizations (NGOs). The first section, "Bringing More Issues to the Table," tells the story of how the environmental stakeholders, a unified group of NGOs from both sides of the border, were able to redefine their relationship with the U.S. Basin states, build a coalition with Mexico's federal government, and add their voices to the binational negotiation process. Next, "Adding Value in Process and Product" describes how, once at the negotiating table, the environmental NGOs aided in the process of the negotiations, as well as its outcome, by generating significant value, well beyond the environmental aspects of the agreement.

Chapter 10, *Protecting and Perfecting*, begins by highlighting how the negotiators were able to work collaboratively to reach agreement while blocking the efforts of various spoilers who wished to derail the negotiations. The section "Dealing with Spoilers" tells the story of how this was achieved, as the negotiators wielded political power, built relationships of trust across the negotiating table, and strategically managed communications with the press. Next, "Leading through Ingenuity" underscores the importance of facilitative leadership, as the key players on each side read the negotiation proceedings in real time to improvise, reassess, caucus, and clarify with each other in small informal settings, with the goal of refocusing and redefining their delegations' strategies. Finally, the section "Testing the Ways to Agreement" explains how the negotiating parties used points of provisional accord in order to maintain momentum, creatively propose options without committing, evaluate multiple packages, and move toward consensus, leading to the ultimate success of the negotiation process.

Summary and Scope of Agreement

On November 20, 2012, the United States and Mexico signed Minute 319, one of the most significant agreements regarding the allocation and management of the shared waters of the Colorado River since the 1944 United States–Mexico Water Treaty.[2] The treaty allocates the flows of the Colorado River between the two countries, providing 15 million acre-feet to the United States and 1.5 million acre-feet to Mexico annually.[3] Throughout the decades, however, the two countries have oscillated between collaboration and confrontation on a number of issues, including infrastructure, irrigation, agriculture, groundwater, development, pollution, and most notably water quality and salinity.[4]

For the first time in 70 years, the two sides have agreed on a mutual set of criteria to adjust these flows in response to conditions of drought and over-allocation of the water resource (for further reference, see images 4–6 in the "Illustrations" section of appendix B). The two countries have also agreed to a set of joint operational measures and cooperative projects to improve conservation, storage, and restoration along the basin. The measures and projects are built around the principle that both countries can achieve better results by considering each other as partners and sharing a more collaborative responsibility in managing the river resource. The landmark agreement also incorporates to the diplomatic binational framework the direct participation of nonfederal actors, including state representatives, water agencies, and NGOs beyond an advisory role, and entrusts them with a seat in the face-to-face negotiations regarding the management of the water resource.

The Minute encompasses a series of steps that the United States and Mexico agreed to undertake during a five-year pilot period, which ends on December 31, 2017. The pilot period is intended to test the framework and to become the foundation for a longer-term agreement. The measures and projects include (1) rules for the reduction of water deliveries to Mexico in shortage conditions; (2) rules for the increase of water deliveries to Mexico in surplus conditions; (3) guidelines for the multiyear storage of Mexico's water in U.S. reservoirs; (4) the delivery of pulse and base flows to support ecosystem restoration efforts in the Colorado River Delta; and (5) joint conservation projects to improve irrigation infrastructure and trade water savings.

In terms of reservoir management provisions, the Minute brings Mexico into the fold with previously agreed-upon strategies among the seven U.S. Colorado River Basin states on how to coordinate reservoir storage and allocate water surplus and shortage. These strategies were negotiated in 2001 and 2007, respectively, between the Upper Basin states (Colorado, New Mexico, Utah, and Wyoming) and the Lower Basin states (Arizona, California, and Nevada), in collaboration with the U.S. Bureau of Reclamation at the Department of the Interior (DOI). In keeping with a commitment to partnership, the two countries have agreed to adapt these strategies to a binational framework in order to share both the benefits and costs of reservoir storage. Following this principle, when one country has a shortage, the other will as well, and when one country has access to surplus water, so will the other.

The reference point is Lake Mead on the Nevada-Arizona border, the primary reservoir in the Lower Basin and the largest reservoir in the continental United States. Under the agreement, during low reservoir storage conditions, water deliveries to Mexico would progressively decrease, in a range of 50,000–125,000 acre-feet, when the surface level of Lake Mead drops below 1,075 feet above mean sea level. This range in reduced deliveries is between 3.3 percent and 8.3 percent of Mexico's annual 1.5 million acre-feet of Colorado River water allocation under normal reservoir conditions. More specifically, if Lake Mead's surface level is ever at or below 1,075 feet, annual U.S. water deliveries to Mexico would be reduced by 50,000 acre-feet. When Lake Mead's surface level is at or below 1,025 feet, annual deliveries would be reduced by 125,000 acre-feet. This means that in the worst-case scenario, Mexico would receive at least 1.375 million acre-feet of Colorado River water on an annual basis during shortage conditions.[5]

During high reservoir storage conditions, water deliveries to Mexico would progressively increase, in a range of 40,000–200,000 acre-feet, when the surface level of Lake Mead rises above 1,145 feet or when flood control releases are required. The increased deliveries would run from 2.7 percent to 13.3 percent of Mexico's annual 1.5 million acre-feet. Therefore, during surplus conditions, in the best-case scenario, Mexico could receive up to 1.7 million acre-feet of Colorado River water annually.

By jointly establishing a set of flexible shortage and surplus criteria, the two countries are responding to current drought conditions and adapting to future climate change scenarios. When the 1944 treaty was signed, the annual average Colorado River flows were estimated to be 16.5 million acre-feet. Current average annual flows are below 14.4 million acre-feet. Moreover, studies carried out by stakeholders on both sides of the border concur that climate change could further reduce Colorado River flows by at least 10 percent in the next 50 years.[6]

In this context, the Minute was a significant breakthrough for both countries, fostering the adaptive management of a critical natural resource. The Colorado River Basin, extending for 250,000 miles, currently provides 5 trillion gallons of water to 40 million people in the southwestern United States and northwest Mexico on an annual basis. More water is exported from the Colorado River Basin than from any other basin in the world, irrigating some of the most productive agricultural regions on the planet, including the Imperial Valley in California and the Mexicali Valley in Baja California. The river's flows are controlled by an extensive system of dams, reservoirs, and aqueducts built over the last 100 years, with a reservoir capacity of over 60 million acre-feet, up to four times the Colorado's annual flows.

However, the practice of engaging in unilateral infrastructure projects and short-term policy fixes, built upon the doctrine of sovereign appropriations (first in time, first in right), had undermined trust between the two countries for decades. Instead of collaborating on fundamental planning from the headwaters in the Rockies to the Colorado's mouth in the Sea of

Cortez, the two sides had imperiled a variety of wetlands, wildlife migra-
tion routes, riparian habitats, and aquifers to fragmented legal and political
jurisdictions, endangering rural and urban settlements across the border.

The new agreement is remarkable precisely because it establishes the
foundation to conceive of the transboundary basin as a cohesive entity. For
example, the best strategy to foster a long-term water supply in a river basin
crossing two countries is to store most of the water in the reservoirs located
upstream in the river basin, where the water-bearing sediment is the deep-
est. When countries do not trust one another, however, downstream stakeholders rely on fixed interbasin transfers to their own water infrastructure,
in spite of how vulnerable their reservoirs may be. Unheard of up until this
point in the binational relationship, the Minute creates a mechanism by
which the downstream riparian (Mexico), can decide to defer a percentage of the annual water deliveries owed to them by the upstream riparian
(United States), to conserve and store these deliveries upstream.

This water deferment, called Intentionally Created Mexican Allocation
(ICMA), allows Mexico to store up to 250,000 acre-feet of its annual Colorado River allocation at Lake Mead every year, under any reservoir conditions, free of charge. Mexico can choose to deliver up to 200,000 acre-feet of
this stored water on any subsequent year, mindful that maximum deliveries
are set to 1.7 million acre-feet each year. The Minute requires that 2 percent
of the stored water volumes be set aside for the creation and delivery of
environmental flows, with additional saline water to be devoted for ecosystem restoration in the Colorado River Delta.

Mexico will be able to use this storage to offset delivery reductions during
future shortage conditions. This is critical so that Mexico can be prepared to
mitigate shortage impacts, as the country lacks the domestic storage capacity to save water on a rolling basis. Moreover, by deferring the delivery
of its water allotment, Mexico acquired more time to repair its damaged
irrigation infrastructure in the Mexicali Valley, which was crippled by a
7.2-magnitude earthquake on April 2010, as the negotiations were ongoing. The damage to water treatment facilities, canals, levees, and dams was
estimated at $300 million.[7] By safely storing a portion of its water at Lake
Mead, which otherwise would be lost due to a lack of infrastructure capacity, Mexico will be able to save it for future needs.

This unprecedented level of trust between the upstream and downstream
riparian has benefits for U.S. stakeholders too. The water that Mexico stores

in Lake Mead will decrease salinity levels and increase surface levels, saving the U.S. National Park Service more than $5 million in annual upkeep costs. Lake Mead is also the source of 90 percent of Las Vegas's drinking water. More predictable and higher reservoir levels will facilitate water management by the Southern Nevada Water Authority (SNWA), helping to reduce the frequency of shortage declarations and providing the SNWA with more time to build an estimated $800-million intake pipe, in light of the decreased average surface levels at Lake Mead.

For environmental restoration purposes, Minute 319 establishes the delivery of 158,000 acre-feet of water to the Colorado River Delta, divided between a pulse flow and several base flows, financed by a three-way commitment between the United States, Mexico, and several NGOs. Both federal governments are responsible for the delivery of 105,000 acre-feet of water to the delta's ecosystem in the form of a pulse flow. The water is derived from part of the water allocation that Mexico stored on Lake Mead to face the aftermath of the 2010 earthquake, and also complemented by joint savings from water conservation measures, as a result of the binational agreement.

The pulse flow was designed to mimic spring runoffs in order to benefit the germination and survival of native trees throughout the delta, and that has already been achieved. From March 2014 to May 2014, the flow hydrograph was timed to coincide with the peak of native cottonwood seed release in the riparian corridor, and it concluded prior to the time that the nonnative invasive tamarisk seed release began. The aim is to contribute to the efforts to revive riparian habitats, wetlands, marshes, and estuaries across the delta, since more than 90 percent of the original habitat where the Colorado River flows into the Gulf of California has been lost in the last 50 years.

In addition, the Minute establishes the delivery of a total of 53,000 acre-feet of water divided into several annual base flows intended to benefit the native vegetation and wildlife restored by the pulse flow. These base flows are financed by a binational coalition of NGOs through the Colorado River Delta Water Trust, which has been purchasing and leasing idle domestic water rights in Mexico for environmental purposes since 2008. The Minute also provides $3 million in funding for on-the-ground restoration activities in the delta, through a contribution by the U.S. Fish and Wildlife Service and the nonprofit National Fish and Wildlife Foundation.

Restoration efforts, on the heels of the base flows, are ongoing at various locations across the riparian corridor, complemented by significant funding from nonprofit sources, in light of the success of the binational pulse flow.

During the duration of the Minute, a team of binational experts recruited from U.S. and Mexican universities, NGOs, and federal agencies is tasked with the joint monitoring and reporting of the ecological and hydrological results of the pulse and base flows. Their responsibility is to track surface water, groundwater, and water quality; evaluate the response of flora and fauna; and improve the understanding of the delta ecosystem in order to propose the next plan for future environmental flows.

The Minute also fosters a collaborative framework for joint U.S.-Mexico investment in pilot projects to improve water conservation on Mexico's side. The United States is providing $21 million, of which $10 million is being disbursed by urban water agencies in the Lower Basin states of Arizona, California, and Nevada. These funds are meant to speed up the process to complete the concrete lining of several unlined parts of the Mexicali Valley irrigation infrastructure. In return, the urban agencies secure water from a one-time installment, whereas Mexico is entitled to all remaining water savings generated by the conservation efforts. The Central Arizona Water Conservation District and the SNWA each receive 23,750 acre-feet of water in exchange for $2.5 million; the Metropolitan Water District of Southern California receives 47,500 acre-feet in exchange for $5 million. The other $11 million is provided by an agreement between the U.S. Bureau of Reclamation and other funding entities, in order to share in the benefits of these water conservation efforts in Mexico. The resulting water savings would finance the entire U.S. government's contribution to the pulse flow and make an additional 124,000 acre-feet available to the United States as a result of a binational water exchange.

The Minute also aims to foster cooperation between the San Diego County Water Authority and Mexico's federal and state water agencies, with the aspiration to eventually coordinate the necessary permitting, pipeline, and environmental infrastructure to create new water for the two countries. By relying on the Pacific Ocean as a drought-proof local supply and seizing on economies of scale, the United States and Mexico are exploring how to work together to jointly finance and build connectivity in a second-stage facility within a proposed seawater desalination plant in Rosarito, Baja California. They are also exploring plans to build a large-scale desalination plant near the Sea of Cortez. As with every other step established in the Minute, both countries agreed to monitor and review the effects of their decisions for five years and negotiate how to improve them by the time the Minute's pilot period ends in 2017.

The negotiations that led to Minute 319 began in late 2007, after the U.S. Colorado River Basin states reached a domestic agreement to equalize reservoir storage in times of shortage. When the binational conversations began, the relationship between the two countries was tense. Both sides were up against a history of frequent water disputes. Moreover, the two parties had recently engaged in a confrontation regarding the lining of the All-American Canal with concrete on the U.S. side, the ensuing reduced seepage to Mexican aquifers, and the lawsuits associated with the potential effects of the extraterritorial application of the U.S. Multispecies Conservation Act. On the heels of this conflict, following the initiative of top officials at the DOI and Mexico's Ministry of Foreign Affairs, the two sides began to meet informally to discuss how to start from scratch and work more collaboratively on the Colorado River.[8]

That conversation assumed that binational cooperation regarding reservoir operations, water storage, water conservation, and environmental restoration was possible (and indeed required) in the face of severe drought. The framework was then brought together in late 2008 under the umbrella of the International Boundary and Water Commission (IBWC). Both the U.S. and Mexican sections of the IBWC were entrusted to facilitate a diplomatic process, in close partnership with the U.S. Bureau of Reclamation and Mexico's National Water Commission (Comisión Nacional del Agua, or CONAGUA). Leaders selected by the seven U.S. Colorado River Basin states, representing the major urban water agencies and irrigation districts along the Upper and Lower Basins, were directly involved as well. Program managers from environmental NGOs provided both countries with strong advisory support.

The discussions continued between the United States and Mexico over the ensuing three years. During the negotiations, the two countries' delegations established work groups, as needed, to help everyone develop a better understanding of the needs and preferences of the other side and then bring proposals back to the larger group and their constituencies. Negotiations intensified in the summer of 2010, in response to the Mexicali earthquake, which crippled Mexico's irrigation infrastructure in the region. The

negotiations kept the same pace in 2011 and 2012, with monthly binational meetings generally lasting three days each, at alternating locations
across the border. An agreement was reached in the fall of 2012.

At the signing ceremony in Coronado, California, U.S. Secretary of the
Interior Ken Salazar described the Minute as a historical milestone that
pointed to the "end of the water wars," in which drought pits one side
against another, with the two countries now "choosing collaboration over
conflict, consensus over discord."[9] Michael Connor, who at the time of
the negotiations was the commissioner of the U.S. Bureau of Reclamation,
and would later go on to become the U.S. deputy secretary of the Interior,
noted that "this deal is the crowning achievement in an unprecedented
three years of cooperation on the natural resources that we share and are
critical to our well-being."[10] Connor further noted that the agreement dem-
onstrates that the United States and Mexico are "more than just neighbors,
we are now partners from here and into the future," with both countries "in
sync to share in the strategies and solutions to the resource challenges that
will only increase with time."[11]

Mexico's IBWC commissioner, Roberto Salmón, concurred, highlighting that the binational agreement was "built on relationships of trust,"
and established the foundation for "future negotiations in order to guar-
antee sustainability in the region."[12] Reflecting two years after the agreement's implementation, Mexico's ambassador to the United States, Arturo
Sarukhán, described to me the negotiation's outcome as "the culmination
of the efforts to break the preconceptions that have hindered the countries'
collaboration in the past," showing that the two countries "can engage
together on the real practice of basinwide thinking."[13]

7   Back to the Drawing Board

From Litigation to Cooperation

Binational controversies around the All-American Canal have a long history. Until the 1930s, the farmland of the Imperial Valley in California received its Colorado River water through the Alamo Canal, which had been built by the United States on Mexico's side of the border, supplying water for farmers in both countries. Mexico charged a minimal fee for this service, but the United States decided to build the All-American Canal so it would not have to depend on Mexico, and indirectly, to claim dominance over the river as well. The All-American Canal was built over dunes flowing south-southwest, such that the seepage replenishes aquifers on Mexico's side. From the 1940s to the 1960s, the Mexicali Valley developed on the basis of pumping groundwater from these aquifers. The Mexican farmers have continued to rely on the aquifers in the ensuing decades, and the seepage is also responsible for sustaining the nearby Andrade wetlands.[1]

In the early 2000s, California had to pursue water conservation strategies, including paying farmers not to grow crops and lining irrigation ditches in the Imperial Valley.[2] The reason for doing this was that each state in the Lower Basin is entitled to an annual allocation of Colorado River water. California's allocation is 4.4 million acre-feet, Arizona's 2.8 million acre-feet, and Nevada's 300,000 acre-feet. However, California's annual use had been more than its allotted 4.4 million-acre feet for decades; from 1950 to 2002, it took 5.2 million acre-feet every single year. That usage was legal, part of the Law of the River (the diverse compacts, federal laws, decrees, regulatory guidelines, contracts, and court decisions underpinning the management and operation of the Colorado River), but when Nevada and Arizona developed to the point of needing to use all their entitled water in 2003, California had to find a way to cut back their use to their 4.4 million acre-feet allocation. As part of these efforts, California decided to line the All-American Canal with concrete to conserve the water that otherwise would be lost to seepage.[3]

Mexico was not consulted in the process that led to the decision to line the canal; it was informed through the appropriate diplomatic means by California and U.S. federal officials after the decision was announced. In light of the imminent lining of the All-American Canal, the two sections of the International Boundary and Water Commission (IBWC) held several meetings to explore binational measures to mitigate the impacts that this action would have on aquifer replenishment.[4] However, the Imperial Irrigation District (IID), which operates the All-American Canal, took a hard-line stance, advocating that it was not the responsibility of the United States to mitigate any cross-border effects. The U.S. government disagreed with this notion, and so did the other irrigation districts in California, Palo Verde, and Coachella, as well as the urban water agencies.[5] These actors are aware of the history that people tend to be elected to IID's board by opposing cooperative solutions, both at home and abroad.[6] In the words of John Keys, commissioner of the U.S. Bureau of Reclamation in the early 2000s, reflecting on IID's approach to Colorado River issues, "the District's right to use Colorado River water has long been recognized; however, wasting water and preventing others from using it is not."[7]

As a result of this refusal to cooperate, both the U.S. federal government and California representatives moved on, discounting this confrontational position from IID as par for the course.[8] In turn, in their conversations with Mexican officials, they continued to discuss mitigation measures to deal with the effects of reduced seepage into the aquifers that serve the Mexicali Valley. These measures included the possibility of building turnouts on the All-American Canal, from which Mexico could deliver water to the city of Tijuana; as well as investing in conservation projects in the Mexicali Valley so that Mexico could try to recover the water that they feared they would lose.[9]

However, as the diplomatic process was ongoing, a binational coalition of farming, irrigation, and environmental interests, in the context of IID's confrontational stance, lobbied federal officials in Mexico City, with support from the governor of Baja California, to instead bring a lawsuit in the United States. The coalition's goal was to block the lining of the canal

based on the potential for its harmful cross-boundary effects on the aquifers, including environmental, health, and safety impacts. The lawsuit was
a controversial course of action because stakeholders and officials on both
sides of the IBWC thought that they had put some good, interesting mitigation proposals on the table. Mexico's Ministry of Foreign Affairs, nonetheless, chose to file the lawsuit in 2005 rather than continue through the
diplomatic avenue.[10]

The case went to a U.S. district court in the Ninth Circuit. Using the
arguments that the final environmental impact assessment had not been
properly conducted and that the National Environmental Policy Act had
been violated, the plaintiffs brought claims against the U.S. Department
of the Interior (DOI) and several regional and local entities. The court of
appeals dismissed the claims because, among other reasons, responsibilities
for cross-boundary effects are hard to account for under current legislation.
This ruling effectively foreclosed further legal challenges and insulated the
lining project from judicial review.[11]

The binational legal confrontation had negative results for all involved:
The parties had to pay high legal fees, the All-American Canal lining was
severely delayed and became more expensive, and no measures to address
the lost seepage were established.[12] As Peter Silva, assistant administrator
of the Office of Water at the U.S. Environmental Protection Agency (EPA),
explains:

The frustration was that we supposedly had this process at the IBWC, but it did not
matter because other people went through their own channels and did something
different with their own political interests. It was very frustrating to lose control
over an issue that we all thought was under ongoing good-faith negotiations. In the
aftermath, the silver lining of that whole confrontation was, and I recall talking in
depth with my friend, the late IBWC Mexican Commissioner Herrera, "We do not
want to go through that again."[13]

In December 2006, a couple of months before Arturo Sarukhán began
serving as the Mexican ambassador to the United States for Mexico's new
administration, headed by President Felipe Calderón, the U.S. Congress
passed bipartisan legislation to complete the lining of the All-American
Canal. Understanding the circumstances, and anticipating the effects that
the lining would have on water stakeholders, Sarukhán, building upon the
Calderón administration's commitment to forge a more collaborative relationship with the United States, and as such President George W. Bush's

administration, made the decision to propose a binational dialogue that would shape "a new paradigm, providing both countries with a clean slate to find effective solutions to jointly manage shared hydrological resources."[14]

To jump-start this process, Sarukhán took the initiative and led the efforts to establish a dialogue with U.S. Secretary of the Interior Dirk Kempthorne, conveying the need to jointly address the social, economic, and political impacts that the lining would have on the border communities.[15] In these efforts, Sarukhán argued, "the two countries had to move forward instead of endlessly discussing the past, doing away with the inertia of conflict that has often undermined binational cooperation."[16]

In the ensuing months, Sarukhán and Kempthorne collaborated to shape a joint declaration. Announced in the summer of 2007, it stated that the two countries were committed to beginning a new episode in the binational relationship. The aim was to "seek synergies and engage in confidence building measures, with a shared vision of the future to responsibly meet the broad array of needs of the Colorado River Basin stakeholders."[17] The message was a significant reset in the binational relationship and provided a much-needed impetus to get past the previous confrontations. As Sally Spener, foreign affairs secretary of the U.S. section of the IBWC, explains:

The joint declaration by Secretary of the Interior Dirk Kempthorne and Mexican Ambassador Arturo Sarukhán was a key turning point. The All-American Canal conflict was very disruptive to the work we wanted to do. Their message basically laid down that the two countries wanted to collaborate. So, we came out of a decade of conflict and litigation, and said, "We are going to try something different: we are going to commit to cooperation."[18]

To set the stage for this new paradigm, Sarukhán and Kempthorne met multiple times in Washington, D.C., "building a high degree of trust with one another, working to understand the best way in which they could reach a mutual agreement about a framework that would empower both countries to look at things radically differently."[19] On the basis of what would become a solid personal relationship, the two leaders studied the concerns and priorities of their domestic agencies and then set out to convince those on the fence about the need to follow a new set of mandates.[20] As Sarukhán explains:

This effort underscored our conviction that the two countries needed to reimagine the terms of reference of the binational dialogue, choosing between either remaining accomplices to failure, or becoming partners for success.[21]

Conscious of the need to break the old narrative through concrete actions, in these efforts, Sarukhán argues that Mexico was "very fortunate that Secretary Kempthorne, and then Secretary Salazar, both chose to trust the proposal to redefine our binational narrative in good faith, and put their weight behind our efforts."[22] Michael Connor, who went on to become the U.S. deputy secretary of the interior, and at the time had recently become the commissioner of the U.S. Bureau of Reclamation, underscores the significance of the mandate from Secretary Salazar to change the relationship between the United States and Mexico in the Colorado River Basin:

There is no doubt that in the Bureau of Reclamation, everybody knew that this was my highest priority. Partly because it was my own priority and partly because I knew my own boss, Secretary of the Interior Ken Salazar, wanted me to invest whatever time and effort was necessary to get an agreement with Mexico. The same thing could be said on the Mexican side. Ambassador Sarukhán certainly knew how strongly he wanted a different relationship with the U.S., and he was relying on his contacts in the Mexican Cabinet to achieve this.[23]

The steadfast support from the DOI and the Mexican embassy in Washington, in coordination with the White House and the Office of the Presidency in Mexico City, disseminated to the U.S. Bureau of Reclamation, Mexico's National Water Commission (Comisión Nacional del Agua, or CONAGUA), and the two sections of the IBWC.[24] The high-level political commitment on both sides was clear: to explore how the two countries could turn the page on the conflict that characterized the All-American Canal controversy.[25] The purpose was to see if the two countries could build, together, a mutually beneficial deal that would improve the management of the Colorado River in the face of drought and reduced flows.[26] As President Calderón notes:

The challenge was to find a way to see our problems and their elements as interconnected. On both sides, we continue to have a very negative tendency to see our problems as constrained and contained in silos. We really have a chance to find meaningful solutions and generate mutual gains when we change our mindset.[27]

Turning Crisis into Opportunity

On Easter Sunday, April 4, 2010, a 7.2-magnitude earthquake struck about 30 miles southeast of the city of Mexicali, near the border separating Baja California from California. The most severe earthquake to occur in the

Salton Trough since 1892, it was felt by 20 million people throughout the western United States and northwestern Mexico. Most of the earthquake's damage occurred in the border cities of Mexicali and Calexico, where 4 people were killed, over 100 were injured, and more than 30,000 families had to be relocated.

The event crippled irrigation infrastructure in the surrounding rural areas. On the U.S. side, significant damage to water storage and irrigation facilities occurred in Imperial County, located on the border between Mexico and Arizona, with an estimated repair cost of $90 million. On the Mexican side, 200 miles of irrigation canals were destroyed, with an estimated repair time of five years and a cost of $200 million, affecting 450,000 acres of farmland and leaving 30,000 acres without water.[28]

The earthquake also fundamentally affected the course of the binational negotiations. Up until that point, farming interests and political players in the Mexicali Valley had continuously opposed and hindered the dialogue with the United States. In this context, from a political standpoint, Mexican negotiators had been heavily constrained in their ability to explore trades between the two countries. As Óscar Ibáñez, the chief of staff for the director-general of CONAGUA, explains:

An earthquake that significantly cripples the infrastructure of an entire irrigation district is going to change the political priorities of the stakeholders involved. People at CONAGUA were suddenly free to explore how to improve the current infrastructure, as well as the operating rules, whereas without the earthquake, for political reasons, the irrigation districts would not have been touched.[29]

When stakeholders are used to behaving within the confines of long-held parameters, crises are sometimes critical to break inertia and provide the parties with an opportunity to rethink what is at stake. The infrastructure damage in the Mexicali Valley altered the calculations and priorities of various Mexican domestic actors. The farming interests in particular, who own the rights to more than 92 percent of the water consumed in the state of Baja California, had to consider collaborating much more with the federal government than they had been accustomed to doing.[30]

All of a sudden, the farmers had no infrastructure and no water. They needed the government's support to resolve these dire conditions because the bulk of the financing for restoration would need to come from CONAGUA. In light of this fact, they could not risk politicizing the situation with confrontational protests, as might have otherwise been the case.[31] The earthquake, therefore, affected the domestic context in Mexico, which, in turn, influenced Mexico's degree of flexibility in negotiating with the United States.

Following the rules set out in the 1944 Treaty, the United States would be required to deliver the annual 1.5 million acre-feet of Colorado River water to Mexico by December 2010. Mexico, however, no longer had the infrastructure to be able to use it.[32] The two countries had to make a decision as to whether to defer delivery. The only way around the treaty's delivery requirements was for the partners to agree to account for that water as if it had been delivered, and then put in place a new approach.[33] It soon became apparent that using reservoirs in the United States to store Mexican water, which had previously been proposed as a mechanism to deal with the ongoing drought, would need to be considered seriously.[34] As Calderón summarizes:

We no longer had anywhere to store the water coming from the Colorado River. If we did nothing, we would not be able to use the water. It forced everyone to look at our domestic circumstances and at the situation with the United States in a completely different way as compared to the past.[35]

Until the earthquake drastically altered Mexico's vantage point, entertaining the idea of storing its own water in U.S. reservoirs had been out of the question for political reasons.[36] However, if Mexico did not change that stance, it would have to face the fact that it would receive its annual Colorado River water allocation, but given its damaged infrastructure, it could not deliver the water to the irrigation districts. As a consequence, a significant part of this water would be lost to the sea.[37] In light of such circumstances, a window of opportunity to enact change presented itself. As Sarukhán notes, "in public policy, countries must never waste a crisis."[38]

The binational negotiations had been moving at a very slow pace before the earthquake, and the two countries remained significantly at odds after the tragedy. However, after one more arduous binational meeting in August 2010, three months after the earthquake, the two sides began to rethink their approach. As Connor describes:

After that difficult meeting, fortunately for this binational process, we had the right people, with the technical expertise in operating the river, asking in side-discussions, "Why don't we start looking at an agreement to deal with Mexico's immediate issue, which is how to not lose the value of water and repair its infrastructure?" So circumstances, and good strategic thinking, allowed us to reset and move forward. We realized that we really needed some success among ourselves, to trust each other, and to give us a little bit of momentum. So all the three commissioners, Drusina, Salmón, and I agreed, "Let's focus on building a deal that will have real value for Mexico and that will simultaneously demonstrate Mexico's agreement to structure water deferment within the framework of how the U.S. operates the Colorado River."[39]

That is what the two countries set out to do before December, during three months of intense, time-consuming discussions. They aimed to enhance trust between the key players by determining effective emergency measures. As Ibáñez explains:

At the center of these efforts was how to find the best mechanism to repair and improve the infrastructure on the Mexican side. Almost everything else was connected to this issue in one way or another, since only if Mexico earned enough flexibility to deal with the water allocations for the farmers in the Mexicali Valley, could both countries work more effectively toward other issues.[40]

This significant change in circumstances and the collaboration that ensued fostered a new sense of trust between the binational actors.[41] The two countries had discussed water storage many times before, but they had never had a shared impetus to implement it successfully.[42] The two sides agreed that Mexico would not take the full allotment of 1.5 million acre-feet while its infrastructure was being repaired. Instead, it would set up a system resembling a bank account in Lake Mead, from which Mexico would be able to take out the water in later years. As John Entsminger, the deputy general manager of the Southern Nevada Water Authority (SNWA), summarizes:

I don't know if without the Easter Earthquake, we get to Minute 319. We were doing some things, we were evolving a bit, but at a very slow pace, and then a sudden change occurred. A catalyst from nowhere, and it accelerated everything we did.[43]

Responding to the earthquake made it easier for Mexico and the United States to discuss how to break the inertia of the previous operating rules. The practical experience in dealing with the earthquake showed the value of turning water that would have otherwise been delivered into a future asset that could be negotiated. With this, a completely new episode in the binational relationship began.

No Negotiation without Representation

On the U.S. side of the Colorado River, the water is owned by the states, whereas on Mexico's side, the federal government owns it. Following the Supremacy Clause, which vests the U.S. government with the exclusive right to conduct international negotiations, the Department of State (DOS) has followed a diplomatic protocol that entrusts the Colorado River Basin states with a significant advisory role but does not involve them directly in the face-to-face binational water negotiations with Mexico.[44] This has frequently created a challenging situation, with the Basin states highly apprehensive about the DOS.[45] This time, however, the states were adamant from the outset that without their direct involvement in the binational negotiation process, no agreement with Mexico would be enforceable. They argued that they should be treated as cosovereigns and must have a seat at the negotiating table.[46] As Entsminger explains:

The states are the entitlement holders. We have the water. We have the facilities. We have the contracts. So, you can make declarations of intent, you can propose celebratory minutes, but if you want to make things happen, to get down on the ground, in order to use and store water from our reservoirs, you have to have our sign-off.[47]

On the heels of the 2007 guidelines negotiations, the Basin states were no longer willing to relinquish control over how the U.S. government would negotiate their Colorado River water supply with Mexico.[48] Moreover, the states argued, many of the elements that the United States could offer, or Mexico could request in a potential agreement, were things that the U.S. government did not have the authority to provide. Involving the Basin states in the formal negotiation process, however, required convincing the Legal Office of the DOS to break the long-standing protocol of country-to-country relations.[49]

Officials within the DOS held different views on the Basin states' involvement in the negotiations. On the one hand, the U.S. section of the IBWC was not against the states being present at the negotiating table. Although it implied a complete departure from the diplomatic protocol to which they had been accustomed since the 1950s, they agreed that having them participate would render the decisions made through the negotiation process more easily implementable.[50] As Carlos Peña, principal engineer of the U.S. section of the IBWC, describes:

We knew that whatever deal we would sign with Mexico had to be previously approved by the states. There was no point in seeking agreement with Mexico without first making sure we knew and protected the states' priorities. You did not want to find yourself proposing something that would be against the states' interests, triggering a situation where they would go and complain with their senators and congressmen, because then the negotiations would have been dead right there.[51]

However, outside of the IBWC, a number of DOS officials actively campaigned against the idea of conducting the binational process with any alteration to the standard diplomatic protocols. They opposed the notion that having sign-off from individual U.S. states on an international agreement should be required. From the Basin states' perspective, however, this opposition made no sense, given the complex structure of water rights and regulations for the Colorado River. As Jennifer Gimbel, director of the Colorado Water Conservation Board, notes:

Several officials at the State Department simply did not understand U.S. water law. If we followed their protocols, nothing was going to get done. It took a partnership between the Basin states and the Department of Interior to convince them otherwise. Getting to that point took an enormous amount of behind the scenes work. [52]

To get the DOS to change its stance, the Basin states counted on the support of the DOI through the U.S. Bureau of Reclamation, which is deeply acquainted with, and in charge of, much of the day-to-day Colorado River operations in the American Southwest. The leaders at the Bureau of Reclamation believed that the states' presence would significantly and favorably affect the binational negotiations, both in substance and process, in a number of ways.[53]

First, it would allow both federal governments to develop a vastly superior and more nuanced understanding of interests and concerns from the perspective of the water holders on the U.S. side of the basin. Second, everyone involved in the negotiations would be able to communicate directly, enabling better, quicker, and more reliable feedback on the proposals being discussed at the negotiating table instead of endlessly shuttling back and forth.[54] As Lorri Gray-Lee, director of the Lower Colorado Region at the U.S. Bureau of Reclamation, explains:

This was a matter of ownership. From the states' perspective, "You, U.S. federal government officials, are negotiating with another country about our asset, our water, and we want to be at the table." So, at DOI, we sought to facilitate an arrangement with Mexico, where at first, we could have one or two state individuals sitting in the room, not at the table, not talking, but at least sitting in the room. Because what I had learned in the past is that we would go into negotiations with Mexico, with only federal government representatives, and when I would go back to report with the states, and give them a blow by blow, there was always a bit of concern, sort of "what is she not telling us," regardless of our good relationship. The state representatives would come at any point and let me know, "It is not that we do not trust you, Lorri, it is just that we have responsibilities." So, by having one or two state representatives sitting in the room while we negotiated with Mexico, then when Reclamation came back to debrief with the state interests, they could jump in and share their take and experience on what we had done. And immediately we could just sense the trust between the group grow so much, because one of their own was telling them the story.[55]

Once there was agreement about the states' participation on the U.S. side, the U.S. federal government approached Mexican federal officials about the need for nonfederal U.S. actors to be active participants in the binational negotiations. This was initially disruptive for the Mexican officials, who had been accustomed to negotiating with their U.S. counterparts.[56] Wary of considering the possibility of the U.S. states sitting at the table, Mexico insisted that the negotiations should be between the two sections of the IBWC, with support from appointed experts from the federal agencies, CONAGUA, and the U.S. Bureau of Reclamation.[57] The Mexican officials argued that the U.S. federal government should figure out a mandate from the Basin states, then come and meet with Mexico. As Charles Cullom, manager of the Colorado River Programs of the Central Arizona Water Project, recalls:

I have colleagues in Mexico who were calling me to ask, "Why do the states want to get in the room? Why don't you let your federal government run the negotiations?" Well, because the states have the water rights and the contracts. And quite frankly, we want to observe how the Upper Basin states drive their issues which might be counter to the Lower Basin, how California might drive negotiations that might be adverse to Arizona, and so on. So we all need to be in the room to watch each other and watch the federal government.[58]

In this context, the U.S. Bureau of Reclamation and the U.S. section of the IBWC spent considerable time and effort to convince Mexican negotiators that the U.S. government would not be able to get anything done without the direct participation of the states.[59] Several Mexican officials, however, were still on the fence. This changed when the catastrophic Easter

Earthquake of April 2010 hit the Mexicali Valley. In the disaster's aftermath, in the process of defining binational emergency measures, the Mexican authorities realized that the involvement of the U.S. Basin states was critical to determine quick, efficient, and implementable actions.[60] As Karen Kwon, first assistant attorney general for the state of Colorado, explains:

Mexico saw that when the two countries need to have something done, and have it fast, as to face the aftermath of the earthquake, to have the states in the room, a few of us, even if only as advisors, to help negotiate the emergency measures, was useful. This was problematic for Mexico because they did not feel that they needed to have state representatives on their side of the room. So we had a very limited number of state people, one or two from the Upper Basin, and one for each three of the Lower Basin states. And as we worked on the emergency measures, we all became familiar with each other and realized we could trust one another and negotiate together.[61]

Although diplomatic protocol requires an equal number of representatives on each side, the Mexican representatives eventually went to their senior leaders and asked for approval to try something different, for an exception to the protocol. They made the case that to foster effective problem-solving in the binational negotiations, it would be best to allow observers from the Basin states.[62] Antonio Rascón, principal engineer of the Mexican section of the IBWC, describes this shift:

Traditionally, we have always conducted binational negotiations between federal representatives, exchanging notes between the two sections of the IBWC, and relying on the expertise of the Bureau of Reclamation and CONAGUA. For these negotiations, it became apparent early in the process that every critical issue would need to be vetted by the U.S. states and that their presence at the negotiating table would enhance and speed up the process. At the same time, we did not want to be overwhelmed by the number of representatives on the U.S. side; we wanted to keep some semblance of symmetry. So at first, the state representatives sat outside the room, to be consulted if needed. As trust was built, they came inside the room. And eventually, they sat at the table.[63]

Including the states in the negotiation process immediately enhanced the communication dynamics between the U.S. government and the seven Colorado River Basin states. It was a significant turn in the binational negotiations, to the benefit of both Mexico and the United States. As Robert Snow, the chief attorney for the Solicitor's Office of the DOI, explains:

For example, before the states were allowed to be in the room, in meeting X, the U.S. would make a proposal, and Mexico might say "no" to that particular request. And so we would go back to the states and say, "We tried really hard, we presented X, and

Mexico said that they could not do it for this and that reason." And the states would kind of scratch their heads, they would not be hostile, but they would wonder, "Did you really try hard enough, did you really do a good enough job to explain that issue, did you really tell them how important it is to us? How could they say no!" But then, when we secured Mexico's permission to have state observers, we would go into negotiations, propose Y, and Mexico would say "no." So, we would go back to the states and explain, and they would start scratching their heads, until the state representative would intervene and say, "Lorri [Gray-Lee] did a wonderful job, she took a crack at it really hard, she tried her best, and it is just not going to fly. You need to listen to her when she says that it's not going to work." And all of sudden the states' mindset moved from disappointment with our inability to achieve X or Y, into problem-solving and say, "Okay, if it is never going to fly, what if we did it this way, what if we did it that way, and what if we packaged it with this other benefit for Mexico." This gave us a way to move past the internal dynamics and focus on the substance.

This acknowledgment of the role of the U.S. Basin states along with the IBWC, the Bureau of Reclamation, and CONAGUA in the binational management of the Colorado River was a critical breakthrough. As Entsminger notes, "Once all sides figured that they would all have to act as cosovereigns, instead of a hierarchy or pecking order, that really paved the way forward."[64] With a more appropriate structure to incorporate the diverse interests of the Basin states in a binational setting, the two countries were able to turn their attention to negotiating an actionable agreement. As Gray-Lee summarizes:

The key is to have an agreement that everyone can buy into. There are so many holes for that marble to go through, everyone has a reject button, so you need to find a way to involve everyone to make sure you can address those holes. It is not about if an answer sounds right. If it is not "their answer," you will not get to the end goal.[65]

8 Broadening Perspectives

Seeing Is Believing

The 1944 United States–Mexico Water Treaty includes a provision that specifies the right of the United States, under conditions of "extraordinary drought," to unilaterally reduce the annual amount of Colorado River water to be delivered to Mexico. The treaty does not include, however, the following critical specifications: (1) the definition of "extraordinary drought," (2) which criteria trigger shortage conditions, (3) the volume of the shortage, and (4) how the reduction will be implemented. These uncertainties needed to be addressed, and unless the United States chose to unilaterally enforce a mechanism and engage in a direct conflict with Mexico, the countries would need to decide together how to handle them. Reaching an understanding, however, would not be easy because the two countries were not approaching the drought from the same vantage point. In this sense, it is critical to understand the domestic circumstances on the heels of which the U.S. negotiators approached Mexico.

On the U.S. side, the period from 2000 to 2007 was the driest eight-year period in more than a century of historical records on the Colorado River. From the fall of 1999 through the fall of 2007, reservoir levels in the Colorado River system decreased drastically, from 55.8 million acre-feet (94 percent of capacity) to 32.1 million acre-feet (54 percent of capacity).[1] The declining reservoir levels and diminished runoffs forced the Upper and Lower Basin states to consider determining, for the first time ever, specific guidelines to coordinate the operations of Lake Powell and Lake Mead, in order to deal proactively with looming shortages in the present and near future.[2] As Karen Kwon, first assistant attorney general for the state of Colorado, explains:

Going to litigation was an option, but the threat of nine justices from the East Coast figuring out what to do with the Colorado River supply, after what undoubtedly would be a very protracted litigation, terrified everybody. We could not know what the outcome would be.[3]

The Upper and Lower Basin states engaged in negotiations for three years, starting in 2004, with the mission to "move away from litigation, be proactive, avoid crises, maximize the gains, and reduce the losses."[4] In December 2007, a Record of Decision was issued to officially adopt the Interim Guidelines for the Coordinated Operation of Lake Mead and Powell, which extend through 2026.

Following the states' consensus, operational rules to better manage the Colorado River water in the context of drought, were set, including the following:

• Three shortage conditions (light, heavy, and extreme), depending on the reservoir levels at Lake Mead, which trigger corresponding reductions in the amount of water available to the Lower Basin states of Arizona and Nevada, and in extreme conditions, California.
• The fully coordinated operation of Lake Mead and Lake Powell, to minimize shortages in the Lower Basin and avoid water use curtailments in the Upper Basin.
• An Intentionally Created Surplus (ICS) mechanism to provide for the creation, accounting, storage, and deferred delivery of conserved water in Lake Mead.
• Limited surplus availability, in select high reservoir conditions, for use by the Lower Basin states.[5]

Therefore, after decades without a coordinated framework with which to deal with drought, the Basin states had reached a consensus that, moving forward, it was better to voluntarily take earlier, smaller shortages to manage the basin's water, rather than experience very large and painful shortages later.[6] This strategy, tied to reservoir levels, would reduce the frequency of shortages by helping store more water and keeping reservoir levels higher.[7] When the U.S. states were defining this approach, they included forecasts of shortages for Mexico in their modeling.[8] As John Entsminger, senior deputy general manager of the Southern Nevada Water Authority (SNWA), explains:

During the domestic negotiations, we sent a cover letter to the secretary of the interior outlining the states' proposal, 90 percent of which became the 2007 Guidelines.

In that cover letter to Secretary Kempthorne, we said, "It is going to be politically impossible for the states to take shortages and have the U.S. federal government simultaneously deliver the full water allocation to Mexico. So, we want to get the Guidelines done, and once they are done, we would like to begin negotiations with Mexico on two things: we want to agree with them on shortages and we want to agree with them on storage."[9]

Hence, over the years, the Colorado River Basin states had developed a process for discussing the problems posed by drought, assessing the probabilities of different scenarios. They had compared, for example, what would happen if they did nothing or implemented plan A, B, or C; as well as what approximate shortages they would face, and with what frequency. Mexico, however, had not developed that level of expertise at all, because it had not been invited to be part of such analysis. As Don Ostler, executive director and secretary of the Upper Colorado River Commission, notes:

Historically, Mexico had not been involved in the discussions about general Colorado River Basin issues. They were not partners but rather customers, with whom the U.S. had a contract for a certain amount of water, and we just delivered it. So there was no real involvement from Mexico in understanding the future problems. We were not working together as a group.[10]

In light of this, a critical hurdle to start the binational negotiations was to work against the assumption by some U.S. stakeholders that Mexico, seen as a customer, would simply support an agreement that established the 2007 U.S. Interim Guidelines into a binational context. Mexico, it was thought, should automatically agree to reservoir levels as the criterion for determining shortage allocations. These assumptions were problematic, as Sally Spener, foreign affairs secretary of the U.S. section of the International Boundary and Water Commission (IBWC), explains:

There sometimes is really a lack of true understanding and appreciation that Mexico is a sovereign nation. We may think that this is the greatest idea in the world, and that it would be in the best interest of both the U.S. and Mexico, but at the end of the day, Mexico is a sovereign nation. Things are not going to happen unless Mexico agrees that it is in their best interest. What the U.S. may think is in the best interest of both, that may simply not be the view in Mexico. In terms of preconceptions, that is something we had to deal with. We would be told, "Why don't you just make them do this?" Well, "because we can't tell them to do anything, Mexico is a sovereign nation!"[11]

Especially in the context of the lack of shared expertise and the historic mistrust between the two countries, starting off with the assumption that

Mexico would agree with what the stakeholders in the United States had previously said Mexico had to agree to was unhelpful. As Charles Cullom, manager of the Colorado River Programs of the Central Arizona Water Project, notes, "speaking in hyperbole, as you might expect, Mexico found that a little bit patronizing. Because Mexico did not have to accept shortages the way the U.S. defines them."[12]

Once the negotiations between the two sides began, Mexico argued that the countries should focus on defining the 1944 treaty's term, "extraordinary drought."[13] The U.S. negotiators explained that they did not consider it feasible to define "extraordinary drought" in such a diverse and expansive basin. They reiterated that the two countries should choose to use reservoir levels as the indicator to determine when shortage would need to be implemented.[14] The Mexican negotiators responded that they would prefer to have shortages tied to one of the well-documented drought indices in the scientific literature, rather than to reservoir levels.[15] The U.S. negotiators replied that drought indicators work well on a year-to-year basis, but they are not as effective for multiyear cases in which there is ample capacity to store water.

The Colorado River system is known around the world precisely because it can store over four times its average annual inflow. The stakeholders make it through periods of drought without shortage for most users, as they have over the last several years, because they can carry over storage from abundant years to use during dry years. So the U.S. negotiators offered the example that one year may see drought in Wyoming, heavy snow in Utah, no rainfall in southern Colorado, and floods in northern Colorado; and no matter how much you analyze precipitation, snowpack, moisture content of the soil, and stream gauges, the most accurate and integrated compilation of all those different metrics is the reservoir levels.[16]

The United States insisted that this was the reason why the operation of Lake Powell and Lake Mead should be determined on the basis of existing and projected reservoir operations. These operations change depending on how full or empty the reservoirs are, and if the United States had found better criteria with which to manage the water, they would likely be using them.[17] Mexican negotiators, however, were skeptical of the use of reservoir levels as the trigger for shortage. They did not trust that reservoir elevations were solely indicative of hydrological conditions. They were also concerned that from an operational standpoint, shortage sharing under low reservoir conditions would not necessarily be strictly proportional. The Mexican officials insisted on measures that could be observed and validated from a neutral-party perspective.[18]

Eventually, the U.S. negotiators comprehended Mexico's concerns and realized that to break this impasse, both sides would need to build trust through shared experience and understanding. With this aim, the two countries established a work group to study metrics that might give Mexican negotiators more comfort as to the overall hydrology of the basin. The seven U.S. states had already gone through the data when negotiating the domestic 2007 guidelines, and they were unable to find a better indicator than the reservoir levels. In repeating this process with Mexico, once again the metrics showed very little correlation to any other marker that could satisfy both sides. As Patrick Tyrrell, head of the State Engineer's Office of Wyoming, notes:

It increasingly became apparent that the only meaningful indicator is in the reservoir levels. It was sort of a process of attrition. At some point, we did not have anything else we could try. I think Mexico started to consider "Maybe we can go forward with the reservoirs as the shortage trigger, because nothing else seems to be working."[19]

Mexican negotiators understood that the reservoir levels are a summary of the hydrological and operational variables in the basin, but still feared that the levels could be manipulated by political decisions.[20] Mexico's worry was that through one mechanism or the other, the levels at the reservoirs would change artificially. The two countries were stuck in a deadlock until the United States redefined its strategy to effectively assuage Mexico's concern. As Carlos Peña, principal engineer of the U.S. section of the IBWC, explains:

We invited the Mexican officials on a tour around the Basin, and we went from Hoover Dam all the way to the Rockies, visiting different reservoirs. Then we gathered with the Mexican officials, and step by step, chronologically, we described the different regulations and Supreme Court decisions that shape our operations. They were rolling their eyes, after multiple four-hour presentations, conveying "Why did you make the Law of the River so complicated?" Yet, at the same time, those explanations were critical to convey the realities of the basin, and to explain that the seven U.S. states do not trust each other. On a personal level, people understand one another, but each state is watching each other. So, we do not need water cops because we have a built-in system where if one state is taking more water than it should, its neighboring state is going to find out, and is going to go to report it to the Department of Interior.[21]

The U.S. negotiators realized that the Mexican stakeholders responded well to the opportunity not only to hear how the United States operates the Colorado River Basin, but also to visit and see how it works in practice. So the United States proposed more tours, inviting the Mexican section IBWC commissioner and his technical staff to a variety of different reservoirs. The aim was to show how the hydrological and environmental data are collected in those reservoirs, how the United States monitors the flows, and how that information is transmitted to a centralized location.[22] Then the U.S. Bureau of Reclamation offered a detailed explanation of how they define "shortage," and how Lake Powell and Lake Mead interact with such an assessment. Slowly, step by step, these efforts had a transformative effect, as Edward Drusina, commissioner of the U.S. section of the IBWC, describes:

These tours had a lot to do with the fact that we had beaten up these topics so much, going over and over, for more than a year, and neither country really seeing a way through. So we proposed to tour the watershed and the reservoirs, as a way to try to inform the Mexican negotiators of how we manage the basin. This allowed them to see and take into consideration what we were saying, and look at it from our perspective; to understand our scientific approach and capital investment to monitor the basin, including the agreements that we have established between the states and the federal government. It was our opportunity to demonstrate our thoroughness in evaluating the watershed, and to show to Mexico that we are not trying to hide something and that everything is out in the open.[23]

Supported by these visits, the trust and understanding across the border that had been missing for many years, and the absence of which had repeatedly hindered the ability to collaboratively improve conditions in the basin, started to develop.[24] For decades, both sides had known very well what the 1944 treaty said, but neither side knew much about what those terms meant in practice for the other side. As Peter Culp, chief attorney at the U.S.-based Sonoran Institute, explains:

Much of the border relationship is built around a mirage that each side has constructed about the other side, about what their values and interests really are. When you bring people together across the border, you find that the challenges on each side are not as different as you think they are; there are a myriad of issues that need to be understood and addressed together. You recognize that in the face of important disparities in terms of power and resources, there needs to be a partnership to build trust and understanding.[25]

The tours to look at canals, dams, reservoirs, and irrigation districts allowed the negotiators to get together, talk through issues, and truly see how water is managed on the other side of the border. The result was an increase in the level of trust between the parties, built upon a greater technical understanding of the system and a more accurate take on the different roles that water resources play in both countries.

Sharing Tools for Better Understanding

One of the challenges in a river system such as the Colorado, where the major infrastructure is located upstream, is that the downstream neighbor, Mexico, has little ability to directly influence the operations that ultimately affect the way in which water is delivered.[26] This situation creates an imbalance of influence, as the actions of one country directly affect the other, but such is not the case the other way around. This challenge is further compounded when the parties rely on a different set of tools to evaluate the conditions in the basin.

In Mexico, both the IBWC and the National Water Commission (Comisión Nacional del Agua, or CONAGUA) manage deliveries and operations in the Mexicali Valley on the basis of the Water Evaluation and Planning System (WEAP) model. This model incorporates surface water delivery, demand infiltration, and groundwater utilization, but it is not as robust on reservoir operations because Mexico has no significant storage facilities. The United States relies on the Colorado River Simulation System (CRSS) model to operate the 10 major reservoirs managed by the Bureau of Reclamation. All of the state and federal stakeholders have fluency in the CRSS, the data that it analyzes, its products, and how this information influences reservoir operations, which is what drives risk in the Colorado River system.[27]

Because Mexico relies on WEAP, and thus cannot account accurately for Colorado River Basin reservoir operations, Mexican negotiators had considerable trouble evaluating U.S. data and trusting U.S. policy proposals at the beginning of the negotiations.[28] This posed a significant hurdle because in the basin, swings in hydrology, which can go from unregulated inflows of 24 million acre-feet in one year to less than 4 million acre-feet a couple years later, can be fully gauged only within the context of reservoir storage that can accommodate up to 60 million acre-feet. Mexican officials needed to find a way to be on an equal technical footing with their U.S.

counterparts to evaluate the reservoirs' data and operations, so that both sides could confidently discuss policy options.[29]

In consequence, the two countries decided to establish a work group composed of binational experts, with the aim of building trust and a technical understanding between the two sides.[30] As Lorri Gray-Lee, director of the Lower Colorado Region at the U.S. Bureau of Reclamation, explains:

The U.S. stakeholders had been talking about dealing with shortage for years. That was not the case for Mexico on the Colorado. So their negotiators had to take a lot of information in and get comfortable much faster. In coordination with the IBWC, Reclamation shared modeling tools so that Mexico would not have to create everything from scratch, so that they could understand what and how we were managing the river, and then shape their own perspective.[31]

The binational work group spent 18 months testing modeling tools, with a focus on CRSS. In that process, the two sides were able to progressively track current and future hydrologic and climatic conditions in the basin from a common framework. Trust was enhanced, as Mexican officials were able to develop a more accurate and nuanced understanding of U.S. reservoir operations. As Adriana Reséndez, technical director of the Colorado River Program of the IBWC's Mexican section, describes:

The work-group process allowed us to understand the modeling that determines the U.S. decisions in a way Mexico had never understood before. It was an enormous change. We started from zero, everything about it was new; we had to process all the new information, test and run the CRSS, and then adapt it to evaluate scenarios that directly apply to us. Progressively, we were able to develop a more nuanced sense of the magnitude and impact of the reservoirs, as they interact with the hydrology of the basin. With the appropriate tools to gauge operations over the entire basin, it became clearer what to seek under a binational framework.[32]

Reaching this shared understanding with regard to the modeling, however, was not without its hurdles. The Upper Basin states originally came into the negotiations with a projection, which they had been using for over a decade, of what their future water use would be. As the negotiations unfolded, in the middle of a work-group meeting, they asked the Bureau of Reclamation to update their water usage schedule. In either schedule, they would come to use their full allocation according to the Law of the River, but in the updated schedule, this takes place sooner. When the parties ran that update in the model, it increased the probabilities of projected shortages for the Lower Basin states and for Mexico. As Jennifer Pitt, director of the Colorado River Project at the Environmental Defense Fund, explains:

That became a real flashpoint, because coming into the process Mexico was not accustomed to using these modeling tools. So, in the context of discussing reservoir operations, the U.S. came in and said to Mexico, "We want to give you a modeling update." Mexico looked at it, and their first reaction was, "You are showing us a greater probability of shortages, what are you doing? You are cooking the system on us!" The Mexican delegation literally stopped the meeting for an hour. There was some intense conversation in Spanish, which some of the U.S. stakeholders could not understand because we all do not have bilingual skills as they do; it happened right in front of us. At some point, somebody from the State of California decided that the best thing we could do to defuse the tension is to have an afternoon snack, and went to the hotel and asked for cookies and coffee. So, as the Mexican delegation was thinking about walking out, the cookies came in, and more so on the Mexican side than the U.S. side, their sense of hospitality is, "If somebody offers you something, you do not refuse it," so they stayed, and that helped us get through the rest of the conversation.[33]

To be sitting at a negotiating table, being asked to consider entering into a voluntary shortage agreement, and having the shortage projections set in front of you actually look worse suggested that the parties did not necessarily think through all the scenarios of how Mexican officials might react to being shown the modeling update.[34] Once the situation was defused, the Mexican negotiators were better able to understand that the modeling update was not meant to trick them. They realized that had the United States been trying to trick Mexico, the Americans would have done the opposite; they would have made it seem as though shortages were less likely to occur in the future, so as to garner agreement.[35]

By empowering Mexico's technical staff to master CRSS as a reliable tool for testing upstream operations, Mexican officials were better able to evaluate how different measures being discussed at the negotiating table could affect the Colorado River Basin, the Mexicali Valley, and the Colorado River Delta.[36] Together, the two sides could precisely replicate the different reservoir operations scenarios that could result from the proposed agreement.[37] This made it easier to shed preconceptions about why the other side was taking a certain position and actually understand the underlying interests at play.[38] This was a critically helpful strategy, as Patricia Mulroy, general manager of the SNWA, explains:

You need to get the technical people in the room and have them speak a common language and understand where the other side is coming from. You need to get the talking heads out of the room, get them out of Dodge! You have to create a space, a safe space, where conversations can be had on the nitty-gritty. So that we attribute the same meaning to the same words and have the same understanding of the same concepts. Whether there are language issues, cultural issues, legal issues, it has worked among the seven states in earlier processes, and it worked internationally with Mexico. Let those who do not have political ambitions, let them have their very technical, very nuanced conversations in their own language, to set the stage. Unless you do that, nothing else moves. Great rhetoric is not going to do it.[39]

Moreover, neither delegation needed to define the right policy to operate the reservoirs right away, but instead both countries were able to jointly test, "If you operate the reservoirs in X manner, it will produce Y results, and if you operate the reservoirs in Z way, it will produce W results." Through that process, the two sides were able to reevaluate natural resource management strategies from a shared technical framework, which increased trust between the two groups of negotiators. As José Gutiérrez, deputy general manager of binational projects at Mexico's National Water Commission, summarizes:

The work group on hydrology, I must confess, became a big family. Great camaraderie developed between us all. Getting to have a deep understanding of how the Colorado River Basin is managed and operated on the U.S. side was magnificent. It allowed us to explore a wide array of issues and to realize that whatever deal we reached, it could really be a win-win package.[40]

Putting Yourself in Their Shoes

In the aftermath of the Easter Earthquake, which happened in 2010 near the border separating Baja California from California, Mexico's Treasury Ministry, which tends to sway discussions in Mexican politics, was especially concerned with finding mechanisms to finance the repair of the damaged infrastructure in the Mexicali Valley.[41] The Ministry argued that Mexico should sell water to the United States in exchange for investment in the country's crippled irrigation infrastructure, as a crucial component of a potential binational agreement.[42] However, the U.S. estimates about the reference prices at which they would be willing to even consider buying some of the Colorado River water that Mexico could no longer use as a result of the earthquake were well below the market rates that Mexico's Treasury Ministry had envisioned.[43]

In turn, the Mexican negotiators explained to their back table that the financial resources that could be obtained in water trades were well below the Treasury's forecasts. They made the case that instead, Mexico should focus not only on rebuilding its infrastructure, but also on improving conservation measures and enhancing environmental restoration, in order to reach a broader agreement in scope, which would then open the door for more opportunities further down the line. As Óscar Ibáñez, chief of staff for the director-general of CONAGUA, recalls:

The facts underscored that the negotiation could not solely hinge on sharing in shortages and engaging in a swap of water. It was necessary to seize the window of opportunity to bring other issues to the table to shape a better package for Mexico. Repairing the infrastructure we already had before the earthquake was not changing the status quo.[44]

Considerable information about the hydrological conditions in the Colorado River Basin is publicly available, so the Mexican officials knew coming into the negotiations that the probability of shortages would only increase in the near future. They were aware that the United States had started to evaluate mechanisms to provide the seven Basin states with multiple alternatives to effectively face a future with reduced flows. The United States has an extensive research program that has highlighted conventional and unconventional approaches to increasing water availability in the future, such as tapping important aquifers in Wyoming and Utah, building desalting plants, paying water users to reduce consumption, and even bringing icebergs from the Arctic.[45] The argument by the Mexican negotiators was that, from Mexico's perspective, the binational agreement had to go beyond determining shortage triggers and financing infrastructure repairs—it also had to focus on increasing the overall availability of water on Mexico's side.[46]

So, as a first step, the Mexican officials conveyed to the U.S. negotiators that the country needed to share in surpluses, from an equity and political standpoint.[47] Surplus sharing was not part of the initial U.S. proposal in the negotiations. Gutiérrez describes the situation:

Mexico could not voluntarily share in shortages without the support of an agreement that involved benefits in a wider set of issues. Otherwise, a "revolution" would occur on our side, and no political actor would support any binational agreement. We needed to be able to show to our constituents that we were sharing in shortages but that in order to prevent that from happening as much as we could, we were going to jointly engage in projects to conserve and create new water resources. It was critical to be able to speak to the farmers and truthfully say, "We tried all these different options, this is what we were able to get, this is what we could not get, and moving forward these are the new conditions." We know, in the context of drought, and future climate change, that the probability of shortage is much larger than the probability of surplus, we clearly know that, but it is important to have a framework that encompasses different scenarios.[48]

The request to share in surplus management and dispersal with Mexico was a hard adjustment for the U.S. negotiators to make.[49] The way that surplus works on the U.S. side is that the water agencies in the Lower Basin states of California, Nevada, and Arizona can take more than their regular annual water allocations in select circumstances, when reservoir levels at Lake Mead are high.[50] However, the Upper Basin states dispute the notion that any surplus in the Colorado River Basin should exist in the first place, so the idea of extending that provision to Mexico, heretofore unprecedented, was tremendously difficult to overcome.[51]

To do so, the U.S. negotiators had to find ways to look at Mexico's request by putting themselves in their shoes, so as to see it from their point of view. This helped them to evaluate whether to adjust their proposal. As Drusina explains:

We would go to the sessions with our own intended outcome of what we were hoping to get, but we would listen, and then try to place ourselves in their shoes. It was hard for some people on our side, very hard. So we would have to caucus, and give those individuals an opportunity to express their opinion. Then normally someone would say, "Don't you think Mexico is taking this into consideration because they have X or Y to deal with?" And yes, from their perspective, "If we are talking about shortage, why are we not talking about surplus?" Water is such a sensitive political issue. It can become a nightmare the moment there is even the slightest impression you are giving away water. [52]

In this receptive dynamic, the Mexican negotiators were able to explain to the U.S. delegation the things that simply could not be proposed to the back tables in Mexico.[53] In this collaborative approach to negotiation, it was critical that both sides clearly and honestly articulate the items that were definitively off the table. The parties recognized that they could not negotiate from a zero-sum, win-lose perspective.[54] They would have to approach it as a win-win and find the trades that worked for both sides.[55] As Entsminger explains:

To allow Mexico to have surplus was one of the hardest things. The only way we figured it out was not having the U.S. be the one that grants surplus to Mexico, but instead having the three Lower Basin contractors, Metropolitan Water District of Southern California, Southern Nevada Water Authority, and Central Arizona Project, give a part of our own surplus. That let the Upper Basin say, "Okay, the total amount of surplus between the Lower Basin and Mexico is not changing, it is just being divided differently." And "the U.S. states are not setting any precedent because the contractors are the ones sharing in surplus."[56]

The three water agencies were willing to share in a surplus because a binational agreement would provide them with the ability to fund water conservation projects in Mexico, from which they could then share in water savings.[57] There is significant potential in those projects, both in terms of the magnitude of water that can be saved and the lower costs at which it can be done, to the benefit of U.S. water users.[58] There are also benefits to be seized from increasing reservoir levels at Lake Mead by storing Mexico's water allocation there, which likely enhances the probability of surplus occurring in the first place. None of this would be possible without a binational agreement in place.[59] As Peña notes:

We were quite conscious that we had to seize a window of opportunity to reach a package deal. Each stakeholder, there were issues where you'd realize, "well, that part of the deal is a little bit rough on the edges, I don't necessarily like that piece much; but that other piece, that looks great for me." The fact it was a whole package, that is what allowed us to move forward, balancing what people could live with, with what people truly needed.[60]

Seizing trades through the differences in infrastructure development and price of doing business helps both sides augment the water supply in ways that they could not do on their own.[61] For example, cheaper conservation projects in Mexico can yield better water savings for both sides. If the United States jointly funds such projects, it gets access to more water, at a lower cost for its ratepayers, whereas Mexico also gets more water, at a lower cost than if it fully funded the projects on its own.[62]

The focus on how to create more benefits by seizing on the fact that costs and benefits are distributed differently across the two countries, while being mindful of how carefully planned trades can allow the two sides to meet their interests more effectively, stands in stark contrast to the deadlock that had previously characterized the binational interactions. This practice allowed the negotiators to evaluate with fresh eyes issues that had been unresolved.

It became more apparent to Mexican officials that there were significant benefits to using the reservoir levels as the trigger measure, not only for shortage, but particularly for surplus.[63] Otherwise, for example, if the two countries were to choose a precipitation index to determine a shortage for

Mexico, then in practice, at a time when the reservoir levels at Lake Mead are high, but it is a dry run-off year in the basin, Mexico would be taking shortage while the Lower Basin states would receive surplus. If each country had a different set of indicators, the countries would be out-of-sync and in constant conflict, in turn creating tremendous political pressure.[64] As Terrance Fulp, deputy regional director of the Lower Colorado Region at the U.S. Bureau of Reclamation, notes:

That conclusion took us months to reach. For equity purposes, when one country is in shortage, taking reductions, both countries should. The flipside is, when one country is getting additional water, both countries should. That really helped us when it came to finding those triggers, as it pertains to the elevation levels in the reservoirs, because such an arrangement made sense, was equitable, and the countries could really sell the concept to their stakeholders: "We are really sharing in these efforts."[65]

The two sides had to make sure to find that sweet spot where they could find a relative balance of benefits for both countries. Ultimately, no matter how solid the deal at the negotiating table, the negotiators would need to sell the deal to the decision-makers and constituents, and they also needed to make sure that the agreement would be perceived as being to their own benefit.[66] As Michael Connor, then-commissioner of the U.S. Bureau of Reclamation, explains:

It took a while to understand what Mexico needed strategically in the big picture, how the deal had to be structured so that they could go back to their constituents and on the merits, show, "This is a good deal and it does not undermine our interests." We needed to have shortages shared. They needed, if they were going to do that, they needed to be able to say, "We have a framework to avoid shortages. We agreed to the concept of shortages, but there are mechanisms here so that we can manage it, that we can create water and that will offset these shortages." So we both had to understand the needs of the key constituencies and how the agreement is going to represent victory for all those folks in the best possible way. I cannot think of anything more important than through open, candid dialogue getting to that framework as early on as possible. When we achieved that, that is when we could start to see how the senior officials could talk of the agreement in a way that captures everybody's key interests, outlining "This is an agreement that reflects binational benefits on as much an equal footing as you can get."[67]

From that perspective, it became easier to understand where the other side was coming from—the values and concerns driving the arguments that they were making in the negotiations. Recognizing that these values and concerns are legitimate, the two sides could think about how to better address them and come to find an approach that would be supported and viewed as a step forward on both sides.[68] This was a significant change in the binational relationship. As Entsminger summarizes:

And the thing is, the small binational team, we probably spent 14,000 hours together, entire days at a time, grinding through, going backwards, going sideways, getting mad, getting back together, and at some point, we started to like each other. We were in a three-day negotiation down in San Diego, and I had to fly home to Las Vegas to run a board meeting. So, I am in San Diego for the first day meeting, fly back home in the afternoon. I wake up, run the morning meeting, and take a flight back to San Diego. I land, and walk back into the binational negotiating room at about noon, and the whole side of the Mexican table, they start clapping, celebrating, and I say to myself, "I love these guys." In that environment, getting to know the priorities of your partners, as if they were your own, that is why we had been successful domestically in negotiating the 2007 Guidelines; I can argue Colorado's position, I can argue California's position; I can argue Arizona's position. But before we did Minute 319, I could not argue Mexico's position. Now I can.[69]

9 Tearing Down Walls

Bringing More Issues to the Table

During the past two decades, through a combination of trial and error, public outreach, coalition building, and adaptive leadership, environmental nongovernmental organizations (NGOs) have significantly transformed the way that they approach negotiations surrounding the Colorado River. This shift began in the late 1990s, following a small rebirth of the Colorado River Delta. Between the mid-1960s and the early 1980s, the delta received little to no water from the mainstem of the Colorado River, and had been declared dead in the scientific literature. After unexpected floods and some wet years in the mid-1980s and 1990s, native cottonwoods and willows suddenly sprouted from the arid riverbanks. This underscored that the ecosystem was more resilient than it had been given credit for. As Taylor Hawes, director of the Colorado River Program at the Nature Conservancy, explains, "That was the startling realization that even though the delta looked like a barren landscape, with a little bit of water, it could be radically revitalized."[1]

As a result of this discovery, research universities and environmental organizations on both sides of the border began to take inventory of the marshes and wetlands in the region. Step by step, environmental experts began to envision a restoration strategy based on pulse and base flows, mirroring the way in which rivers in this arid region work. At the time, however, nobody knew how to make this happen from a political and legal standpoint. As time went by, it became clear that receiving water for environmental restoration from any involved government entity would be quite difficult because all the water rights in the Colorado River Basin had been allocated long ago.[2]

Therefore, the NGOs' efforts centered on identifying water sources for sale, wastewater from municipalities, and farming water sitting idle. This eventually led to the creation of the Colorado River Delta Water Trust, a binational effort led by Pronatura and the Sonoran Institute, among other partners, to create an environmental water bank. Their next step was to secure small federal land concessions to monitor and simulate base flows in a few pilot restoration sites in the delta. These restoration efforts were successful.[3]

Yet the NGOs knew they would need access to public infrastructure, such as reservoirs and dams, if they ever were going to be successful in creating a pulse flow that would have an impact over the whole delta. This meant that they needed to build relationships with public officials on both sides of the border in order to create a rapport and understanding about its potential benefits.[4] This was no easy task in either country.

On the U.S. side, the NGOs had not had a positive relationship with the states, urban water agencies, and irrigation districts for a long time. They had been stuck, with little success, working under the paradigm of environmental activism that relies on lawsuits to trigger environmental action. Confrontations about water rights had been costly, difficult, brewed mistrust, and achieved little in the way of results.[5] In light of this, a small group of NGOs gradually realized that they needed to try to move away from the adversarial stance of pursuing litigation. Instead, they would promote conversations about how to address environmental challenges collaboratively, working within rather than against the extensive body of laws, decrees, regulations, contracts, and court decisions that make up the Law of the River. This new approach, they concluded, would be a better way to reach implementable solutions.[6]

In these efforts, in the early and mid-2000s, the NGOs produced several publications describing their restoration aims, outlining actionable proposals.[7] In their publications, the NGOs underscored that there was a consensus in the environmental community, based on years of research and workshops, about what could be done to restore ecosystems for the benefit of the border communities beyond the priorities of environmental interests.[8]

The Bureau of Reclamation of the U.S. Department of the Interior (DOI) welcomed these recommendations and considered them an important piece of the puzzle of how to enhance sustainability in the Colorado

River Basin.[9] Subsequently, during the second term of the George W. Bush administration, as the Upper and Lower Basin states negotiated what would become the 2007 Interim Guidelines, the NGOs restated their recommendations to high-ranking officials from the DOI, including official written communications with Secretary of the Interior Dirk Kempthorne.[10] By the time the Obama administration came to office, the perception about the NGOs was beginning to change. The NGOs were often in the room during U.S. federal-state interactions, more so than a decade before.[11]

To understand this move toward a more collaborative dynamic between government officials and environmental advocates, it is also necessary to look at how the NGOs became more involved on Mexico's side. The bureaucratic organization of public agencies often results in the independent consideration of issues that, in practice, are inevitably connected and would be better managed in a cohesive manner.[12] This had long been the case in Mexico, where water management and environmental restoration had been dealt with separately for decades. As Osvel Hinojosa, director of the Water and Wetlands Program at Pronatura, explains, in the late 1990s, when the Mexican NGOs attempted to meet with the National Water Commission (Comisión Nacional del Agua, or CONAGUA) about water for environmental restoration, "it was almost impossible to find an official willing to talk to them."[13]

The first significant step toward overcoming this hurdle was a federal legislation reform in 2004. During President Vicente Fox's administration, CONAGUA was entrusted, for the first time ever, with the legal responsibility of protecting the environment as part of its water management mandate. This reform encouraged officials to work within a broader framework, mindful of environmental protection.[14] But finding ways to prompt domestic government agencies, as well as water users, to look at things differently was no easy task. The bureaucratic tendency to move very slowly usually hinders change, however beneficial the change may be, and such was the case in Mexico. Therefore, the vast majority of the CONAGUA staff remained focused on balancing the needs of the agricultural irrigation districts and municipal water agencies.[15]

When President Felipe Calderón came to office (2006–2012), his administration provided greater emphasis on environmental interests due to three factors. The first factor was the background of the people whom he appointed to lead CONAGUA and the International Boundary and Water Commission (IBWC). Prior to being appointed director-general of CONAGUA, José Luis Luege had been Mexico's attorney general for the Environment and secretary of the Environment and Natural Resources in the Fox administration.[16] Because of this experience, he was familiar with the issue of restoration in the Colorado River Delta. Luege understood the priorities of the NGOs acting in the region, as he had collaborated with them to protect endangered species in the Sea of Cortez. Through this involvement, he had built a relationship with Pronatura, along with additional NGO partners in Mexico and the United States. The commissioner of Mexico's IBWC section, Roberto Salmón, had also previously worked with Luege.[17]

The second factor was that during this period of time, both countries had endured the aftermath of the All-American Canal conflict, with the ensuing acrimony and significant financial losses from the litigation. As a result of the severe drought conditions that the Colorado River Basin had been experiencing since the turn of the century, domestic stakeholders started to consider options to change the status quo that would perhaps otherwise not have been explored. It is in this context that the NGOs found a more receptive audience to their message that moving away from the zero-sum mindset would be critical to the successful and sustainable management of the basin's water resources.[18]

The third factor was that after the 2007 U.S. Interim Guidelines were negotiated, when the United States approached Mexico about voluntarily sharing in Colorado River shortages, Mexican officials found themselves in a bind. If they refused to accept the shortages, they would risk unilateral water restriction from their upstream neighbor. However, if they were to agree to the shortages, that would spell political suicide domestically.[19] In this scenario, recognizing the lack of alternatives, Mexico's federal government started to realize that including the interests of the NGOs could infuse much-needed flexibility into the binational negotiations.[20]

Arguing in favor of environmental restoration offered the opportunity to make the case for a principle of fairness that went beyond domestic interests. It gave an international dimension to the negotiations that surpassed the binational context, as the Upper Gulf of California and the Colorado River Delta had been designated a Biosphere Reserve by the United Nations

Educational, Scientific and Cultural Organization (UNESCO). As Salmón explains:

Including an environmental aspect in our proposal was critical. It provided us with legitimacy to discuss issues beyond the two traditional items, water for the cities and water for agriculture. By involving environmental restoration as a third element, we were bringing to the table an element that inevitably has no borders. This would in turn broaden the discussion about water management. And by requesting an environmental component, from a governmental perspective, the NGOs' proposals would be considered more thoroughly, which rendered their input more effective.[21]

In turn, Mexican officials articulated very early in the negotiations that they valued working toward restoring the delta.[22] This was rather perplexing for many U.S. states, which were coming to these negotiations to talk about shortage in the context of reduced water supplies.[23] Their concern was that an additional consumptive use, even if for environmental purposes, could only hinder the efforts to fight the drought, putting more demand on the system.[24] Mexico countered that if the two countries enhanced conservation efforts, there would be enough flows to protect and enhance the environment, which in turn would benefit everyone, as it would increase aquifer replenishment.[25]

The seven states, however, did not want to suggest that there was a duty to provide Mexico with water for environmental purposes. They did not want to set any precedent along those lines.[26] Moreover, they were highly suspicious of Mexico's request because they believed it was a ruse, an effort to secure water that would in fact be diverted for agricultural purposes.[27] They were concerned because the Mexican agencies did not have a track record of protecting the environment. As Patrick Tyrrell, head of the State Engineer's Office in Wyoming, describes:

We needed to trust them on the fact that environmental flows would not be snatched and then be directed to irrigation. The reason for that is that area around Mexicali is a breadbasket for Mexico. It would be a great temptation if water comes down the border for environmental purposes, to be grabbed for irrigation. So our preconception was that the water would never be used but for irrigation.[28]

To assuage these concerns, the Mexican officials invited U.S. stakeholders on field trips to visit environmental restoration sites across the delta in the Mexicali Valley. They put together a binational field trip, rented a bus, and toured the Mexicali Valley. The U.S. visitors could see firsthand what the irrigation system looked like and what opportunities for water conservation were available in Mexico. Seeing this in person was incredibly helpful. Charles Cullom, manager of the Colorado River Programs of the Central Arizona Water Project, describes the impact of these visits:

Initially, Mexico was saying two things that seemed to be in conflict. One was, "We have growing water needs in our border communities and our irrigation districts, so we need more water." The other was, "Water for the environment is an important issue, so we need environmental flows." From our perspective, it could feel like Mexico was talking about environmental flows because it could leverage more water for human health and safety. So, it took some teaching from Mexico to show us that indeed environmental protection was a priority, that it was following an amendment to their Constitution, and responding to the priorities of the administration of President Calderón. The Mexican negotiators highlighted the institutional framework that would support the pulse flow, and conducted several tours for us, to show us their investments in restoration projects across the Colorado River Delta, using human wastewater and supporting local youth to plant cottonwoods in the summer.[29]

As a result of these visits, more of the U.S. states' negotiators began to consider the possibility that they could pursue voluntary shortage with Mexico, while at the same time finding effective solutions that included environmental restoration.[30] Inevitably, this meant fighting certain preconceptions on their own side, such as the suspicion among the Upper Basin stakeholders that the request for environmental flows was a plot by the Lower Basin and the NGOs to send Upper Basin water downstream. Jennifer Gimbel, director of the Colorado Water Conservation Board of the state of Colorado, explains how the U.S. negotiators worked against this notion:

We approached top water leaders, governors, board members that were knowledgeable about the law and about policy, and we worked very hard with them. We got initial reactions: "There is no way we are going to talk to Mexico, no way we are going to do this pulse flow, we are in a drought!" So we had to bring them along through a step-by-step effort. You let them vent. You let them overreact. You bring them back. You talk to them. You make them consider things. Then we brought in specialists from Reclamation, stakeholders from other states, to try to explain the process, try to convey instead why this would help protect our interests. Through these behind-the-scenes conversations, we slowly gained, not a willingness to move forward, but an "Okay, we'll give it a try." That is all we needed, a "Let's just see if we can get there."[31]

In fact, the Lower Basin states supported involving the NGOs, not because of a hidden agenda, but because the NGOs were proposing that

Mexico should be able to store the water for environmental purposes in Lake Mead.[32] Keeping reservoir levels higher meant a lower probability of shortage and a higher probability of surplus, which was in the interest of Arizona, California, and Nevada.[33] As Karen Kwon, first attorney general for the state of Colorado, explains:

The water users with senior rights over the Colorado River headwaters came in saying, "No, no way we are devoting water for environmental purposes!" It was not until we were able to peel back, to discover what our barriers were and what we would be able to accomplish, that we moved forward. It took a big effort to communicate to them that if we do not solve the problems of the Lower Basin and in Mexico, and choose to proactively be a part of the solutions to the problems they are experiencing, once problems erupt, and we engage in the risk of litigation, it is uncertain what will come out of it all, even if we have senior water rights. So you need a lot of publicizing to convey this, and then you need negotiators on the other side, willing to make a good-faith effort to understand the obstacles, political and legal, that you face, instead of ignoring and arguing, "This is what we need and we don't care." If you go into negotiations with the latter attitude, it is not going to work. A win-lose strategy in transboundary discussions is never going to be effective.[34]

For this reason, prior to the negotiation process, the NGOs remained committed to openly debriefing with different constituencies about the proposals that they would be bringing to the negotiating table, if they were involved.[35] An attitude of "This is what I want, and I will not budge," was absent because they knew that, given the complexity of the system, that strategy would not work. As Carlos Peña, principal engineer of the IBWC, notes:

The environmental stakeholders would come up to us, and say, "This is what we would like to see, what do you think about it?" They did not come up and say, "We want the pulse flow, no matter what!" So the discussions would include our technical experts discussing, "Well, your idea is great, but here is a problem, and this is an issue." This openness helped us all out, because people were coming in with the mindset that the goal was to build a negotiation process that worked for everyone.[36]

Once the U.S. states' negotiators convincingly explained to their back tables, as well as to one another, that environmental restoration was a real desire on both sides of the border—something that Mexico needed and for which it had a policy and institutional framework—it was then easier for both countries to agree and say "Yes, let's work on this and find a binational environmental solution.'[37]

Adding Value in Process and Product

The NGOs came into the binational negotiations convinced that the way for them to achieve meaningful environmental results would be by gleaning an accurate picture of what the other stakeholders in the basin needed. They believed that they could promote significant change by effectively understanding the interests of the other stakeholders, and in turn, intertwining such interests with their own.[38] As Jennifer Pitt, director of the Colorado River Project at the Environmental Defense Fund, explains:

We knew what our bottom line was, pretty simple, getting environmental flows on the delta. We understood we could not get that in isolation, that the people in charge of managing reservoirs and dams would only do it in the context of a package that would address a number of needs for agricultural and municipal water users. Environmental issues do not find their way to the top of the agenda of agency commissioners. In order for them to really focus on restoring the delta, it would need to be considered within a broader context of issues. So we knew that we had to figure out how to best reach our goals through the map of needs the other stakeholders had.[39]

The NGOs knew that from a political and operational standpoint, the successful restoration of the Colorado River Delta would need to occur under the umbrella of a binational agreement. Informed by witnessing years of conflict, the NGOs surmised that such an agreement could occur only if the binational relationship between the two governments evolved into a partnership around water management, with a broader mandate fostering more trust and a deeper understanding.[40]

To accomplish this task, the NGOs reaffirmed their argument that it was necessary to address multiple factors concurrently, so that all the stakeholders knew that making progress on one issue would not preclude progress on another. Their idea was that everything should be contingent on everything else, providing the negotiators with a safe space to consider all the issues and to look at multiple packages. As Peter Culp, chief attorney at the Sonoran Institute, describes:

It's difficult to get to comprehensive solutions of complex issues unless you have a strong sense of conflicting interests and priorities, as well as the opportunities to bridge and trade across them. You need to connect all the different important issues. You cannot talk about potential shortage conditions without addressing reservoirs for surplus conditions. It is very difficult to make an argument for binational infrastructure investment without talking about binational water exchanges. You will not be able to devote water for environmental restoration unless it happens under the umbrella of actions that address multiple issues simultaneously.[41]

During the negotiations, the two countries formed various work groups to discuss the criteria by which to define and improve binational measures regarding drought and shortages, hydrology and operations, water conservation, new water sources, and environmental restoration.[42] The NGOs were involved in all five working groups, though there were occasions during the process in which only federal and state stakeholders were permitted to remain in the room.[43] The aim of involving the NGOs was to have them contribute to the full suite of proposals and help shape a better package, which every stakeholder could go home and show as a win for their constituents.[44]

In achieving that goal, the NGOs played several roles beyond their substantive expertise in environmental issues, which included (1) proactively securing funding to cofinance the restoration efforts; (2) functioning as informal channels of information, which government officials could use to send signals to the other side in ways that were not necessarily possible in the formal sessions; and (3) helping to resolve misunderstandings in the formal negotiating sessions.

Though not explicitly articulated from the beginning of the negotiations, the NGOs understood that a private commitment to help finance the purchase of water rights for environmental flows, in addition to government support, would be more convincing. This financial commitment would be seen as the NGOs proposing a solution, not requesting that others solve the problem. By shouldering an equal financial burden (33.3 percent each), they would be joining as a third partner, along with the federal governments of Mexico and the United States, in the environmental restoration efforts.[45]

There had been a recent precedent for this. In the context of drought, the U.S. Colorado River Basin states had wanted to operate a desalting plant in Yuma in order to increase the water supply, rather than having infrastructure sitting idle.[46] This would diminish water inflows to Mexico, however, where the wetland of Santa Clara lies. Since the desalting plant had almost never been operated, the water had been regularly discharged down, short of the Upper Gulf, feeding that wetland, a protected area within a larger Biosphere Reserve. After constructive dialogue, the two countries acknowledged the concerns on both sides, and in April 2010, they resolved that Mexico, the United States, and the NGOs via the Colorado River Delta Water Trust would each contribute a third of the water that was required to maintain the wetland during the pilot test run of the desalting plant.[47]

This decision to share responsibility was viewed as a precedent for Minute 319. This time, however, the NGOs went a step further by proactively coming to the negotiating table with significant financial resources, even before a deal was signed. As Hawes explains:

The Nature Conservancy got a loan from the Packard Foundation, under a confidentiality agreement, for $1.3 million, so that we could be ready to buy water rights the moment a binational deal would be struck. It was a clear sign that we were ready to hit the ground running, that we were putting our money where our mouth is, to make sure that we could meet our responsibility on the environmental part of the agreement. That pushed both countries to move forward; Mexico was already much on board, and it helped the U.S. authorities to realize, "Well, if the environmental community can find money to support this agreement, I'm sure we can on our own."[48]

Being able to make that financial commitment early on and show constructive engagement boded well for the NGOs. The fact the Packard Foundation, which had previously provided loans to the Nature Conservancy, did not have to conduct the financial clearance that would otherwise be required with a new organization, was also important. The loan was an investment program; it was an advance on the amount of money that the NGOs thought they would be able to raise. The NGOs were confident that with a signed binational agreement in hand, they could approach potential contributors and make a compelling case for them to help support the Colorado River Delta Water Trust. In fact, that turned out to be quite true. They set themselves a goal of raising $10 million by 2017, and by late 2014, they were already at $9.5 million.[49]

This was a bold move, for when the negotiations were ongoing, even though the NGOs had insider information that a binational agreement was a possibility, it would have still been very hard to make the case to receive financial backing from a sponsor with whom they did not have a previous relationship. Even the Packard Foundation was initially uneasy about giving the NGOs the money outright, but Culp made the convincing argument that if the NGOs could put money on the table, it would enhance their credibility in the negotiations.[50]

The NGOs contributed to devising solutions to another significant hurdle in the negotiations—namely, easing the mistrust between the two countries. The NGOs had a unique vantage point on this because they had been advocating collaboratively across the border for many years. From their perspective, the NGO representatives could see that while no government agency was acting deceitfully from either country, the officials did come up against areas of misunderstanding frequently.[51] The NGOs understood that they would not achieve their environmental aims until the two countries were able to move beyond arms-length interactions and unilateralism.[52]

In that process of exchanging perspectives, the NGOs demonstrated that they could be trusted by the states and the federal agencies, particularly where information that should not cross the border was concerned.[53] As Pitt explains, the people directly representing environmental interests were absolutely sure of each other as environmental colleagues, as well as patriots:

We had a very clear common goal. We talked about this as a group. That our Mexican colleagues would be included in a Mexican domestic conversation, or we would be included in a U.S. domestic conversation, where we felt we were given information we could not share with each other, and respected that. We did not move it, to the point that we became, for both sides, agents to relay information back and forth outside of the formal process. It was a form of citizen diplomacy, definitely a unique situation to be in.[54]

In consequence, at multiple times during the negotiations, when government officials did not feel that they had a direct way to communicate with their counterparts on the other side, they would rely on the NGOs as a conduit to send informal messages in both directions.[55] As Peña explains, one recurrent strategy to overcome a technical or political impasse was to talk to the U.S. NGOs, who in turn would talk to the Mexican NGOs, who would then speak with the Mexican officials, and so on:

This worked as shuttle diplomacy, where people could float ideas, suggesting, "Well, if you agree to that, I believe the other side will agree on this, particularly if you put this concept on the table." The NGOs helped a lot in that sense, particularly because government and state representatives always have people to report to. But with the NGOs, if you are dealing with a program manager, this person does not have a boss, there is nobody else to go to, so the person speaks with authority, and that enhances trust. The NGOs knew that if this agreement were not to be made, the pulse flow would fall apart. They had a vested interest in making sure a binational deal went ahead, and also knew that the agreement had to work in practice.[56]

The NGOs also contributed to resolving critical misunderstandings in the formal negotiating sessions.[57] In early 2012, the two countries had reached a point at which people had been talking a long time about the different elements that should be included in the agreement, but it was not really clear what a feasible package would look like.[58] So the mutual decision was made to have each country prepare a version of what they thought the elements of an agreement should look like. The United States prepared one draft proposal and sent it to Mexico, and Mexico prepared another draft proposal and sent it back. Those two drafts, according to the translation, made it seem like there was very little room for agreement.[59] The United States had put something on the table, and it was clearly critical for them. Mexico seemed to be responding "No" without hesitation. The documents seemed to suggest there was nothing more to discuss. However, as Hawes recalls:

What salvaged things was that Peter Culp, who was in close coordination with NGO partners in Mexico, and had had previous back channel conversations on the issue, detected the fact [that] the translation was not accurate. He could clearly see that the translation from Spanish to English, which had been made by a U.S. agency following diplomatic protocol, had omitted many of the reasons why Mexico was proposing what it was proposing. This made it seem like each side was talking past each other. In the Spanish version, however, Mexico went on at length describing why they were asking for some things and why they were refusing others, which in any negotiation is critical to know. But that was not present in the translated text.[60]

The U.S. delegation was ready to walk away from the table on the basis of the poorly translated document. But the NGOs were able to remedy the situation. They explained the translation errors and omissions, informing the sides that they were not in disagreement with each other to the extent that they thought.[61] In fact, the two proposals were using different language to describe related elements, and it appeared as though some of the important messages that each side was sending warranted further discussion. In turn, the NGOs were able to convince the U.S. delegation that they needed to ask for another translation. Once the U.S. stakeholders got a new, complete translation, they agreed to continue the negotiations with Mexico. As Culp describes:

The problem was to understand the relationships that people on each side saw between the different elements. We were trying to get the countries to finally move away from positional bargaining, where each side picks a number and you try to meet at the middle. Instead, what we were proposing to do is to form a partnership, allocating benefits and burdens, in an equitable fashion. So, if you want to have a shortage provision in the agreement, what are the other elements that have to be part of it in order for the shortage agreement to look good to the other side? If you want to have an environmental component, what other elements are needed to make the agreement work? The same applies to binational investment. So, using the two drafts to tease out how each side understood the relationships between those elements, we actually got to a much better conversation about what a final package could really look like. Because essentially the two sides were speaking a different language, literally and figuratively, where they were telling very different stories about the agreement based on the priorities and cultural understanding each side had. Once we moved past an arms-length-exchange of drafts and got to interpretation, "Okay, this is what they are trying to say, and vice versa," it made all the difference.[62]

Fostering relationships of trust, the NGOs contributed to the efforts on both sides to sustain a commitment to see the binational negotiations through to the end.[63] They were critical in breaking impasses at different points in time, enabling both sides to move forward.[64] They were also able to engage in high-level political dialogue and help devise implementable solutions.[65] As such, the NGOs were key in emphasizing the benefits at stake and the fact that, on balance, more was to be gained than lost in working together.[66] As Gastón Luken-Aguilar, president of Pronatura, summarizes:

The process took on a life of its own, and hinged on inspiration and a lot of perspiration. The same way in which you plant a seed and then patiently care for it until it blossoms.[67]

10   Protecting and Perfecting

Dealing with Spoilers

During the binational negotiation process, various simultaneous negotiations were taking place. In addition to the negotiation table with the governments and stakeholders of the United States and Mexico on either side,
the U.S. Basin states were negotiating with the U.S. federal government
separately. That process had its tense moments as well, which threatened
to derail the negotiations between the two countries.[1] As explored in chapter 7's "No Negotiation without Representation," the U.S. section of the
International Boundary and Water Commission (IBWC) fairly quickly supported the idea that the Basin states should be a part of the binational negotiations.[2] From the outset, however, several officials at the Legal Office of
the U.S. State Department (DOS) in Washington, D.C., opposed the states'
request to participate as cosovereigns.[3] They resisted the states' involvement, in spite of the fact that their federal government colleagues at the
Bureau of Reclamation at the U.S. Department of the Interior (DOI) were in
full support, having outlined the reasons why including the states would
be to everyone's benefit.[4]

From a legal standpoint, the DOS officials argued that in 99 percent of
cases, the exclusive jurisdiction of negotiating treaties with other governments is conferred upon the U.S. government, and the DOS in particular. That was true in this case. However, in practice, the DOS did not have
the authority to offer many of the elements that Mexico needed to have
in the binational agreement in order to satisfy the interests of their own
back table, such as water storage in the aftermath of the 2010 Mexicali Valley earthquake, access to surplus, and coordinated reservoir operations to
release the environmental pulse flow.[5] The federal agency does not own the

water rights, so they needed the Basin states to agree to the requests from Mexico. They also needed the Metropolitan Water District of Southern California, the Southern Nevada Water Authority (SNWA), and the Central Arizona Project, among other water agencies, to be on board with Minute 319's measures.[6]

Nevertheless, throughout the negotiation process, DOS officials were reluctant to support several of the adjustments that the two countries made to the diplomatic protocol.[7] More important, DOS officials were against approving a domestic memorandum of understanding that acknowledged that the Basin states must sign off before the United States could sign the binational agreement, and that the federal government would need the consent of the Basin states before it could extend or amend the Minute in the future. Such an arrangement was in stark contrast with the traditional diplomatic protocol. When the text agreement between the two countries was finalized in late 2012, the Basin states and the DOS had yet to get on the same page. As John Entsminger, senior deputy general manager of the SNWA, describes:

That was the single most difficult issue in the waning days of the binational nego-tiations. Everyone looks back as if the Minute was a foregone conclusion, but there were many days in which it looked like it was not going to happen. We were in the last meeting, in a very small room, Commissioner Connor, Commissioner Drusina, Bob Snow, Jerry Zimmerman, the State Department representative, and I. We are all reviewing the binational text agreement and our own domestic documents. The DOS representative is still refusing to agree to the sign-off clause between the states and the federal government. And in the room upstairs, we can hear the Mexican rep-resentatives are already celebrating, they are taking pictures. So, finally, I told him, "If we walk out of here without you saying yes to the clause, you are going to have to go upstairs and tell the Mexicans that the deal is off, and I am going to call my boss [Pat Mulroy], I have her on speed dial, and before you get back from upstairs, my boss will have called Senator Reid, and Senator Reid will call former Senators Salazar and Clinton, and the dead cat is lying at your door."[8]

In turn, the DOS official, also under pressure from the DOI, finally acqui-esced. This was not, however, the first time during the negotiations that the Basin states were able to successfully flex their political muscle and as Entsminger underscores, "remind officials at the Legal Office of the State Department that there are three branches of government."[9] At the very beginning of the binational process, the negotiation representatives from the Basin states flew to Washington, D.C., and walked into the office of high-ranking officials across the U.S. government in order to vigorously complain about the lack of cooperation from the DOS. They did so armed with a signed letter from both U.S. senators from Arizona, California, Colorado, New Mexico, Nevada, Utah, and Wyoming.[10] This sent a very clear message that the states were quite serious about securing their direct involvement in the process, from beginning to end. As Patricia Mulroy, general manager of the SNWA, recalls:

They have the final pen. So, if officials at the State Department were going to get creative at the end, to try to slip something in on us in the final draft, all it would have taken was for our 14 senators to declare that the binational agreement with Mexico would require the full vote of the U.S. Senate as opposed to a Minute. Big difference. We can do it. We had proved it previously. The party lines fall away, and they are a block! Which is really scary for the Executive. Even more when one is the Senate majority leader [Harry Reid (D-NV)]. And another one [John Barrasso (R-WY)] is the Chairman of the Subcommittee [on Economic, Energy, and Environmental Policy] that makes the decision at the Committee on Foreign Relations on whether a full vote will be required. So life gets pretty interesting! This went a long way in checking federal mischief.[11]

The political power of the Basin states, through the U.S. Congress, also played a critical role in insulating the binational process from outsiders not directly involved in the negotiations, without a real stake in the outcome but with relative power to try to tilt the results in another direction for their own purposes. Such was the case with several players located on the Rio Grande. The 1944 United States-Mexico Water Treaty, which allocates the Colorado River waters between the two countries, simultaneously allocates a part of the shared waters of the Rio Grande. The Rio Grande case is extremely complex, and a full discussion of its context is beyond the scope of this book. However, a brief look at part of the history of the Rio Grande, the conflicts, and challenges, is available in appendix B. In summary, over the last two decades, the tensions and confrontations have been significant between the state of Texas on one side and Mexico on the other. In the context of drought, Mexico has significantly delayed its water deliveries to the United States, as allowed by treaty guidelines. These delays have created disputes, as farming, irrigation, and political leaders in Texas have argued that drought or no drought, Mexico should deliver the full allotment. The allocation itself, which entitles Texans to 50 percent of the annual flows even though only 30 percent of the river is on their side, does not make things easier.[12]

So, for political and economic reasons, during the Colorado River nego-tiation process and afterward, a number of bills were introduced by Texas's congressional delegation seeking to link the Rio Grande with any potential agreement on the Colorado River.[13] Given the stark contrast between the operating rules, conditions, and challenges of the Colorado and Rio Grande rivers, permitting such a linkage would effectively kill any prospect of suc-cess in collaboratively managing the Colorado River between the United States and Mexico. The seven Colorado River Basin states, however, would not allow that to happen, and they made sure to enlist their congressional delegations to block Texas's efforts. As Mulroy notes:

There was a skunk that was standing outside the room that bled into this. In the 1944 Treaty, the Rio Grande and the Colorado River are both linked. We in the Colo-rado River Basin have always been worried that a solution in the Rio Grande gets tied into a solution in the Colorado River. You put it into the context of the Rio Grande, and all the acrimony between the Texans and Mexico. We almost had that acrimony spill over to our negotiations. But we kept that at bay. And that is where the power of seven states to go over and speak with 14 U.S. senators cannot be underestimated.[14]

The political power of the seven Basin states was useful not only to block domestic spoilers, but also to deter spoilers on Mexico's side of the table. Particularly at the beginning of the negotiations, officials at the Mexican section of the IBWC and at the National Water Commission (Comisión Nacional del Agua, or CONAGUA) were in a complex political situation because they were also responsible for overseeing the dynamics of the Rio Grande. In broad terms, Texans would say that the states of Chihuahua and Tamaulipas were manipulating the Rio Grande reservoirs and that they were deliberately not allowing water into Texas. The states in Mexico, on the other hand, would say that the Texans were trying to take advantage of the disparities in economic and political power between the two countries, and that in the context of drought, Mexico's federal government was doing the best it could. To make matters worse, the river is overallocated and mis-managed, during normal conditions, on both sides.[15]

In this context, at the beginning of the Colorado River process, some Mexican officials were asking themselves, "When the U.S. Colorado River stakeholders are talking about shortage, do we really believe that this is a real shortage, or are they simply manipulating the reservoirs in the Upper Basin in order to create an illusion of shortage, to force a different outcome in the Rio Grande?"[16] Not until the Mexican officials realized that they actually shared interests with the Colorado River Basin states, and the last thing that either side wanted was to go into shortage, did Mexican officials relax about engaging in negotiations. Knowing that the Basin states would go all the way to the U.S. Congress to prevent a linkage between the Colorado River and the Rio Grande was extremely important.[17] As Entsminger highlights:

The fact is, in Texas they have 2 senators. We have 14. So we can do things through the Legislative Branch that even our executive branch, IBWC, and Interior, could not get done. That is another example of the value of being involved as cosovereigns in this binational negotiation process.[18]

The efforts of the Basin states to prevent the linkage of the negotiations of the two rivers provided the Mexican negotiators with more maneuvering room.[19] It also helped to work against a narrative of mistrust that runs deeply through Mexican politics, where many feel that in order to protect national interests, one must be anti-U.S., and if one is not decidedly against the United States, one cannot be trusted.[20] As Roberto Salmón, commissioner of the Mexican section of the IBWC, notes:

There continues to be in Mexico a sizeable subset of stakeholders who have an odd sense of patriotism, with a heavy historical burden that solely considers the U.S. under the lens that since the U.S. took away half of Mexico's territory through war [in the 1860s], and incidentally most of the Colorado River, "whatever water we share with them, whatever water we store, the U.S. will eventually find a way to keep it for themselves, because it is in their nature." It is very difficult to face any binational process with such a mindset. We made a good effort to make sure that did not permeate our negotiations, but it is certainly something we had to struggle with as it pertains to some domestic constituencies.[21]

In this narrative, people living near the U.S.-Mexico border tend to be viewed apprehensively as well. This is because it is assumed that whenever they achieve local benefits, that must signal either that they have sold out Mexico's national interest or have been deceived by the United States. As Carlos de la Parra, environmental consultant for the Mexican section of the IBWC, explains:

This is a lose-lose proposition for border stakeholders because any solution we reach is automatically questioned. It is very tiresome to have to explain that living on the border and finding solutions for both sides does not make us any less Mexican. Quite to the contrary, we actually choose to stay in Mexico. For example, at one point in the negotiations, there were high-ranking Mexican officials to whom I had to describe our progress and they sternly suggested that if the U.S. was offering storage, "it was because they were going to use it for energy generation." This made no sense but they would not believe me. So I had to go back and ask the Bureau of Reclamation for data to convince our very own officials in Mexico City that Mexico's stored water would only increase levels in Lake Mead by some inches. Quite a conclusive sign to show the storage had no connection with hydroelectricity![22]

This is an example of the extent to which certain irrigation district managers and federal officials in Mexico City refused to change their preconceptions and were dead set against any agreement, opposing it no matter how beneficial it could be.[23] However, as discussed in Chapter 7's "From Litigation to Cooperation," the fact that the leaders at the IBWC and at CONAGUA were decidedly in favor of reaching an agreement under a collaborative framework with the United States went a long way in providing the binational negotiation process with the political momentum to move forward.[24]

Moreover, in light of the terrible results from the confrontational route pursued during the All-American Canal controversy and in the aftermath of the earthquake, these domestic spoilers were no longer in a situation to mount serious political opposition. They were in dire need of assistance from the Mexican federal government to figure out a way to save the water that would be lost as a result of the earthquake's destruction of their irrigation infrastructure.[25]

Another critical way in which the binational efforts were shielded from spoilers was by ensuring a very careful approach to shaping the public communications throughout the negotiation process. As discussed in chapter 7's "Turning Crisis into Opportunity," the Mexican negotiators came into the negotiations with an interest in securing joint investment to finance conservation projects and improve the irrigation infrastructure in the Mexicali Valley.[26] One of the measures to this end, on which the two countries agreed and interests on both sides were served, is that the United States was to invest in the improvement of Mexico's irrigation infrastructure, such that Mexico conserved more water and was able to store some of it at Lake Mead, and in return, the United States received a part of the conserved water.[27]

However, both sides knew that reporting on this measure in the media was unlikely to provide the necessary nuanced explanation. Both sides had to manage the politics of their back tables and were apprehensive about how the negotiations would be portrayed in the news. On the Mexican side, the negotiators needed to carefully prevent any conserved water exchange from being described, inaccurately, as selling water, in light of the political narrative of mistrust of the United States.[28] On the U.S. side, it was difficult to explain to domestic water users how they would benefit from investments related to water conservation in Mexico instead of investments in the United States, without also having to explain the full context of the international negotiations under which those investments were being decided. Moreover, at the very time when the two sides were trying to forge a binational partnership around managing the Colorado River, the front-page news coverage was heavily focused on immigration and border security legislation controversies.[29] The negotiators on both sides of the border had to find the right way to frame the Colorado River issues, as well as the right time to communicate their progress. As Peter Culp, chief attorney for the Sonoran Institute, notes:

In many, many cases, we were very concerned that reporting about the binational conversation going on would set us back by alienating one side or the other. So, having the ability to ensure a safe space and ensure that our conversations would remain confidential was very important. It would have been very difficult for either side to put on the table some of the key elements that triggered the agreement if they had to do so publicly from the beginning. It is impossible to take those kinds of risks or commitments if you are going to be reading about them in the newspapers the next morning. It was only possible to agree to them once you had a package, and you could explain. Once everything was in place, and where each side could tell a story about why it was that it was the right thing to make these agreements, even if it included things to which you were opposed in the past. You could not talk about those things publicly until you were ready.[30]

Because the level of nuance that is generally communicated in public media tends to be quite low, the two countries agreed to a process whereby they carefully constructed and reviewed press releases, giving both sides an opportunity to determine what and how information would be disseminated.[31] They were extremely disciplined, communicating as little as possible to the public, so as not to jeopardize their progress.[32] This strategy was used in both countries and extended beyond the negotiations to include the rollout of the measures associated with Minute 319, as well as their implementation.

Mindful that news travels quickly between the two countries, the Basin states had to be very cautious about how news about the binational agreement would break in the United States, for fear of how Mexican spoilers could respond. On the U.S. side, the urban water agencies have different rules about how they must communicate final decisions, such as a binational agreement, to their boards of directors. In the Lower Basin states of Arizona and California, they are able to announce their decisions and the agreement details in closed meetings. Nevada, on the other hand, has stringent "sunshine" laws that require information to be made publicly available.

Attentive of how the announcement of Minute 319 could be depicted in the U.S. press, the negotiators at the SNWA had to take the binational agreement to their board of directors and essentially tell them, "Do not ask us a thing about it. If you have a question, I will talk to you one on one behind closed doors." If not handled in this careful manner, misinterpreted details of the agreement could show up in the local papers instantly, and then quickly make their way to Mexico. As Mulroy describes:

So, when we were about to host our board meeting, I sat down with the editor of the *Review Journal,* and with the editor of the *Las Vegas Sun,* and the heads of the TV stations, and said: "Here is what you cannot say, here are the phrases that you cannot use because it will kill it on the Mexican side." So the story is under control, they have been calling back and forth; I know what the story is going to say. And I wake up at three o'clock in the morning, I will never forget this, it is two days before the meeting, I know the story is going to break the day of the board meeting, and all of a sudden it dawns on me, that someone else writes the headline. And the headline could be a killer. Six-thirty in the morning I call the editor of the *Review Journal,* and I said, "Bob, I have never done this, but we have to control that headline, I want to control what that headline says before it shows up in paper, and they worked with me." And we controlled it to the last inch, because this sunshine law made the Mexican negotiators so uncomfortable, because California could do it under attorney-client confidentiality; Arizona did it in a closed meeting of the board; not us, we had to do it wide out in the open. I got a lot of gray hair and lost a lot of sleep over that one. Fortunately, the members of the press understood the importance of the narrative for the public. This town better than probably most others gets how absolutely integral water is to its economic success. So they had a lot of confidence in us, and we had to cash in those chips for Minute 319.[33]

This degree of caution was exercised equally on Mexico's side. The day of the release of the environmental pulse flow, more than 15 months after the binational agreement had been signed, media outlets from the communities around the Colorado River Delta were paying considerable attention, to celebrate the environmental milestone.[34] There was no national media presence, however, because the IBWC and the nongovernmental organizations

(NGOs) had decided that such coverage would risk bringing the news to Mexico City. They did not want the good results to get tangled with political interests for whom the delta is not a priority. This was a deliberate effort on their part. As Gastón Luken Aguilar, the president of Pronatura's Sea of Cortez office, explains:

The Pronatura office in Mexico City wanted to convey the environmental meaning of the pulse flow and we had to fight hard and convince them not to do so. People have a large degree of skepticism and suspicion about what authorities announce, and media outlets will often charge a fee for announcing anything. So, why risk getting involved in controversy? Why waste money in such efforts? Instead, communicate your success to the foundations and nonprofits, with the aim to highlight concrete results, and engage them to support your future efforts. This is effective communication; the purpose must be to increase your ability to move quickly and effectively, remaining independent from political swings. Communicate succinctly, and only with people to whom the results are meaningful. Do not empower an enemy to come out of the woods.[35]

As such, by flexing political muscle, forming relationships of trust across the table, and being strategic and disciplined in interactions with the press, the negotiators on both sides of the border were able to work as a unit and better insulate their negotiations and agreement against spoilers.

Leading through Ingenuity

In the United States, the many Colorado River actors have a fairly similar view of the long-term challenge in the Colorado River Basin: that maintaining current practices without adaptation to changing conditions will undermine the sustainability of the river.[36] These actors, in coordination with officials at the Bureau of Reclamation, include state officials, urban agencies, and environmental organizations, all of which are in constant dialogue at many levels and have solid relationships.[37] Reclamation, therefore, had a well-informed understanding of what could make a binational agreement work from the U.S. perspective.[38] As Michael Connor, who went on to become the U.S. deputy secretary of the interior, and who during the negotiations was commissioner of the Bureau of Reclamation, explains:

Our initial perspective was "How do we take the next step from the 2007 U.S. Interim Guidelines, how do we move forward to increase certainty, how do we address our relationship with Mexico, and how do we avoid conflict?" What is very interesting is that, over time, there are aspects where everyone changed their initial perspectives. Reclamation did, the states did, the NGOs did, and Mexico did, through the intense dialogue that we had, reaching a better understanding of what the other side needed. It is a process that I think is structured, but it has some fluidity to it. From the federal government perspective, we had to be advocates for the whole deal. Sometimes I would feel, reading the context and the situation that I would need to be an advocate for the states with Mexico, or an advocate for the NGOs respective to the states, or an advocate for Mexico itself. I remember specific instances, calls, and meetings. In practice, there were several principles that we were trying to achieve as a federal government, but beyond that, we were functioning as facilitators, working in favor of an agreement that would be good policy and a good structure to deal with long-term challenges.[39]

The IBWC had been responsible for the facilitative role on a binational level in the past, while the DOI, and Reclamation in particular, had been performing this role more recently on a domestic level, from the Bill Clinton administration through the George W. Bush administration.[40] This created an opportunity for the leaders and senior staff of these agencies to continue and expand this role as part-advocate and part-neutral party, in order to incorporate and empower as many stakeholders as they could in the search for an agreement that would meet the core interests of the diverse array of actors in the basin.[41] As Terrance Fulp, deputy regional director of the Lower Colorado Region at the Bureau of Reclamation, notes:

You have to recognize people understand an issue at different points in time. You need to recognize that, be aware, and not jump ahead of them. Because if you do, they feel left behind, they will dig in, and they will actually believe that where you are headed is wrong. It happened on both sides, and we needed the skill to recognize it and in real time, not going where you want to go, not pushing it, because you cannot force it, you have to back off, and let it evolve, try a different approach, different examples, different language; there are all sorts of ways around it. And in these situations, it certainly helps to have practice. Some people don't have it, I have had people on my team that are brought in to these kind of negotiations, and you try to teach them, you try to help them, and for various reasons they either just don't want to do it or cannot do it. So, fundamentally, you want people willing and with the instinct to listen carefully, process quickly, and react appropriately. It is some combination of innate learning and practice over time.[42]

In this sense, the senior leadership at Reclamation and both sections of the IBWC had to be committed to finding ways to look at the issues being discussed at the negotiation table from as many different angles as possible.[43] Leading their own delegations under the premise that the more that all parties understood each other's concerns, the more likely that the two sides could define implementable actions, they persevered in figuring out how to speak the "other side's language."[44] These efforts did not go unnoticed among the stakeholders and set a constructive tone. As Lorri Gray-Lee, director of the Lower Colorado Region at the Bureau of Reclamation, highlights:

You need leaders willing to take a risk. And that risk is recognizing that they do not know what they do not know. The three commissioners were willing to do things like go on tours, sit down with technical folks, and listen to briefings, not because they had to, but because they wanted to understand where everybody was coming from. That willingness to recognize they do not know everything, that humbleness, was very valuable.[45]

There were multiple ways in which this commitment to facilitative leadership took shape, playing out in several guidelines that structured the negotiation process. One of these was related to caucuses. Since people tend to interpret things differently, when a controversial theme would come up, the negotiators had to make sure to huddle to discuss the diverse interpretations of what was being put on the table.[46] The stakeholders abided by a series of unwritten rules: (1) no country delegation could initiate more than three caucuses in a day; (2) there was a time limit for each caucus; and (3) whichever delegation called for a caucus would be the one that would briefly step out of the negotiating room.[47] As Sally Spener, foreign affairs secretary of the U.S. section of the IBWC, explains:

The water rights framework in the U.S. is very different from Mexico. If you deal with CONAGUA, you deal with the people that have the water. In the U.S., you have seven Basin states with a different water rights framework, each with competing interests between the Upper and the Lower Basin. We all had to be very cognizant of these issues. One way we dealt with this is that we had caucuses. An issue would arise, and we would look at each other, and think, "Well, that is interesting, would California agree to this? Will Colorado? How does it affect Arizona?" So we would tell Mexico, "We need a caucus." We would break, hash it out with our domestic stakeholders, and come back to the room with a response. That was a consistent and very helpful way of operating during the negotiations.[48]

The issues at stake were incredibly complex, so sometimes people would lose sight of the forest for the trees. They could get bogged down with particular details, so the chief negotiators would rely on caucuses to get through those instances and remind their delegations of the big picture— the overall aims that they were trying to accomplish.[49] On most occasions, the negotiators would come back from a caucus with a clearer understanding of which aspects were workable and which might need revision. As Salmón explains:

> At the core is how you conduct the process. You need openness, you need to listen to every proposal carefully; even if you immediately realize it is not something you agree with, take the time to analyze it, to weigh its different elements, and then come back with a counterproposal. This offers the other side two things: the respect they deserve for their efforts, and an opportunity to receive in exchange an offer that may even be better than what they proposed.[50]

The path toward greater understanding was facilitated not only through caucuses, but also through side-talks. On several occasions, in the formal sessions, a delegation would make a proposal or argue in favor of a concept, which puzzled the other side.[51] There were times when, even after careful reflection, the arguments from one side would remain incomprehensible to the other.[52] In those moments, it was critical to have an informal conversation, at a reception, café, or over dinner, to try to understand the "why" behind these arguments. Only if people understood the reasons, they could try to unpack some of the seemingly insurmountable impasses.[53]

People generally interact differently in informal settings than in formal ones. In private, they may be willing to discuss trading items that they might not be able to propose in public. This is because in a formal setting, either the stakeholders cannot have such a nuanced conversation or the politics that each side must manage do not allow such a proposal. Therefore, having the ability to ensure a safe space for open dialogue was very important.[54] It would have been very difficult for either side to put some of the key elements that led to agreement on the table in a public manner from the outset.[55] As Culp notes:

> You need people to be able to engage in side-talks and talk informally with one another in between sessions. Because then, in the formal sessions, instead of focusing on the points of disagreement, both sides can come back and come up with a script where, "You guys say this, then the other side will say that, and then we can work through it."[56]

During the negotiations, this was particularly useful on occasions when a delegation would make a proposal or argue in favor of a concept that proved to be so contrary to the other side's concerns or mindset that it prompted members of the other side to consider ending the negotiations entirely.[57] At these moments, the senior leaders would have to seek their counterparts, talk outside, and figure out a way to reframe the mandate or issue at stake.[58]

For example, the IBWC meeting procedures have a strictly formal protocol. The two IBWC sections chair the meetings and speak in their respective languages. When the discussions would turn to hydrology and complex technical aspects of river management, this process could be quite slow, requiring a lot of diligence and patience.[59] Even though the two sides would work hard to make sure that they were expressing themselves clearly, in order to get the main points across in an easy-to-follow format, some points did get lost in translation, especially with the delay in the interpretation.[60] This could lead to potentially serious disagreements.

Such was the case when the two countries were trying to define the terms of reference for the negotiations, all the way back when they were laying the groundwork for comprehensive binational discussions. During a meeting in Mexicali, people on both sides seemed to be talking past each other, and at one point, the translation from Spanish to English was spoken through the headphones, roughly conveying "Mexico does not like the U.S. principles." That seemed to be the last straw. As Commissioner Connor and Commissioner Salmón recall:

Connor: Everyone in the U.S. delegation was stunned, both the federal and state representatives. We start to ask ourselves, "What are we doing here if we cannot even agree on the high-level principles we are trying to achieve?" People are ready to go home and call the whole negotiations off.[61]

Salmón: I am reading the faces of our American counterparts, and their reactions are of surprise and disappointment. I do not understand why. So we adjourn, and one of our NGO colleagues tells me that "the U.S. is puzzled about Mexico's change in stance." I am puzzled too! "What do they mean?" My colleague explains that the U.S. understood "We had always said X, and now we were saying Y."[62]

Connor: So, the commissioners, we go to a little café in Mexicali, and on our side, we start explaining, "We are not going to get much traction in these discussions if Mexico does not accept these fundamental principles, which we thought were pretty mundane and fair." And Commissioner Salmón says, "What? We did not say that at all." "Really? Because that was the translation."[63]

Salmón: This is when we confirmed that the translator was probably tired and certainly omitting critical information. I did not wear the translation headphones, so I could not know that the translation was not effective. I assumed it was. So we had to sit, with a beer in hand, and go all over the morning conversation to resolve the misunderstanding.[64]

Connor: So we had a long conversation, and over drinks, in a casual atmosphere, at the end of the evening, we were laughing about it. We then reported back to the states that "Okay, it was a translation problem." And if we had not thought about having an informal discussion in a very small group, I do not think we would have been able to continue the binational negotiations. It was looking very bleak. And from that point on, we knew, if we get to a severe disagreement, we have an outlet, an informal discussion.[65]

Salmón: Subsequently, for many parts of the negotiation process, and most certainly in the end, we made sure that all the critical negotiating sessions were carried out in English. Such an effort on our part was deeply appreciated by the U.S.[66]

Connor: Personalities matter. My first reaction to Commissioner Salmón was, "This is a very engaging, very bright and candid colleague, this is a person you like to have these discussions with." And of course there were moments in the negotiations where we would meet for a side-talk, and "Yes, it turns out that was not a translation problem, there was a strong negative reaction to something we proposed!"[67]

In consequence, these informal side-talks became a necessary and integral element of the success of the binational negotiations. As another tool in the facilitation efforts, they allowed each side to get a sense of whether its points were being effectively communicated across the table, building trust and resolving misunderstandings, while also providing an opportunity for leaders to jump in, tweak, and adapt their delegation's focus when necessary for the ultimate success of the negotiation process.[68]

Testing the Ways to Agreement

Throughout the negotiations, the two sides worked from general accords on the various issues at stake, and then focused on the details and connections between these issues.[69] When the two delegations reached a broad agreement, they would call it a *point of tentative agreement (POTA)*. They documented the POTAs at each meeting, which in turn provided them with clear points of departure for proceeding meetings, fostered momentum, and helped to move the negotiations forward.[70]

For example, as discussed in previous chapters, Mexico came to the table willing to negotiate shortages, but requesting to do so based upon a drought indicator that could be observed by a neutral party, and also making sure that they could share in surpluses.[71] The United States believed that there was no better drought indicator than the elevation levels at Lake Mead and did not agree that Mexico should receive any surplus.[72]

The two delegations were in a deadlock until they redefined their approach to the situation. They reached a broad agreement that they wanted to deal with shortage sharing, and simultaneously to deal with surplus sharing, because from a political standpoint, this would be the only feasible avenue to pursue.[73] This particular POTA may appear simple in retrospect, but it was not obvious to all the parties, on either side.[74] As Entsminger explains:

This goes back a bit further than the controversy of the lining of the All-American Canal. It goes to the 1999 U.S. Surplus Guidelines, of having surpluses available for the Lower River Basin states, and not allowing Mexico to participate. From Mexico's perspective, the U.S. had strung together a number of snubs. So, undoing that historic animosity and getting to the point of tentative agreement, where we are equal both for shortages and surpluses, that was huge.[75]

Using this POTA as the starting point, both countries were able to then discuss the specifics. If they were to share in shortages, when would they be applicable to Mexico, and under which conditions? If they have high reservoir conditions, how much water is Mexico to access, and what do the Basin states need to do to enable this?[76] The POTA made it easier not to lose sight of the principles that should underpin the measures to which the two sides should agree. In turn, it became clearer that reservoir levels, as the trigger indicator for shortage and surplus, would best meet both sides' core interests.[77]

The use of points of tentative agreement also played a critical role in allowing stakeholders to know that when a topic was discussed, it was not the last time that they would be able to review or talk about that item.[78] Stakeholders would walk away from meetings with a sense that an agreement had been reached on X, Y, and Z subjects, but with the clear understanding that they were giving each other the opportunity to change their opinions after digesting the POTAs in the days and weeks following the meeting.[79] As Carlos Peña, principal engineer of the U.S. section of the IBWC, notes:

We wanted to make sure that we were highlighting when we had agreed upon something, but not stop there, and instead recognize "Let's put it aside, and as we discuss these other issues, we may go back and have to tweak that." We also knew that any discussions we had, we would all need to go back and check with our principals to make sure that they were okay, even when if we had a sense they would. This worked equally for both sides.[80]

On some issues, after careful and sustained deliberation, the parties might agree on 90 percent but disagree on 10 percent. So the negotiators would put those issues on hold, note them as POTAs, and move on to the next issue. They knew that by analyzing other items, they could discover insights, trades, or circumstances that would allow them to go back and bridge the gap on that 10 percent disagreement. As Salmón explains:

It helps a lot to begin by searching for optimal solutions, without hindering the brainstorming process by political and diplomatic considerations that inevitably will later need to be discussed. The reliance on points of tentative agreement was critical because it took a legal and emotional burden away from everyone involved, that otherwise would prevent you from thinking outside the box. You need to be able to discuss ideas without the fear that by discussing them, you are committing to them. The fact that what you say is not binding creates the space to explore a wider array of issues, and allows you to revisit them at different points in time. When people can speak freely, they become more creative.[81]

During the negotiations, the two sides shared the notion that opportunities for progress would need to be based upon fair and equitable contributions.[82] They surmised that there would need to be agreement on the operations of the reservoirs. There should be investment in infrastructure. An environmental component was also necessary. It was important to make sure that these three pillars were crafted in relative balance. Within this framework, the focus was on creating value first, before identifying the criteria with which to divide it.[83]

The POTAs, therefore, played a significant role in this sense, as they facilitated the negotiators' efforts to identify the most promising projects from a basin perspective.[84] This was a stark break from past practices. As José de Jesús Luévano, secretary of Mexico's section of the IBWC, describes:

From the get-go, we asked all technical work groups to focus their efforts on identifying all possible solutions and suspending criticism, not judging proposals from the perspective of one country or the other. The mandate was that in the search for solutions, the driver should be what works best for the Basin as a whole. "Do not worry about who will pay for it, who will benefit the most." This was done with the understanding that once the wide array of options was on the table, then the two countries would engage in diplomatic and political considerations. For our past experience was that if you have work groups in which each delegation is solely focused on their own interests, it is very hard to move forward.[85]

In addition, the POTAs were essential for both sides to avoid being trapped for too long by impasses that undermine momentum, where frustration grows and where people may seriously consider leaving the negotiations altogether.[86] As Robert Snow, the chief attorney for the Solicitor's Office of the DOI during the binational negotiations, describes:

Everything is linked with everything. You do not have a deal until you have a deal on everything. Those points of tentative agreement tend to build up and generate momentum. So capturing them, as many times as possible, is critical to show that you are making progress.[87]

The use of POTAs allowed the negotiators to evaluate the stakes from different angles and incorporate new lessons as they moved through the different rounds of the negotiations.[88] This helped the parties to enlarge their thinking. In turn, a higher degree of flexibility and improvisation to explore mutually beneficial trades arose, allowing them to shape better packages for everyone involved.[89] As Karen Kwon, first assistant attorney general for the state of Colorado, explains:

A common saying through our negotiations was, "It is all part of a package, and unless we get a package, that element is not going to come through." For example, our initial negotiating stance, on occasions, was, "that does not need to be a part of the package," but Mexico was adamant, "No, no, it does, we are not doing shortage sharing unless we do surplus, unless we do environmental flows, and infrastructure investment." So we would answer, "Well, we are not doing those unless we get some water compensation." We have a more robust agreement as a result of that process.[90]

By relying on points of tentative agreement, the stakeholders were able to break complex water problems into manageable pieces. This made it easier to invent without committing. It also allowed the parties to evaluate a wider array of options that directly exploited the differences in interests between the two delegations. This facilitated the creation of value, by allowing the negotiators to bundle options into multiple packages and test these different packages with their constituencies until it became clear that the benefits of reaching a binational agreement outweighed the costs. This in turn was critical for both countries to be able to come to consensus.

Part IV: Strengthening Negotiation Practice

11   Enhancing the Prospects for Finding Agreement

The previous chapters of this book have explored two negotiations that led to landmark agreements between the United States and Mexico: the first regarding the shared energy reservoirs in the Gulf of Mexico, and the second regarding the shared waters and environmental resources of the Colorado River. For more than seven decades, the United States and Mexico found themselves pursuing unilateral action on a frequent basis. This often led to deadlock and a succession of binational confrontations. In 2012, both countries altered course and were able to reach significant agreements. In turn, the two sides have committed to codevelop and jointly manage these transboundary natural resources as partners. Both agreements have been implemented effectively.

The purpose of the research underpinning this book has been to examine how the negotiators on both sides shaped these two landmark agreements, and explore in what ways they contributed to the resolution of these long-standing binational disputes. The evidence from both cases suggests that the modes in which developed and developing countries decide to conduct transboundary resource management negotiations can contribute to altering the prospects for finding agreement.

In this sense, it is useful to comparatively revisit the strategies and decisions that the negotiators made in the Gulf of Mexico and in the Colorado River, in light of the four areas of insight discussed at the beginning of the book: dispute resolution, adaptive leadership, collaborative decision-making, and political communication. While intersecting in many ways, they are often discussed separately from one another, both by scholars and practitioners. Exploring the combination of several propositions from these four areas of insight can contribute to the development of a number of interdisciplinary practices. These practices, in turn, can assist stakeholders in the active resolution of high-stakes transboundary energy, water, and environmental conflicts.

Dispute Resolution

Ceasing Confrontation

Critics to the zero-sum approach to dispute resolution suggest that approaching conflicts in the public arena through the lens of win-lose interactions only breeds more opposition and instability.[1] They argue that this mindset undermines trust between the parties and credibility with the public at large, prolongs disputes, wastes stakeholder resources, and leads to suboptimal outcomes.[2]

For over 70 years, the United States and Mexico frequently framed their conflicts regarding the shared natural resources in the Gulf of Mexico and the Colorado River from a zero-sum perspective. When confrontations erupted, they often pursued unilateral action with a fixed-pie mentality.[3] In the Gulf of Mexico, for instance, the two sides could not agree not only on how, but also whether to cooperatively explore and develop hydrocarbon reservoirs across their maritime boundary. For decades, rather than pooling investment, seizing economies of scale, and sharing infrastructure and expertise, they clashed with one another with a win-lose mentality. The United States held to the rule of capture, pursuing unilateral offshore energy development, whereas Mexico stuck to strict constitutional rulings, forbidding any meaningful energy partnerships between the international oil companies (IOCs) and Petróleos Mexicanos (PEMEX), Mexico's national oil company (NOC).

Caught between the rule of capture, on one side, and the threat of litigation following the constitutional rulings on the other, the reservoirs were locked behind a development moratorium well into the 2010s. This effectively froze any commercial activity related to the hydrocarbon deposits, whereas in other parts of the world, in spite of comparable (or greater) political and economic disparities, more than 30 countries had reached agreements to codevelop similar offshore energy resources since the 1950s.

In the Colorado River, the two sides clashed equally under a zero-sum, upstream versus downstream riparian approach. For decades, in spite of the existence of the International Boundary Waters Commission (IBWC) as the forum to pursue binational solutions, the two sides found it frequently difficult to agree on how to coordinate the Colorado River Basin operations beyond allocating water deliveries on an annual basis under the umbrella of a client-customer relationship. Lacking a more cooperative framework, neither side was able to proactively address several unintended cross-boundary effects resulting from the unilateral development of infrastructure and overallocation of the water resources.

This led to a number of problems, including spikes in salinity levels, disruptions in agricultural productivity, hazardous waste dumping, aquifer depletion, and the weakening of several ecosystems, including the virtual disappearance of the Colorado River Delta. Along with the episodes of binational conflict, the seven Basin states on the U.S. side (Colorado, New Mexico, Utah, Wyoming, Arizona, California, and Nevada), also from a zero-sum mindset, incurred considerable costs in litigation with each other, while simultaneously fighting with the U.S. federal government and environmental organizations. This pattern of confrontation between stakeholders in the basin, on both sides of the border, continued well into the 2000s, as exemplified by the All-American Canal conflict and its associated costs.

The history and evidence from both cases underscores the fact that, in both the Gulf of Mexico and the Colorado River, under a win-lose mindset and stuck at repeated impasses, each country spent considerable effort arguing to induce the other to do what it wanted, when it wanted, with little success. Under the threat of force or litigation, both countries ended up worse off, prolonging disputes, wasting resources, and producing suboptimal outcomes.

Widening the Scope

Proponents of the mutual gains approach to dispute resolution suggest that by broadening the scope of issues at stake, as well as the angles from which they are considered, the parties can discover linkages that had not previously been apparent and are thus able to consider new and mutually beneficial trades.[4] In turn, by trading across these differences, the parties can create more value and satisfy their interests more effectively.[5]

In both transboundary negotiation cases explored in this book, new issues were brought to the table, which then enabled extensive value creation and facilitated fruitful and unexpected trades. For example, in the Gulf of Mexico case, the U.S. Department of the Interior (DOI) was at first unconvinced that negotiating with Mexico would prove beneficial, on account of the facts that it could jeopardize the reach of the rule of capture and require agency staff resources beyond their capacity during the reorganization of the Minerals Management Service (MMS). However, after a careful back-table dialogue led by high-ranking officials at the U.S. State Department (DOS), officials at the DOI became more comfortable with the idea that coming to an agreement with Mexico on how to codevelop transboundary hydrocarbon reservoirs would have numerous ancillary advantages beyond the immediate issues at hand.

The United States proponents foresaw that such an agreement could (1) provide the private U.S. oil industry with a way to break into Mexico's hydrocarbons sector; (2) improve U.S. energy security by codeveloping reservoirs in conjunction with Mexico, rather than relying on oil imports from more geopolitically risky nations; and (3) have positive impacts on other issues of concern between the two countries, such as immigration, trade, and security, by increasing Mexico's overall economic and social stability.

In the Colorado River negotiations, various issues were brought to the table that had not been included previously. While the Basin states, in order to face drought conditions, had wanted to entice Mexico to share in water shortages in exchange for water storage in U.S. reservoirs, Mexico conveyed that it could be convinced to reach agreement only if they also shared in the surpluses. Mexico also requested including binational measures that would increase water availability on its own side of the border (i.e., improving irrigation infrastructure, building desalination plants, and restoring the Colorado River Delta).

These were issues that the U.S. Basin states had not entertained before and to which they were initially opposed. As the negotiations evolved, however, they realized that agreeing to share in surpluses with Mexico would allow the United States to secure in turn the elevation levels at Lake Mead as the indicator to trigger shortage conditions in the basin. Moreover, by investing in conservation efforts in Mexico, seizing on the economies of scale, the United States would bring more water to the Lower Basin agencies and its customers at a lower cost than if the investments were done in the United States. Also, by including the matter of environmental restoration in the binational discussions, both sides would benefit from the involvement of the nongovernmental organization (NGO) representatives, with their decades of expertise on how to enhance aquifer replenishment, ecosystem resilience, and water availability from a comparative perspective.

The evidence from both the Gulf of Mexico and Colorado River cases highlights that bringing more issues to the table provided stakeholders on both sides with the opportunity to see new and more nuanced connections between several potential measures. This allowed them to shape better trades across their differences and establish more compelling packages. In turn, the negotiators were able to reach more effective and sustainable policy outcomes for all involved.

Embracing Flexibility

Advocates of the Water Diplomacy Framework (WDF) suggest that upon negotiating complex resource management decisions, in order to better address the uncertainty, nonlinearity, and feedback loops involved, decision-makers should (1) expect persistent boundary crossing among domains (i.e., social, natural, and political) and scales (i.e., spatial, temporal, disciplinary, and jurisdictional); 2) conceive of problems as highly sensitive to perturbations; and (3) account for the possibility that the same actions in a particular place and time will not have the same results in another context.[6]

Both negotiations present instances of persistent boundary crossings between domains and scales. In the Gulf of Mexico case, we see that the multidisciplinary education and succession of experiences (i.e., undergraduate engineering degree, professional expertise managing well logs in offshore oil field exploration in the Indian Ocean, law school degree, and conducting diplomatic relations for the DOS across the globe) of one of the lead U.S. negotiators, David Sullivan, enabled him to proactively grasp the complexity of what would be required to find an agreement that was both technically feasible and politically implementable. This understanding inspired Sullivan to propose a series of binational workshops, in which the two countries could evaluate and learn about the many intricate issues at stake, instead of negotiating from a "draft, counterdraft" practice right away. Such a step involved going against the traditional diplomatic protocol and meant fundamentally altering the initial path of the negotiation to account for a wider set of social, natural, and political considerations.

In the Colorado River case, the two sides had to come to grips with the realization that the jurisdictional entities responsible for the management and ownership of the water were quite distinct between the two countries. Whereas in Mexico, the federal government both owns and operates its share of the Colorado River water, in the United States, the seven Basin states own the water and share management responsibilities with the U.S. Bureau of Reclamation. These differences had significant political implications, including the fact that if the two sides wanted to reach an actionable agreement, given the myriad issues at stake, they would need to break the standard diplomatic protocol of nation-to-nation negotiations by including representatives from the U.S. Basin states.

We also see examples of how sensitive both conflicts have been to perturbations. In the Gulf of Mexico case, the Macondo oil spill of 2010, along with the simultaneous reorganization of the MMS, served to delay the official launch of the negotiations. The U.S. delegation, in the midst of managing these two disruptions, was unable to prepare a counterdraft in response to Mexico's original draft agreement proposal. With the Mexican delegation in Washington, D.C., ready to begin face-to-face negotiations, this time bind was the other principal reason for Sullivan to suggest that the countries participate instead in what would prove to be highly productive, collaborative workshops.

In the Colorado River, California had been using more water than its annual allocation since the 1950s, as allowed by interpreting the Law of the River (i.e., the numerous federal laws, compacts, decrees, regulations, contracts, and court decisions defining the management and operation of the Colorado River), since the other two Lower Basin states were not using their full water allocation. However, in the early 2000s, when Nevada and Arizona came to require the use of their full water allotments, California was forced to quickly devise ways to conserve water and make due with its annual allocation. In a domino effect, this led California to propose lining the All-American Canal with concrete in order to prevent seepage. This would conserve water for California, but it also would limit the replenishment of Mexican aquifers, on which the farmers in the Mexicali Valley depend. Thus, the parties ended up in a contentious litigation, with damaged relationships and significant loss of time and money.

The need for flexibility in handling natural resources, as the same action will have different impacts according to the shifting circumstances, is also present in both cases. In the Gulf of Mexico, forbidding cooperation with IOCs and placing a moratorium on the development of transboundary oil exploration did not necessarily pose a significant problem at first, in the context of Mexico's productive onshore and shallow-water fields. As decades passed, however, production from these wells began a sharp decline, and Mexico was left with the need to find new sources of revenue, most of which were located offshore, in deepwater fields for which it needed access to a level of investment, risk-sharing practices, and technological expertise that would be possible only through a binational partnership and the removal of the moratorium.

In the Colorado River case, a clause in the 1944 United States–Mexico Water Treaty that allowed the United States to unilaterally reduce water deliveries to Mexico in conditions of "extraordinary drought" (without defining the term, its associated volume, or triggers) was permissible to both countries at a time when no immediate risk of drought loomed. However, once the two countries faced severe drought as a reality, which was only predicted to worsen, the lack of specificity regarding how and when to define "extraordinary drought" led to an urgent need to find a solution. In the context of overallocated water resources, increasing demand, and reduced flows, figuring out how to resolve the impasse and avoid costly confrontation became critical.

The evidence in these case studies underscores that effective natural resource negotiations tend to require a great deal of improvisation in order to adapt to an ever-changing world. The examples from both cases provide support for the three tenets of the WDF, highlighting the extent to which countries stand to benefit from fostering a negotiated environment that embraces boundary crossings, accounts for perturbations, and enhances flexibility.

Adaptive Leadership

Detecting Judgment Hurdles

Several leadership scholars argue that people (and the organizations they belong to) are regularly subject to several harmful biases in judgment. They make the case that addressing these patterns is crucial for conducting effective problem-solving efforts.[7] These biases tend to include:

• Plunging into disputes without having a shared framework to determine how and what information to gather.
• Making insufficient adjustments from past references, even after these references are no longer relevant.

• Focusing disproportionately on data that confirm one's assumptions without seeking evidence to the contrary.

• Giving more weight to short-term considerations without linking to medium- and long-term concerns.

• Evaluating solutions on the basis of past results without acknowledging new circumstances.

• Making decisions that account for only one potential outcome, and therefore not preparing for multiple scenarios.[8]

In the energy resources case, for instance, the two countries spent many decades without a shared framework with which to evaluate and decide whether transboundary reservoirs existed in the first place. Seismic information, which is necessary to determine the exact location and scale of the hydrocarbon deposits, was proprietary on both sides. Without mechanisms to share data between the two countries, and without cooperation between the IOCs and the NOC, neither side could have a full picture of the reservoir realities on either flank of the maritime boundary.

The United States claimed that the existence of the reservoirs was doubtful. More important, they posited that even if cross-boundary reservoirs were to be found someday, given the narrow geological formations in the region, extracting activities on their own side of the maritime boundary would not result in the drainage of hydrocarbon reserves on the other side. Mexico was convinced to the contrary on both points. They argued that the existence of cross-boundary reservoirs was highly likely, and that the United States did not recognize these facts precisely because the IOCs aimed to drain the shared reservoirs. In this context, neither side looked for mechanisms to disconfirm their long-held assumptions, many of which were based on outdated references derived from decades-old political posturing.

In the water resources case, short-term considerations had continuously been given primacy over medium- and long-term concerns, with parties adhering to the "first-in-time, first-in-right" doctrine. Moreover, neither country had agreed to a structure through which to prepare for scenarios that had not been drafted into the 1944 treaty allocating the waters of the Colorado River between the two nations. Making matters worse, several studies suggested that the period that was used as the reference to determine the average flows of the river (1900s–1920s), thus dividing the waters between the Upper and Lower Basin states and subsequently between the United States and Mexico, was characterized by abnormally high rainfall.

In turn, as the 2010s began, the two countries had yet to develop a coordinated set of binational measures to respond to severe drought and the looming effects of climate change.

Based on evidence from the two cases, in both the Gulf of Mexico and the Colorado River, the two countries spent decades mired in disputes in part due to the following circumstances:

• They lacked a shared framework to assess the full picture of the extent of their problems in the first place.
• They were stuck on past references, even after these references clearly needed to be updated.
• They were fixed on defending their assumptions without seeking evidence to the contrary.
• They placed too much weight on short-term considerations in spite of the long-term risks.
• They failed to account for multiple scenarios, many of which were pressing and deserved careful consideration.

In light of this, I argue that these judgment biases were not only prevalent, but also compounded under a zero-sum frame of mind. This hindered the effective resolution of their transboundary disputes until, as part of these landmark negotiations, these biases were finally acknowledged, addressed, and overcome.

Breaking the Deadlock

Practitioners of adaptive leadership argue that parties to a dispute will frequently prove risk-averse, overestimating the likelihood of losses and underestimating the potential for gains.[9] Such distress and resistance are said to hinder problem-solving efforts by the stakeholders and to narrow the possibilities for finding mutually beneficial agreements.[10]

At various stages prior to and during the two negotiation processes, parties on both sides succumbed to the common trap of overestimating the potential losses and underestimating possible gains. For example, in the Gulf of Mexico, Mexico, the relatively weaker party, originally proposed to negotiate a binational agreement from a defensive perspective, with the aim of blocking the United States from unilaterally draining the shared reservoirs. In this frame, based on a fear of loss, Mexico was unable to convince the United States to come to the negotiating table, as the latter saw nothing to gain by engaging in binational negotiations in which they were presumed to be deceptive from the outset.

The United States, for its part, simultaneously overestimated the potential losses that could result from moving away from the unilateral rule of capture as its legal guideline and establishing instead a new transboundary framework with Mexico. The United States feared that such a shift would set a precedent, thus undermining their position in other international negotiations, and would subject the scope of action of its private IOCs to a complex web of binational politics with Mexico. However, creating a framework to foster codevelopment through unitization partnerships, as it pertains to offshore cross-boundary hydrocarbon fields, has long been the international best practice to effectively and efficiently produce oil resources. Unitization partnerships better allocate operating risks between the parties and increase output from the reservoir, thus resulting in higher revenues for all involved.

Mexico's concerns about being deceived by the United States, fears founded on the two countries' difficult history, arose in the Colorado River case as well. Mexico originally overestimated the potential dangers involved in agreeing to store its water in U.S. reservoirs. Many of the country's back-table groups argued that the United States must have ulterior motives for offering to store Mexico's water, such as hydroelectricity generation, and that the United States would inevitably take advantage of it. But when an earthquake struck the Mexicali Valley in Baja California in 2010, forcing Mexico to reconsider its hesitancy toward storing water in the United States, it found that such fears had been unfounded. In fact, Mexico discovered that it had underestimated the benefits of such a situation. Storing its water in the United States enabled Mexico to prepare for times of drought by securing reliable water storage in the upstream U.S. reservoirs, at no charge and without the need to expend large sums to construct reservoirs on the Mexican side of the border.

On the U.S. side, the Upper Basin states were extremely hesitant about collaborating with the environmental NGOs. Based on a history of confrontation and litigation throughout the American Southwest, the states initially overestimated the costs of such a partnership. Especially in times of drought, they worried that allocating water for environmental purposes would be politically infeasible. As the negotiations unfolded, however, they realized that the NGOs, through their decades of binational expertise and relationships, brought great value to the process beyond the expected technical insights. More specifically, the NGOs helped to resolve political misunderstandings between the two countries by functioning as informal, trustworthy channels of information through which government officials could send messages across the border in ways that were not necessarily possible in the formal sessions.

The evidence in both transboundary negotiations underscores that when the parties were able to move past the disproportionate focus on potential losses, as well as the underestimation of benefits, they were able to progress toward mutually advantageous outcomes.

Facilitating Renewed Outlooks

Adaptive leadership proponents suggest that individuals in positions of authority should facilitate processes that empower stakeholders to carefully question their own assumptions and relationships.[11] They suggest that a proactive effort to spur parties to critique, reprioritize, and update their interests in light of renewed perspectives is critical to deal effectively with complex problems.[12]

In the Gulf of Mexico case, for example, David L. Goldwyn, at the time the highest-ranking official for international energy affairs at the DOS, was critical in facilitating a fruitful process to change preconceptions within the U.S. back table. He did so by carefully structuring discussions and meetings between government officials at the White House, the DOS, and the DOI, in order to slowly change assumptions about what negotiating with Mexico would entail. Gaining full support from Secretary of State Hillary Clinton, Goldwyn was able to help shape a broad mandate for the U.S. team—a mandate that sought to create an agreement based on mutual gains, in stark contrast to the narrow view that had characterized the adherence to the rule of capture. Later, empowered with this mandate, Sullivan at the DOS was able to propose his idea of holding binational workshops, which allowed representatives from both countries to fundamentally critique and update their interests as they gained a better understanding of the other side's political, legal, and commercial constraints.

On Mexico's side, a decision by the leaders at the Ministry of Energy and PEMEX to invite U.S. officials to PEMEX's state-of-the-art, three-dimensional visualization room for a key meeting was a game-changer. There, Mexican experts presented proprietary seismic data that the U.S. representatives had not seen previously. This gesture encouraged the U.S. negotiators to reassess some of their assumptions in light of this new data. And, most important, the gesture functioned as a critical signal of Mexico's willingness to approach the complex problems at stake in the binational negotiations with transparency. This data presentation served as a confidence-building measure, fostering a new sense of trust and laying the building blocks for a more collegial relationship between the two sides.

In the Colorado River case, throughout the negotiations, the U.S. Bureau of Reclamation took on a facilitative role, advocating on behalf of the interests of different stakeholders at different points in time, to allow parties to redefine their assumptions and relationships. For example, Michael Connor, the commissioner of the U.S. Bureau of Reclamation, in collaboration with his colleagues at the DOI, was part of the effort to convince the Upper Basin states, on behalf of the NGOs, that the proposed water for environmental restoration purposes was not a ploy by the Lower Basin states to get more water for their own purposes, nor would Mexico divert environmental restoration water for its irrigation needs.

Conversely, Connor argued on behalf of all the Basin states, encouraging the DOS officials to revisit their opposition to having the Basin states participate as cosovereigns in the binational negotiation process. He argued that, although not in line with traditional diplomatic protocol, the only way to an actionable agreement would be through the face-to-face direct involvement and approval of the Basin states, as they were the ones who, in practice, own and comanage the Colorado River waters with the DOI.

Similar efforts occurred on the Mexican side. The work by Roberto Salmón, the commissioner of the Mexican section of the IBWC, in collaboration with his colleagues at the IBWC and at the Office of the Director General of the National Water Commission (Comisión Nacional del Agua, or CONAGUA), was essential to spur several domestic stakeholders to reprioritize some of their interests. For example, several members of the Ministry of the Treasury and of CONAGUA were convinced that the binational negotiations should primarily focus around acquiring as much U.S. investment as possible in order to repair the crippled infrastructure left in the wake of the Easter Earthquake in Mexicali. However, Commissioner Salmón and his colleagues were mindful that the Mexican Treasury estimates about the financial resources that the U.S. stakeholders would make available for such investments were markedly off.

Therefore, instead of requesting this support outright, they made the case to look at the potential binational agreement as the way to jump-start collaboration on other fronts, from environmental restoration to water conservation measures to building desalination plants, as a means to start dealing with the complexity of the challenges at stake and to reap more benefits further down the line. Specifically, they succeeded in increasing water availability on Mexico's side, beyond what the infrastructure repairs could have achieved on their own.

The two cases present ample evidence to support the tenet of adaptive leadership that highlights the importance of having leaders encourage stakeholders to reassess their presumptions and relationships with the other side. Such commitment, behind the scenes and across the table, helped to set a tone through which both countries were able to learn from one another and redefine how to best meet their interests. This was to their mutual advantage in light of the complexity of the challenges in the Gulf of Mexico and in the Colorado River.

Collaborative Decision-Making

Working from a Shared Baseline

Collaborative decision-making experts frequently argue that higher-quality outputs, in the form of more flexible guidelines, standards, and policies, derive from mutual understanding, shared problem frames, agreed-upon baselines, and technically informed scenarios.[13] As such, they emphasize the need to devote significant resources, preferably up front, to understand the core interests of the parties.[14]

In the Gulf of Mexico, for example, the two sides needed to devise a framework to resolve potential dispute scenarios regarding the existence of transboundary reservoirs, the division of production responsibilities, and the redetermination of voluntary and compulsory allocations. Given that PEMEX is a state-owned company and the IOCs are private entities, the countries were challenged to make their initial dispute resolution perspectives compatible. They were significantly at odds about what type of framework would effectively deter potentially serious conflicts between hydrocarbon developers on either side of the maritime boundary.

On one side, fearful of the disparities in relative political and economic power, Mexico requested the inclusion of a binding international arbitration clause to settle potential disputes, as part of the binational agreement. The United States was opposed to this because both the U.S. Congress and the IOCs requested not to use binding arbitration, preferring to settle out of court instead. In this context, the prospects of reaching an understanding appeared bleak until the two countries started to work side by side to get at the underlying interests of each country pertaining to the purposes of the dispute resolution framework itself.

By working together, they discovered that Mexico's main concern was to have a mechanism in place ensuring that the IOCs would not exploit the transboundary reservoirs unilaterally; and the U.S. concern was to make sure that commercial activity in the maritime boundary was not frozen as a result of protracted binational disputes in the hands of international arbitrators. Upon this realization, they concluded that the best path would be to include a series of incentives in the agreement, which would simultaneously ensure codevelopment and obviate the need for binding arbitration.

From this agreed-upon baseline, they built a three-tiered dispute resolution process (senior-management-level dialogue, mediation, nonbinding arbitration), that closely mirrored the joint operating contracts that the IOCs are used to, but involved a clause whereby, if the IOCs and NOC do not reach an agreement, either of the two governments could step in to stop production. The significant financial losses that would result from being required to halt production, when hundreds of millions of dollars are at stake, ought to provide a more-than-adequate incentive, driving the parties to reach an agreement without binding arbitration.

Reaching this creative understanding was possible by combining the expertise, both as an oil engineer and as a lawyer, of Sullivan, the head of the U.S. negotiating team, with the involvement of a highly regarded industry observer on the U.S. side, Keith Couvillion, the deepwater land manager of Chevron, representing the IOCs. Couvillion had prior relationships with expert PEMEX and Mexican officials, so he was able to openly discuss which types of measures would incentivize the IOCs to act in particular ways and why, while also understanding and responding to the constraints and priorities of PEMEX.

A shared technical understanding was also required in the Colorado River case. One crucial example is the initial discrepancy in the water management modeling systems utilized in each country. Mexico had long employed the Water Evaluation and Planning System (WEAP) modeling tool to manage its share of the Colorado River waters. This model suits the conditions in the Mexicali Valley, as it effectively incorporates surface water delivery, demand infiltration, and groundwater utilization. It is not as robust, however, on reservoir operations, since Mexico has no significant storage facilities. The U.S. Basin states and the DOI, however, use the Colorado River Simulation System (CRSS) model, which aids in the management of several large reservoirs, as well as the various dams and canals that underpin operations on the U.S. side. So, by relying on WEAP, Mexico was unable to effectively test how different policy options being discussed in the binational negotiations would affect basin operations on the U.S. side, and in turn water deliveries to Mexico.

Only by working together for more than a year in a binational work group, during which time Mexico's technical experts were able to learn and master the use of the CRSS model, were the two sides able to engage in serious policy discussions about the different alternatives at stake from a hydrological, operational, and environmental standpoint.

Through this process, which was also aided by in-person visits to major infrastructure sites along the Colorado River Basin, a mutual understanding arose about the nuances of the drought scenarios with which the Basin states had been working. The two countries also identified how the Basin states' insights could be incorporated into binational measures in such a way as to provide Mexico with confidence that the upstream reservoir operating measures would be subject to a mutually beneficial set of checks and balances for the downstream riparian.

The evidence in both cases underscores that only once the negotiators shared mutually agreed-upon frames of reference were they then able to produce critical parts of the agreements to truthfully suit each side's core interests. The shared problem frames, agreed-upon baselines, and technically informed scenarios that resulted from a long, nuanced, in-depth, and collaborative decision-making process produced higher-quality outputs. This enabled the creation of mutually beneficial solutions in the form of more accurate, feasible, flexible, and effective guidelines and policies.

Trusting Each Other

Proponents of collaborative decision-making suggest that the practice enhances interpersonal and institutional linkages, rendering conflict resolution better informed by the relevant stakeholders.[15] When, as in most cases, clear solutions are not evident but there are various alternatives benefiting different parties in different forms, reaching better, wiser, and more equitable decisions is more feasible on the basis of relationships that foster reciprocity and trust.[16]

In each of the transboundary cases, building a solid rapport through collaboration was a critical component to shaping an effective negotiation process. In the Gulf of Mexico, the leaders of the negotiating delegations from the United States and Mexico, David Sullivan and Arturo Dager, were able to develop a deep sense of respect for and trust in one another. Regularly engaging in side-talks at various points in the binational process, they depended on each other to protect the collaborative spirit of the negotiations and to ensure their ultimate success. For example, on occasion, a politically well-connected figure would come to the binational negotiating table, and without recurring involvement beyond a couple of sessions, would display a dissonant, hard-bargaining approach. This happened on both sides and created unnecessary tensions.

In such circumstances, during the breaks between the morning and afternoon meetings, the leader on the side of this errant interloper would ask the other, through private conversations, not to pay mind to this behavior, to simply let the person rant and move on. Whereas the confrontational hard-bargaining approach could have otherwise put the negotiations in jeopardy by weakening the links that were being formed across the different agencies represented at the table, this strong foundation of trust and reciprocity enabled the two leaders to protect the process and inform their delegations not to become angered or derailed by such aggressive tactics.

The negotiators in the Colorado River case also built relationships of trust with each other in a number of ways. One manner in which this was accomplished was by inviting the other side on tours of relevant infrastructure and natural areas. Mexico, for example, did not initially trust that the surface elevation levels at Lake Mead should be the trigger for shortage conditions, as they feared these levels would be artificially manipulated. Instead, they wanted a hydrological index that could be observed by a neutral third party. However, the U.S. Basin states and the U.S. Bureau of Reclamation, after years of research and negotiations among each other, knew from direct experience that the elevation levels were indeed the best measure to gauge conditions in such a large and diverse river basin.

After the sides had been at odds for more than a year, arguing back and forth in work groups, the U.S. section of the IBWC proposed to break the impasse by carrying out extensive tours for their Mexican colleagues of the U.S. infrastructure and data collection centers in different Basin states. Through these visits, the United States demonstrated to Mexican officials that the system of water management relying on elevation levels was highly objective and was crafted so as to have checks and balances in place that would prevent any one state from manipulating the levels without the other states finding out. Seeing how the reservoirs function in practice was invaluable in building the necessary trust that eventually led Mexico to agree to use the elevation levels in Lake Mead as the primary indicator of shortage and surplus.

These dynamics also worked the other way around. Mexican officials at the IBWC invited U.S. representatives on tours of the Mexicali Valley and Colorado River Delta to assuage their concerns regarding Mexico's requests for environmental flows in times of drought. The U.S. negotiators were able to see that the Mexican federal government was indeed dedicated to environmental restoration projects across the delta, and that no water sent to Mexico with that purpose would be diverted for agricultural uses. They also saw the state of the infrastructure and recognized the abundant opportunities for conservation projects. These tours enabled the two sides to form bonds, empathize with their counterparts, and figure out ways to agree upon mutually beneficial solutions.

The evidence from each of these two cases supports the argument that the practice of collaborative decision-making enhances interpersonal and institutional linkages. By actively fostering relationships of trust and reciprocity, the negotiators were able to make informed decisions between multiple alternatives and craft more stable agreements that served to benefit both sides.

Involving the Right People

Scholars of collaborative decision-making argue that to foster and sustain the effective resolution of disputes in the public arena, government officials must overcome several assumptions about the parties to a public dispute.[17] Crucial among these is the narrow preconception that stakeholders ought to have little role in devising and implementing solutions, beyond providing comments, lobbying lawmakers, or challenging them in court.[18]

In each of the transboundary negotiations discussed here, the serious involvement of stakeholders who had not been included in previous efforts was a significant turning point in resolving the disputes. In the Gulf of Mexico case, the U.S. negotiators received a mandate from the White House to create a framework that would produce offshore energy from the transboundary region, and to do so in a safe and efficient way. The assumption on the U.S. side, however, was that everyone in the environmental community would be hostile to the notion of a binational agreement on transboundary hydrocarbon reservoirs. In light of the catastrophic Macondo oil spill, and with a Democratic Party majority in the Senate, it was hard to imagine why the environmental interests would ever allow new acreage for offshore drilling in deep water to be opened for development.

Yet, under these circumstances, instead of waiting for the NGOs to lobby or litigate against a potential agreement, the U.S. negotiating team conducted an extensive outreach campaign from the outset, to consult with the NGOs and figure out solutions. The challenge was clear: the cornerstone of Mexico's public financing lies in oil revenues. Due to plummeting productivity in their current fields, Mexico was inevitably going to move into deepwater exploration and production on their side of the maritime boundary. The United States had two options: to continue to abide by unilateral development under the rule of capture or to figure out a framework to codevelop the reservoirs with Mexico.

The latter strategy, through unitization partnerships, would decrease the number of wells built and would improve the technology that is put in place. Moreover, in the process of consulting with the NGOs, the U.S. negotiators devised an inspection regime, which ultimately formed part of the agreement and is unique to this binational accord, in which inspectors from either side can call attention to situations to which they believe authorities on the other side are turning a blind eye. This occurs in such a way as to not compromise national law, yet be enforced under international law. Through this mechanism, the two countries circumvent any issues of sovereignty while providing an additional safety check to lower risks to life, serious personal injury, and damage to the environment. With this package in place, the environmental organizations expressed that while they obviously would not advocate for passage of the agreement, neither would they step in to oppose it.

In the Colorado River case, traditionally, only federal government officials were to negotiate binational water issues. After much convincing on the part of the seven Basin states and the DOI, the DOS and Mexican authorities finally permitted U.S. state representatives into the process. This occurred in confidence-building stages: first, these new stakeholders were in an adjoining room ready for consultation; then they were permitted to be in the negotiating room as observers, though not at the table; and ultimately, they were seated at the table. As the Basin states own the Colorado River water on the U.S. side, their contribution was fundamental in breaking deadlocks, devising the content of the agreement, and ensuring its successful implementation and follow-up monitoring.

The involvement of the Basin states proved to be critical on numerous occasions. For example, in the aftermath of the Easter earthquake that crippled Mexico's irrigation infrastructure in the Mexicali Valley, the presence of the Basin states was essential to quickly devise the emergency measures that allowed Mexico to store a significant share of that year's Colorado River water allocation in Lake Mead—water that otherwise would have been lost if it had been delivered.

Another example is that by allowing the Basin states to participate as cosovereigns in the negotiations, the Lower Basin water agencies, such as the Southern Nevada Water Authority (SNWA), the Central Arizona Project, and the Metropolitan Water District of Southern California, were able to explain firsthand the ways in which their interests differ from the agencies of the Upper Basin. The water agencies in the Lower Basin are geographically and institutionally much more inclined to joint investments in conservation projects and desalination plants on Mexico's side of the border, in order to facilitate water savings and exchanges, seizing on the lower costs to bring more water to their ratepayers.

Last but not least, the active leadership of state representatives, such as Pat Mulroy, president of the Association of Metropolitan Water Agencies, and John Entsminger, senior deputy general manager of the SNWA, both close to Senator Harry Reid, fundamentally altered the internal balance of power to which U.S. federal officials were subject. This in turn protected the course and outcome of the negotiations between the United States and Mexico. Flexing the political muscle of the seven Basin states, through the combined might of their 14 senators, was fundamental to block the spoiling efforts led by diverse interests in Texas, which could have otherwise derailed the Colorado River negotiations by trying to link them to the Rio Grande disputes.

The evidence from each of the natural resource cases supports the argument that breaking standard protocol and ensuring a broader and more meaningful stakeholder engagement brought a significant benefit to both negotiation processes. It removed the threat of litigation from opposing parties, empowered them to address emergencies, was critical to block potential spoilers, and vastly improved ownership and implementation of the agreements' measures.

Political Communication

Changing the Narrative

Long-held narratives emphasizing conflict and mistrust, though frequently popular with the media, often hinder the resolution of disputes in the public arena.[19] Practitioners of effective political communication argue instead that actively integrating more balanced perspectives into the public discourse is critical to enabling the first steps toward reconciliation and remedy.[20]

For both the Gulf of Mexico and Colorado River cases, shifting the narrative of mistrust to one of collaboration was foundational to creating mutually favorable agreements. For example, with the Gulf of Mexico, and specifically across Mexico's energy sector, the narrative for decades had long centered on a deeply held mistrust of the United States. There was a widespread preconception that not only would the United States and its private industry find a way to drain oil belonging to Mexico out of the transboundary reservoirs, but that if a cooperative agreement were ever reached, it would inevitably be tilted in favor of the United States. The Mexican negotiating team, however, seized upon this "mission impossible" and believed that negotiating a fair agreement to benefit the social and economic development of both countries was feasible.

The mistrust across the table also ran in the other direction. Several members of the U.S. private industry and U.S. government had long considered the rule of capture to be their best line of defense to not become entangled in the complex web of politics that tends to underpin the operating decisions of PEMEX, as a state-owned company. So they were hesitant about supporting any collaborative process with Mexico, delaying and curtailing interactions.

However, through extensive informal conversations that began in the last two years of the George W. Bush administration and intensified during the first two years of the Obama administration, the two sides were able to reach an accord to make a concerted effort to move forward in a new, constructive, and collaborative binational process. This dialogue took place between high-ranking officials at the DOS and the DOI and Mexico's Ministry of Energy and Ministry of Foreign Affairs, as well as the IOCs and PEMEX.

This shift to a new process was later cemented by the presidents of both countries, with Barack Obama and Felipe Calderón stating, at the conclusion of a binational summit in Washington, D.C., that the two sides were exploring how to build a safer, more efficient, and more equitable bilateral energy framework. Soon thereafter, the two countries announced the formal launch of the negotiations through another joint public statement, which clearly defined the new mandate from both presidents: to find a way to safely and effectively develop the shared reservoirs across the maritime boundary. The negotiators themselves noted the importance of this high-level public encouragement in carrying them through the negotiations. It signaled that the public narrative was shifting from viewing each other as threatening to undermine national sovereignty to seeing each other as critical energy partners to enhance their mutual economic vitality.

Similar examples about significantly changing the narrative can be noted in the Colorado River case. The Mexican ambassador to the United States, Arturo Sarukhán, initiated a series of informal discussions with the U.S. secretary of the interior, Dirk Kempthorne, regarding the need to specifically build a new binational narrative in order to create a collaborative framework through which the two countries would be able to address the many serious challenges of the Colorado River Basin. Following the All-American Canal conflict, the ambassador argued that the countries could remain accomplices in failure or become partners in success.

Based on the understanding that the two countries were able to reach as a result of this high-level dialogue, which took place over a couple of years, they then released a set of joint declarations that set the tone for the respective government agencies to engage in a cooperative negotiation process. Officials from both sections of the IBWC, as well as the U.S. Bureau of Reclamation, confirmed the significance of these declarations in starting anew after years of contentious conflict.

This tone continued once the Obama administration came into office in 2009. Under the auspice of this new narrative, the U.S. authorities and Basin states were able to conceive of working with Mexico, as they never had tried before. Through the negotiation process, they reached a new level of mutual understanding and regard, which is best captured by the fact that both sides now publicly consider Mexico not as a customer to whom they must deliver water, but rather as a partner in managing the Basin.

The evidence from these cases highlights that the two countries had to supersede a narrative of mistrust, which had long shaped the interactions between them in relation to these transboundary disputes. They had to be more sensitive to the intensity with which different constituencies hold certain values and acknowledge the legitimacy of their interests; then, they had to refocus their attention not on how the two countries could ever get along (framing it as an impossible dream), but rather on how they could thrive together. Once an initial agreement on this shared goal had been reached behind the scenes between the two sides, in each case, it proved very useful that top leadership from both countries publicly acknowledged the mistakes of the past and announced that they were committed to figuring out, together, how to move ahead constructively. In both negotiations, therefore, by bringing new perspectives into the public discourse, the two sides enabled the first steps toward reconciliation and remedy.

Fostering Appreciation and Connection

Communication scholars, building upon brain and cognitive science, underscore that reason works under the significant initiative and guidance of emotions.[21] They make the case that emotions influence what we focus on, thus underlying our imagination, reflection, and judgment. Regardless of the technical components underpinning a dispute, we ignore emotions at our own peril; we should rather work to increase appreciation and camaraderie among the stakeholders mired in confrontations in the public arena.[22]

Each of the cases explored in this research provide examples of the importance of the emotional aspect of negotiation. In the Gulf of Mexico case, a story of mutual respect unfolded, with negotiators on each side moving away from a narrative of mistrust and getting to the point of describing their counterparts as trusted colleagues: willing to invest the time to debate the technical underpinnings of the issues at hand and ready to strongly advance their delegation's interests, while still receptive and flexible enough to empathize with the core concerns of the other side.

For example, toward the end of the Gulf of Mexico negotiations, the Mexican officials admitted to the U.S. representatives that at first, they had thought that the U.S. proposal to hold binational workshops before proceeding to negotiate from a text agreement was simply a delaying tactic. They were able to experience how critical those monthly workshops proved to be, however, as they empowered both sides to get to know one another, build rapport, and learn about numerous complex themes simultaneously.

These positive developments facilitated opportunities for the negotiators to consider how they could solve their problems in a collaborative way among trusted colleagues rather than through hard-bargaining tactics. This enhanced level of appreciation and confidence, garnered through the workshops and continued in informal interactions between sessions (i.e., coffee breaks, lunches, and dinners), was an important aspect that enabled an agreement to be reached in a considerably shorter amount of time compared to other similar international negotiations. The negotiators on both sides explain that they were no longer second-guessing the motivations or reasoning behind the other side's proposals as much as they would have in the absence of those shared experiences.

A very similar journey, from mistrust to mutual respect, took place in the Colorado River case. Over the course of more than three years, the people involved in these negotiations had repeated opportunities to connect with each other on a personal level, through informal interactions, tours, and work-group meetings. There were several episodes in which the negotiators describe how, after a coffee break, sharing a walk, or spending time together over dinner, they were more willing and able to put themselves in the other side's shoes, and better appreciate their constraints and interests.

Entsminger, one of the lead negotiators for the Lower Basin states, representing Nevada, exemplifies this level of enhanced connection. Known for his no-nonsense approach, he thought to himself, after being greeted with warm applause by the Mexican delegation upon his return to a binational work-group session after an absence of less than a day, how much he really cared about the people with whom he was negotiating, in spite of butting heads recurrently after having spent days, weeks, and months trying to craft binational solutions.

There is also the story of Connor, the commissioner of the U.S. Bureau of Reclamation, in which he recounts that after meeting in a side-talk early on with Salmón, the Mexican IBWC commissioner, to resolve a significant miscommunication that threatened to derail and halt the negotiations from the outset, he felt that the Mexican leader was a person whom he could genuinely trust. The Mexican officials spoke similarly of their U.S. counterparts, painting a picture that emphasized feelings of shared respect and admiration.

Similarly, the environmental NGOs were able to bring their close personal and professional ties to colleagues on the other side of the border, contributing to the binational negotiation process in crucial moments. They took on the role of trusted neutrals to move information between government officials from one country to the other, prompted stakeholders on both sides to reconsider confrontational stances, and actively resolved cultural and language miscommunications that could have derailed the signing of the agreement.

The evidence from both cases, as seen through the unfolding of relationships based on congeniality and assurance, supports the notion that positive emotions of affiliation and connection critically influenced the negotiators' reflections and judgments. Providing negotiators with opportunities to build these personal and emotional bonds empowered parties to put themselves in the other side's shoes more often and more effectively, to the significant advantage of both countries.

Focusing on the Benefits

Experts in effective communication in the public arena suggest that when stakeholders emphasize the sacrifices rather than the opportunities at stake—solely the costs instead of the benefits—constituencies tend to reject the message.[23] They argue that the political message should focus instead on empowering the parties to seize the gains that will clearly leave them better off.[24]

The negotiators in both cases were aware that media coverage of the proceedings (and potential agreements) was likely to construe the negotiations (and associated measures) in an incomplete or negative light, rather than focus on the benefits to both countries. As a result, they actively worked together to stem this challenge from the outset.

In the Gulf of Mexico, given the history of mistrust about U.S. involvement in Mexico's energy sector, the two countries agreed to communicate solely through joint declarations (and to keep these to a minimum). Press releases focused on emphasizing the benefits of a new era of collaboration. The aim was to minimize opportunities to spoil a binational deal, particularly by domestic Mexican actors who, for political purposes, would try to accuse Mexican government officials of betraying their country, regardless of the solutions at stake in the negotiations that would directly address the weaknesses of Mexico's energy sector.

PEMEX, simultaneously, recognized the need to build public awareness of the realities associated with Mexico's declining oil fields, as well as the need to address this challenge proactively. The NOC devised a media campaign that, without mentioning the ongoing binational negotiations, stressed the fact that many of the country's landmark shallow offshore oil fields were nearing the end of their cycle. PEMEX conveyed that to make the transition to promising new fields, most of which were to be found in deep water, new mechanisms through which to associate with international energy companies would be necessary. The message was simple: the country stood to gain substantially if PEMEX were able to rely on better technology, foreign investment, and international partnerships. The increased oil tax revenues would then serve to finance the country's investments in education, public health, and security, areas for which the general public could agree that additional funds, derived from collaboration, were necessary.

In the Colorado River case, the negotiators also had to manage their interactions with the press carefully. The two sides similarly agreed to a joint communication strategy in which stakeholders in each country had the opportunity to review and approve the press releases of the other. Throughout the negotiations, conscious that stakeholders tend to reject the idea of burden-sharing, the two countries kept media briefings about their progress to a minimum. They knew that it would be very difficult for either side to put on the table several of the key trades that eventually enabled the agreement if they had to do so publicly from the beginning or as the negotiations were ongoing, before a winning package had been fully established.

Both countries were also very concerned that media reports misconstruing the binational conversation could set the negotiations back by creating added pressure and alienating specific constituencies on one side or the other. As news travels quickly across the border, close attention was paid not only to how the local public would respond to reports in the media, but also how stakeholders from the other country would react once their own media outlets interpreted these reports.

Careful notice was given to the phrasing of newspaper headlines and television broadcasts, as described in detail by Mulroy. She recounts memorable tales of meetings with the heads of the television stations and newspapers in Las Vegas, with the purpose of delivering an announcement of the landmark binational agreement that would be well received and understood on both sides of the border. Great attention was paid to the content and headlines, assessing how these would be received not only by the public in Nevada but by the audience in Mexico. In these meetings, she made sure to stress the benefits of the agreement, while also avoiding specific phrases in English that could be entirely misunderstood if translated literally into Spanish.

This painstaking messaging was evidenced not only by government stakeholders, but also by the NGOs. They steered their communication campaigns to a select group of foundations, purposefully avoiding widely publicized announcements and resisting pressure to broadcast news in the media, throughout the negotiations and even after the binational Colorado River agreement had been signed and implemented. As described by Gastón Luken-Aguilar, president of Pronatura, the goal was to communicate effectively with concerned stakeholders who could weigh the nuances and benefits of the binational collaboration and in turn commit their resources to deliver results in the implementation stage.

The evidence from both cases underscores that the United States and Mexico focused on emphasizing the benefits rather than the costs of the binational negotiations. Through simple, brief, jointly reviewed, targeted, and carefully timed messages, both sides were able to outline the mutual gains at stake for concerned stakeholders. This commitment protected and enhanced collaboration throughout the entire negotiation process, providing stakeholders with the space and time to find effective trades and deliver results on the ground, empowering both countries to provide their constituencies with a mutually beneficial agreement.

12   Steps to Effective Transboundary Negotiations

The four different areas of insight through which the cases are analyzed in the previous chapter, while overlapping in many ways, are normally examined as distinct from one another. Inspired by integrating these four perspectives, and based on the lessons learned from the field, I provide here a set of strategies to contribute to the preparation, negotiation, and resolution of transboundary resource management disputes. This prescriptive advice is intended primarily for leaders working to resolve energy, water, and environmental conflicts, but the principles and strategies may prove useful in other sectors and contexts as well. The suggested 12 steps flow in approximate chronological order, from well before a negotiation is initiated to follow-up measures after an agreement has been implemented.

1.   Persuade the Other Side to Negotiate

Upon recognizing a conflict for which negotiation is deemed necessary, the first step entails enticing the other side to come to the negotiating table. The other side may hesitate or may not believe that negotiation is needed or in their best interest. Whether coming from a position of greater or lesser relative power, one must make a compelling case as to the benefits to be reaped from initiating negotiations and reaching agreement. In order to impart this to the other side, one would need to employ a combination of the following tactics: (1) present insights to which the other side has not previously been privy; (2) build alliances with members of the opposing side's back table, to nudge them to the negotiations; and (3) bring more issues to the discussion beyond the immediately central matters. In these ways, one can demonstrate to the other side that if they choose not to negotiate, they will lose a significant opportunity to benefit from a positive outcome, with more repercussions, and in more areas, than they may have thought at first.

2. Overcome Past Grievances

Leading up to the negotiations, and once they have begun, the parties in many instances must cope with long histories of confrontation. To move beyond a difficult past, it is helpful to have top leaders single out the specific former and current practices that have contributed to deadlock. The purpose should be to reach across the table, through informal conversations, to discover if there are ways in which both sides believe that, together, they can take concrete steps to improve their dispute resolution practices and move beyond past and present failures.

This should entail two approaches, to address both the rational and the emotional underpinnings of the narrative of mistrust. In order to engage the aspect of reason, one must point to the technical components that have led to an impasse. Leaders should emphasize the costs that have resulted from (1) a lack of access to the full array of relevant information, (2) a failure to properly map and link issues, and (3) breakdowns as a result of not looking at problems ahead of time and for the right amount of time. From an emotional standpoint, negotiators should raise awareness about how the preconceptions on both sides have affected what they say and how they interpret what they hear. At least at first, all sides should try to be aware that their conceptions are likely to be colored by the arduous shared history, with each side doubting the other's motivations and trustworthiness and blaming the other rather than looking to themselves.

3. Declare the Mandate

Only once an informal decision to work together constructively has been reached between the leaders on both sides should a formal public announcement to launch the negotiation process be made. The formal announcement should come from the highest authorities possible. Simple and memorable, it should clearly state that the mandate is to foster a collaborative process in order to allow both sides to reap more benefits than either would be capable of achieving on their own. It is beneficial to display the high-level buy-in publicly, so that further down the line, if

complications arise, the negotiators can refer back to the formal announcement to remind themselves of the need to work things out as their main
diplomatic responsibility.

4. Adapt the Protocol

Building upon the informal consensus and the formal announcement to
move forward cooperatively, the two sides should develop a comprehensive
map of the key stakeholders who, if involved in a transboundary process,
would be eager to contribute to the negotiation proceedings and eventual
agreement. Leaders in the public sector should be willing to break standard
protocol to ensure that the right people are sitting at the table. Whenever
such a protocol precludes the ability to engage relevant stakeholder expertise, it should be reassessed and adjusted. Rather than maintaining a relationship based on lobbying and litigation, wasting time and resources for
everyone, it is best to significantly involve the relevant stakeholders in the
negotiation process so that they can contribute their knowledge and relationships to shape more stable and robust decisions.

The more effective the stakeholder involvement, the clearer communications will be between the various parties and back tables. Depending on
the circumstances of the case, it may be best for the relevant public, private, and nongovernmental stakeholder groups to be consulted informally,
participate as observers, and/or sit at the negotiating table. In most cases,
all three forms of engagement will be necessary at different stages, with
one building upon the next. As a result of an effective engagement, by
fostering relationships of trust, the stakeholders will ask crucial questions,
provide meaningful insights to address technical and scientific queries, foster a deeper understanding between diverse constituencies, and develop a
greater sense of ownership and commitment to the potential agreement.

5. Send the Best Representatives

Another crucial lesson relating to protocol flexibility is to allow the best-
suited negotiators for a given case to take the lead, no matter the agency
in which they are based. Often, critical expertise or leadership ability
lies within an agency that would not normally manage such negotiations. Be mindful of this possibility and react accordingly. No matter their

department affiliation, leaders who genuinely have the expertise and believe in a mutual gains approach should be provided with the opportunity to make the case, build the team, and lead the way. Such forward-thinkers are the most likely to ask the critical question "How can we make this happen?" while also being willing to spend the necessary time and resources to sustain this collaborative vision. Grant these people authority through a broad mandate, so that they have the necessary flexibility to think outside the box in order to offer, develop, and respond to more nuanced proposals.

6. Expand Your References

Once negotiation leaders have been selected, they will need to empower their negotiating teams to properly prepare for the upcoming negotiations. Throughout these steps, the preparatory actions should be actively seen as part of a larger outreach and coalition building effort to develop ties and a deep understanding of the core concerns of the stakeholders on one's own side, as well as the other side's back table. Such preparatory work should include research to understand how others have previously attempted to address similar problems, along with an in-depth exploration of the alternatives to the negotiated agreement for both sides. In addition, it can be helpful to recruit subject matter expert consultants who are recognized, known, and welcomed by both sides, so that they may illuminate blind spots along the way.

7. Get on the Same Page

Upon beginning the negotiations, the first order of business should be to build a process through which the parties can work side by side, teasing apart the complex web of interconnected issues at hand. It is usually best to avoid beginning the negotiations with a "draft-counterdraft" strategy. Attempting to negotiate details too early in the process, before having more in-depth knowledge of the other side and their concerns, makes the negotiations more difficult because the participants become more prone to posturing.

Rather, it is more effective for the negotiators on both sides to first work and learn together, to develop a more comprehensive understanding of how things function on the other side (i.e., markets, operating rules, and political context). This is not to say that research into these areas is not necessary in the preparatory stage—it is—but the aim in working collaboratively is to gain an intimate knowledge as to how core issues affect the other side in practice, as well as to figure out how the other side values and ranks distinct items. It is also to one's advantage that the other side understands how these factors influence one's own interests and constraints, for this provides clarity to everyone regarding the items that are crucial in shaping an actionable agreement.

Particular practices that effectively foster a better mutual understanding include thematic workshops, expert-driven workgroups, and in-person tours of sites of interest (i.e., infrastructure, facilities, and natural areas). These types of activities create a safe space in which negotiators can (1) share sensitive information to get a better grasp of the challenges at hand; (2) explore potential trades without the restrictions of the formal process, by testing options one on one or in small-group interactions between scheduled official events; and (3) lay the foundations for continued relationships, which may even become friendships.

8.   Highlight the Benefits

Once the negotiators have fostered a common understanding and built trust, they can be proactive and move more easily into the value creation stage. When discussing the components of a potential deal, it is best to generate as many feasible options for consideration as possible to enable trades across differences. This can be done by working with points of tentative agreement, which empower negotiators to suspend criticism, invent without committing, and revisit issues at different stages and from varying angles.

In many cases, it is helpful to work with proposals in a two-stage process. First, the negotiators should be able to produce options from a shared knowledge base (i.e., data, terminology, and modeling tools), so as to assure that all sides consider these diverse options to be technically sound ways to address the underlying problems. Next, bundle these options into different packages to test them with the back tables, which will judge them according to various considerations (i.e., political, diplomatic, economic, and environmental). Shape the packages around incentives rather than requirements, thus maintaining the stakeholders' focus on the benefits to be seized.

9. Lead Thoughtfully

In addition to finding ways for the sides to learn and invent alternatives together, thoughtful leadership is critical to successful negotiation. Make sure to empower your negotiators to put themselves in the other side's shoes and develop the reputation for taking this task to heart. Foster leadership practices that defuse tensions, build trust, and widen viewpoints. These practices include finding a way to facilitate caucuses on a regular basis and engage in side-talks. Caucuses provide a chance to integrate the various interpretations of the proceedings thus far and enable the negotiators to regroup and adapt strategies in response to changing information. Side-talks allow leaders to clarify miscommunications, break impasses, and take a step back in order to keep sight of the big picture.

10. Seize the Day

When unpredictable circumstances arise during a negotiation process for which the parties are unprepared, leaders should embrace the opportunity to rethink current practice. During times of upheaval, the other side may be more receptive to proposals to devise new processes (or at least amend the existing ones), creating an opening to pursue solutions that may not have been feasible before. In a changing context, the sides should emphasize working together to test confidence-building measures in order to foster momentum that can eventually lead to better relationships and a more robust agreement.

11. Communicate Strategically

To protect the negotiation process and potential agreement from those who would aim to spoil it, negotiators should be particularly strategic concerning interactions with the press and the public. Both sides should commit to a joint communication strategy, including each side's review and approval of the other's press releases and announcements beforehand. Because negotiators may be able to discuss options privately that cannot be considered publicly, at least not until a comprehensive package is in place, they should work in tandem to keep the progress and details of the negotiations under wraps. Assurance of confidentiality in the negotiation process is a critical aspect of the aforementioned phase of inventing without committing, in order to provide negotiators with a secure environment in which to gather as many solutions as possible for consideration.

Once an accord is reached, be equally mindful of how the agreement is presented to your back table and to the other side's constituents. To foster a sustained commitment and stability, work together to make sure that the communications provided to the stakeholders on both sides highlight the ways that they are coming out ahead. Focus on the trades across differences that would not be possible if working separately. Target outreach to the communities that have a stake, are specifically going to see improvements, and whose continued involvement will benefit all parties moving forward. Communicate in ways that resonate on an emotional level. From the headlines to the fine print, empower the other side to return home with a winning story.

12.   Follow through for Success

Just as the negotiation process and the contents of agreement itself must be carefully crafted, so too must the means for follow-through. This structure should include a dispute resolution framework to take account of multiple possible scenarios. With such a framework in place before any conflict arises, both sides may be assured that they have recourse and a fair forum in which to settle disputes. The follow-up framework should also put incentives in place to encourage the parties to take action and work collaboratively before a crisis erupts. By ensuring that proactive measures are built into the framework from the outset, contentious conflicts can largely be avoided.

Given the high degree of uncertainty in natural resource management negotiations, flexibility to address changing circumstances should also underpin the composition of the agreement. The accord should enable both sides to monitor the progress of the agreement's measures and adjust and fine-tune them accordingly. One useful strategy that provides the opportunity for monitoring and reassessment is to test a new course of action during a pilot period. Such a trial can be used to garner support, as this approach eases fears of the unknown by securing an end date from the outset. Once the pilot is underway, stakeholders can experience its impacts firsthand. Should the pilot result in more benefits than costs, the stakeholders will become advocates for a longer-term agreement.

Afterword: Building Negotiation Skills

After laying out steps to assist and enhance transboundary natural resource management negotiations, the focus here will be to envision, in broad terms, how these steps might be effectively explored, refined, practiced, and disseminated collaboratively between interdependent developed and developing countries. The aim is to give an example of how to bring together various disciplines in order to build capacity at the intersection of public dispute resolution, adaptive leadership, collaborative decision-making, and political communication.

Expanding the pool of individuals and organizations that are practitioners of a mutual gains approach to problem solving, through the lens of these four areas of insight, could assist energy, water, and environmental stakeholders to achieve better negotiation processes and outcomes on behalf of their interests at home and abroad. Such capacity-building efforts should focus on offering negotiation tools to government officials, industry representatives, environmental advocates, and community stakeholders. The overarching aim would be to provide venues where the stakeholders can test and practice, together, how to move beyond hard-bargaining tactics and avoid the ultimatums that accompany the presumptions that there are not enough resources to go around and that one side must win and the other must inevitably lose.

Developing a Negotiation Pedagogy

As an illustration on how to put into practice the insights and steps discussed in the book, I present here a strategy to contribute to this goal, entailing the development of executive negotiation training modules and dispute resolution syllabi. These materials would be combined and customized according to specific energy, water, and environmental conflicts. Such modules, based upon the theory and practice of the mutual gains approach to negotiation and the areas of scholarship upon which this research is based, could be developed in collaboration with an advisory board composed of government officials, industry experts, civil society stakeholders, and faculty from multiple universities and disciplines (i.e., environmental science, engineering, business, law, public policy, international relations, and urban planning).

The executive training modules would be divided into two major types. First, opening sessions would be crafted to serve as a general introduction to the theory and practice of the mutual gains approach to negotiation. The introductory sessions would focus on major themes such as negotiation strategy, the psychology of negotiation, dispute resolution tactics, and the impacts of negotiation. These interconnected themes, building upon each other, would explore, among many other fundamentals of negotiation, issues such as framing and anchoring, handling cognitive and motivational biases, addressing power imbalances, breaking social and organizational barriers, managing uncertainty in science-based disputes, dealing with mistrust and anger, communicating persuasively, exploring reconciliation in values-based disputes, charting the structure for multiparty negotiations, and facilitating consensus.

Second, specialized training modules would be added and combined with the introductory modules to form a cohesive and custom-designed program. In the specialized sessions, a series of tools would be highlighted, such as different ways to foster adaptive leadership, enhance collaborative decision-making, and strengthen persuasive communication about specific energy, water, and environmental challenges. The modules' exercises and cases would focus on natural resource management challenges faced by decision-makers and technical experts in governing, industry, and nongovernmental bodies, including among others:

- Water management and conservation
- Infrastructure investment
- Energy transition and planning
- Prospecting, production, and marketing
- Climate preparedness and resilience
- Technology diffusion and adoption
- Sustainable land use planning

- Facility siting
- Hazardous waste disposal
- Public health risks reduction and mitigation
- Environmental restoration

One key component of the executive trainings would be tailored negotiation role-play simulations. These negotiation exercises would be based on the evidence of in-depth case studies, such as the ones outlined in this book, which allow participants to test insights in a learn-by-doing approach. The negotiation role-play simulations would raise questions about, and allow participants to explore in real time, various ways of managing issues during a negotiation, such as moving past a draft-counterdraft strategy, building coalitions with constituents across the table, going beyond partisan experts, engaging in joint fact-finding, leveraging trades across differences, and resolving the tensions between value creation and value distribution.

As the training modules and accompanying materials are crafted, they would need to be evaluated and then presented at the most senior organizational levels, in both academic and professional settings. By piloting the trainings, they would be made more effective based on lessons learned and feedback from experienced stakeholders.

Establishing a Negotiation Center

The ideas outlined, the development of executive negotiation training modules and dispute resolution syllabi, are being implemented between the United States and Mexico, including the establishment of a binational negotiation research center. Mexico's National Council on Science and Technology and the Ministry of Energy selected this initiative through a competitive process, thus launching a long-term, interdisciplinary, public-private partnership between universities, public agencies, and research institutions in both countries, including MIT and Harvard.

The aim of the training modules and syllabi, as well as the research center, is to contribute with materials and a venue for government officials, industry representatives, nongovernmental leaders, and both graduate and undergraduate students, to test, practice, and hone in their skills. The mission is to enhance capacity building for a mutual gains approach to negotiation between neighboring countries, contributing to both innovative research and effective management of shared water, energy, and environmental resources.

The pedagogy of the center, developed in binational collaborations, will emphasize exercises and cases that enhance understanding and implementation of prescriptive negotiation insights, including those discussed in this book. The training materials will be complemented with other existing role-play simulations, many of which I have been fortunate to test and work with firsthand as a member of the faculty at MIT, teaching executive, graduate, and undergraduate negotiation workshops at its School of Engineering and School of Architecture and Planning, as well as at the Program on Negotiation at Harvard Law School, the Harvard School of Public Health, and the Fletcher School of Law and Diplomacy at Tufts University.

These negotiation-training sessions are being piloted in Mexico, in partnership with leading Mexican research and governing institutions, including PEMEX and the Ministry of the Environment and Natural Resources. The executive workshops have involved large groups of high-ranking representatives from the public, private, and nongovernmental sectors with extensive expertise in natural resource management. The response of the stakeholders has been highly encouraging. Senior government officials, along with corporate leaders and nongovernmental experts, have emphasized the shared benefits to be seized from identifying, nurturing, and strengthening human capital in order to assist in the negotiations shaping the regulation and implementation of landmark national reforms in Mexico's energy, water, and environmental sectors. This includes the training not only of negotiators, but of independent mediators as well, all of whom are to be entrusted with assisting stakeholders in conducting effective environmental and social impact assessments in high-stakes resource management projects across the country.

The overarching mission of the binational collaboration is to strengthen both countries' efforts in sustainable resource management by empowering stakeholders to enhance their negotiation and decision-making tools. In the long run, the dispute resolution, leadership, collaborative decision-making, and persuasive communication insights outlined in this book, along with the training and research conducted by the negotiation center, could lend themselves not only to transboundary natural resource management, but also to other areas of importance to the United States and Mexico.

The two countries are well positioned for continued coordinated domestic and international development, with increasing shared responsibilities throughout the region and beyond. Given their respective roles in North America, the Caribbean, and Latin America, and their affiliation with the Asia-Pacific Economic Cooperation and the G-20, a commitment to practicing a mutual gains approach to negotiation could be valuable beyond the immediate topics of energy, water, and the environment.

In the face of their significant and pressing social and economic disparities, devising ways to empower stakeholders to contribute to fairer and wiser decisions in the negotiation and allocation of both countries' resources is meaningful for communities on either side. This is a challenge that all developed and developing countries face, to diverse degrees and across various sectors, both at home and abroad. Figuring out how to contribute to changing the mindset and the practice of negotiation, in order to actively seek to win together, is a step in the right direction.

Appendix A: The Gulf of Mexico Case Background

Geographic and Economic Overview

The Gulf of Mexico is a roughly oval ocean-basin covering 615,000 square miles. It is 810 nautical miles wide, with more than half of its area formed by shallow continental shelf waters and filled with sedimentary rock. It is bounded in the north by 1,680 miles of U.S. coastline from the states of Florida, Alabama, Mississippi, Louisiana, and Texas. In the south, it is bounded by 1,750 miles of Mexican coastline from the states of Tamaulipas, Veracruz, Tabasco, Campeche, Yucatán, and Quintana Roo. The Gulf of Mexico narrowly connects to the Atlantic Ocean through the Florida straits between the United States and Cuba. It also connects to the Caribbean Sea through the Yucatán Channel between Mexico and Cuba.

The United States and Mexico are important partners in energy trade, and the Gulf of Mexico plays a vital role; the following information, representative around the time of the negotiations, provides a brief snapshot. In the United States, the responsibility for managing ocean energy resources falls within the purview of the U.S. Department of State (DOS) and the Bureau of Ocean Energy Management (BOEM) of the U.S. Department of the Interior (DOI). The BOEM manages more than 8,000 offshore active leases through five-year outer-continental-shelf oil and gas programs, with 90 percent of the leases located in the Gulf of Mexico. The region accounts for roughly 25 percent (over 3 million barrels a day) of total U.S. domestic oil production (over 12 million barrels a day), and 15 percent of total U.S. domestic gas production. These offshore energy projects generate, on average, $7 billion in annual public revenue.

Mexico is among the 10 largest oil producers in the world, generating an average of 2.9 million barrels per day of total liquid oil, with over 85 percent coming from crude oil; earnings from the hydrocarbons industry account for over 30 percent of total government revenues. Oil production in the country declined by 25 percent between 1995 and 2010 but began to stabilize at the time of the Gulf of Mexico negotiations. Over 75 percent of Mexico's annual oil production occurs offshore, northeast and southwest of the Bay of Campeche in the Gulf of Mexico, through the

Cantarell, Ku-Maloob-Zaap, Abkatun-Pol-Chuc, and Samaria-Luna centers and their satellite fields.

The United States receives over 70 percent of Mexico's annual oil exports due to its proximity and the specific capacity of the U.S. Gulf Coast refineries to process heavier crude streams, which constitutes most of Mexico's output. In 2014, Mexico exported 1.2 million barrels of oil per day to the United States, placing third behind Canada and Saudi Arabia, to contribute to the U.S. consumption of 19 million barrels of oil per day.

Political, Legal, and Environmental Timeline

1819	The United States and the Spanish monarchy sign the Transcontinental Treaty, setting the boundaries between the United States and the Viceroyalty of New Spain (Mexico). The boundary is the Sabine River from the Gulf of Mexico to the 32nd parallel north, then due north to the Red River, west along the Red River to the 100th meridian west, due north to the Arkansas River, west to its headwaters, north to the 42nd parallel north, and west along that parallel to the Pacific Ocean. The treaty settles the boundary disputes lingering from the Louisiana Purchase. (For further reference, *see image 1* in the "Illustrations" section.)
1821	Spain and Mexico sign the Treaty of Córdoba, ending the Mexican War of Independence.
1828	The United States and Mexico sign the Treaty of Limits, confirming the borders between the two countries, as established by the Transcontinental Treaty. The United States keeps Florida, Louisiana, and Oregon; Mexico keeps Texas, New Mexico, and California.
1836	Angered by conflicts about property taxes, tariffs, and the abolition of slavery, legal and illegal settlers, led by Stephen Austin and Sam Houston, start a secession movement in Texas. The Mexican forces fight the revolt and are defeated when Mexico's de facto dictator, Antonio López de Santa Anna, is captured at the Battle of San Jacinto. As a prisoner, in exchange for his life and without constitutional authority, he signs the Treaty of Velasco, recognizing Texas's independence and setting the boundary at the Rio Grande. This is 150 miles farther south than the traditional border, at the Nueces River. Mexico does not recognize nor ratify the treaty.
1844	In the context of an increasing struggle pitting Northern states against Southern states, James K. Polk narrowly defeats Henry Clay for the U.S. presidency. Texas is soon incorporated as the 28th state of the Union, on the heels of a doctrine of territorial expansion and manifest destiny. The annexation violates the Treaty of Limits between the United States and Mexico.
1846–1848	Conflict erupts over the contested territory at the Nueces Strip. War between the two countries ensues. The United States conducts military campaigns across the Mexican territory. The war ends with the capture of Mexico City. As a consequence of military defeat, through the Treaty of Guadalupe Hidalgo, Mexico cedes 850,000 square miles of territory to the United States. This includes the present-day states of Arizona, California, Colorado, New Mexico, Nevada, and Utah, as well as most of Kansas, Oklahoma, and Wyoming. In consideration of the territories acquired (550 million acres), Mexico is paid 5 cents per acre ($15 million total). The market price at the time was $1.25 per acre ($500 million). (For further reference, *see image 2* in the "Illustrations" section.)

1854	The two countries sign the Treaty of Mesilla. For the purpose of building a potential transcontinental railroad, a 30,000-square-mile tract of land south of the Gila River and west of the Rio Grande is purchased by the United States from Mexico for $10,000. The international land boundary between the two countries is set. Overall, it will remain the same from the mid-nineteenth century to this day. It extends for nearly 2,000 miles and consists of two types of limits: a natural boundary formed by the Rio Grande that runs 1,250 miles from El Paso, Texas, to the Gulf of Mexico; and an artificial boundary of 700 miles defined by coordinates of latitude and longitude in New Mexico, Arizona, and California. (For further reference, *see image 3* in the "Illustrations" section.)
1902-1906	Maritime boundaries constitute acts of States, subject to international law. Accordingly, maritime limits are usually defined by agreements between contracting States forged before the international community. Mexico moves from an original territorial sea of 3 nautical miles (1902) to a territorial sea of 6 nautical miles (1906). The United States acquiesces, keeping a 3-nautical-mile-territorial sea, which had been established since the late 1770s. Due to the curvature of the earth, beyond 3 nautical miles, from a traditional rampart, people could not see whether a ship was coming to their shores. The 3-mile reference, now largely obsolete as a concept, was derived from the range of cannons fired from land.
1917	On the heels of the Mexican Revolution, the new political Constitution of Mexico establishes that all resources in the country's subsoil and seabed are owned by the State. However, the already-existing contracts with international oil and gas companies, leasing Mexican hydrocarbon reservoirs since 1876, are recognized under the law.
1938–1945	Seizing on civil and political unrest, highlighted by oil workers' strikes, Mexico becomes the first country in the world to expropriate all hydrocarbon resources and facilities previously owned by international companies. A presidential decree is issued to create a single national entity, Petróleos Mexicanos (PEMEX), which gives Mexico exclusive rights of exploration, extraction, refining, and commercialization of hydrocarbons. In response, the Standard Oil Company and Royal Dutch Shell demand compensation, both for their investments and for the full amount of reserves still underground. Mexico offers to compensate for the loss of facilities, but not for the value of the reserves. The private companies boycott Mexico to prevent the acquisition of the machinery and chemicals necessary for refining petroleum, and the U.S., Dutch, and British governments establish an embargo on Mexican oil exports. As World War II unfolds, wary of the impact of Mexico selling its oil production to Germany and Italy, the parties settle. U.S. president Franklin D. Roosevelt recognizes Mexico's right to expropriate the hydrocarbon resources, in exchange for a compensation package to the private companies that centers on selling them oil production at below market prices.

1950s	In the ongoing debate between developed and developing countries, on the heels of the Santiago Declaration by Chile, Ecuador, and Peru, a number of countries begin to make maritime claims extending to 200 nautical miles the sovereign control of resources off their coasts. Major maritime countries, including the United States, oppose these claims as intruding on the freedom of the high seas.
1969	Through a presidential decree, Mexico establishes a 12-nautical-mile belt along its littoral. This is later ratified by Article 3 of the United Nations Convention on the Law of the Sea (UNCLOS), to which Mexico is a party but the United States is not.
1970	The two countries explore how to resolve the cumulative impact of natural phenomena such as floods, changes of course, and formations of islands, which are altering the directions of the Colorado River and the Rio Grande, with associated social and diplomatic disruptions on the international land border. In the process of finding practical solutions for the transboundary rivers (resulting in the Treaty to Resolve the Pending Boundary Differences and Maintain the Rio Grande and the Colorado River as the International Boundary), the International Boundary and Water Commission is tasked with defining the maritime boundaries between the two countries, starting at the center of the mouth of the Rio Grande in the Gulf of Mexico, and at the westernmost point of the mainland boundary in the Pacific Ocean. Both countries agree to establish the maritime boundaries on the basis of a series of straight lines, following the principle of equidistance provided by the United Nations Geneva Convention on the Territorial Sea and the Contiguous Zone (1958), to which both the United States and Mexico are parties. Both countries recognize these maritime boundaries up to 12 nautical miles off their respective coasts.
1973	Addressing global claims over the waters, submarine areas, seabed, ocean floor, and subsoil of the continental shelves, UNCLOS creates the concept of the exclusive economic zone, which is composed of 200 nautical miles. This development has a number of legal implications to the continental shelf and the international seabed area.

1976	On the heels of the Fishery Conservation Management Act and the ongoing UNCLOS negotiations, the United States and Mexico begin negotiations to delimit the continental shelf in the Gulf of Mexico and the Pacific Ocean. The purpose is to settle the overlapping claims of jurisdiction resulting from the potential establishment of 200-nautical-mile exclusive economic zones, which could supplant the 12-nautical-mile boundaries. The U.S. Department of State (DOS) and Mexico's Ministry of Foreign Affairs negotiate throughout the spring into fall without success. The two countries exchange diplomatic notes to further recognize the 12-nautical-mile maritime boundaries and acknowledge the need for more technical work to decide how to delimit the continental shelves.
1978	The two countries sign the Treaty on Maritime Boundaries between the United States of America and Mexico. The maritime boundaries established have three segments: (1) In the Western Gulf of Mexico, the maritime boundary extends eastward from the international land boundary separating Texas from Mexico, up to a point 200 nautical miles off the coasts of the two countries. (2) In the Eastern Gulf of Mexico, the maritime boundary begins at the westernmost point at which the 200-nautical-mile zones off the coasts of Louisiana and Yucatán overlap, and then extends to the easternmost point in which these zones continue to overlap. (3) In the Pacific Ocean, the maritime boundary extends westward from the international land boundary separating California from Mexico, up to a point 200 nautical miles off the coasts of the two countries.
	At the time, the international community involved in the UNCLOS negotiations has not agreed on a definition of the outer edge of the continental margin, and neither have the two countries. In the Gulf of Mexico, this means that the maritime boundaries are formed by two separate and interrupted lines, leaving two undefined gaps, colloquially known as "doughnuts," in the areas in which the coasts of the two countries opposite each other are more than 400 nautical miles apart. The undefined reach of waters is 130 nautical miles in length. (For further reference, *see image 4* in the "Illustrations" section.)
1979	The PEMEX Ixtoc oil well in the Bay of Campeche, 60 miles off shore, collapses as a pressure buildup sparks an explosion. At a rate between 10,000 and 30,000 barrels a day, crude oil spills from the semisubmersible drilling rig into the Gulf of Mexico. Over the next 10 months, 140 million gallons of oil are dispersed into the ocean-basin, rendering the event the largest oil spill in the world to date, affecting estuaries, lagoons, bays, and coasts across the ocean-basin. The Ixtoc spill remains to this day the third-largest oil spill in the world, behind the Deepwater Horizon spill (200 million gallons) and the Gulf War spill (240 million gallons).

1980	The U.S. Senate Foreign Relations Committee reports favorably on the Treaty on Maritime Boundaries between the United States and Mexico. In July, it recommends, unanimously and without reservations, ratification to 'ensure that important U.S. fishery and seabed and subsoil mineral rights are protected.' The treaty is scheduled for consideration by September by the full Senate when, on the heels of objections by business, advocacy, and political groups, it is pulled out from the calendar. The argument goes that 'recommending ratification of the treaty is recommending the needless giving away of 1 million acres of the most-promising undrilled seaward petroleum territory to which the U.S. has rightful claim.' This geological interpretation suggests islands off the coast of the Yucatán Peninsula should not be included in drawing the equidistant boundary between the two countries, which would result in moving the maritime boundary further south. The U.S. relies on the Florida Keys and Dry Tortugas, however, to draw the maritime boundary with Cuba. Without a vote, the treaty is not ratified by the United States. In response, Mexican officials voice their concerns over the possibility that U.S. companies will use submarine horizontal drilling to extract Mexican hydrocarbons from the U.S. side. They call it the "Suck-Up (Straw) Effect." The image lingers in Mexican politics for the next three decades.
1990–1994	The United States seeks negotiations to settle one of the two undefined gaps, the one known as the Western Gap (i.e., the Eastern Gap is not addressed because it requires a three-party negotiation with Cuba), but Mexico refuses to negotiate until the 1978 Treaty on Maritime Boundaries between the United States of America and Mexico is ratified by the U.S. Senate.
1997–1998	Mexican officials learn that the U.S. Department of Interior (DOI) is auctioning submarine tracts in the continental shelf of the Western Gap, in an area that would correspond to the United States if the maritime boundaries gaps are assigned on the principle of equidistance. Pursuant to customary international law, Mexico sends a diplomatic note to the United States stating that it objects to any attempt to acquire submarine areas by unilateral possession, and that it will not recognize the adjudication of licenses for the exploration and exploitation of hydrocarbon resources by private companies. In turn, the U.S. oil sector successfully lobbies the U.S. Senate to ratify the 1978 Treaty 20 years after it was signed. Advocates note the untapped reserves of crude oil and natural gas along the 200-nautical-mile boundary and highlight the technology that will allow U.S. companies to extract and produce from these reservoirs.

| 2000 | The Treaty on the Delimitation of the Continental Shelf in the Western Gulf of Mexico is signed between the United States and Mexico. It defines the limits within which each party may exercise its sovereign rights over the Western Gap. The total area comprises 5,000 square nautical miles (i.e., the area amounts to 6,600 square land miles, relatively similar to the area of the state of New Jersey). The United States receives 38 percent of the total area (1,900 nautical miles) and Mexico receives 62 percent (3,100 nautical miles). The decision follows the principle of equidistance from their respective 200-nautical-mile exclusive economic zones. (For further reference, *see image 5* in the "Illustrations" section.) |

Through Articles IV and V, both countries define a series of cooperative measures to explore the possible existence of transboundary hydrocarbon reservoirs; facilitate requests from the other party to authorize geological and geophysical studies; notify each other about the discovery of any reservoir; and solve any dispute by negotiation or other peaceful means that may be agreed upon by the parties. The definition of these oil and gas reservoirs, their boundaries, and the manner in which the resources contained may be allocated remain pending matters. The treaty establishes, however, a 10-year moratorium on hydrocarbon drilling, lauded in Mexico as a diplomatic triumph that prevents unilateral extraction by the United States.

| 2001–2010 | The United States begins to lease 9-square-mile hydrocarbon blocks in the Western Gap. Research in the Alaminos Canyon, the Sigbee Deep, Lakach, and the Perdido Fold Belt, near the maritime border in the Gulf of Mexico, carried out by U.S. and Mexican stakeholders, further suggests the existence of large transboundary hydrocarbon reservoirs. (For further reference, *see images 6, 7* and *8* in the "Illustrations" section.) |

| 2010 | High-pressure methane gas from a well expands into a driller, igniting an explosion that engulfs the Deepwater Horizon oil rig, operating in the Macondo prospect in the Mississippi Canyon in the Gulf of Mexico. More than 200 million gallons of crude oil—62,000 barrels per day—are pumped into the Gulf of Mexico for more than 80 days, making it the largest oil spill in U.S. history and the second-largest in the world. A total of 68,000 square miles of ocean are affected, as well as the coastline in Texas, Louisiana, Mississippi, Alabama, and Florida. BP, the operator of the rig, is responsible for $40 billion in fines, clean-up costs, and settlements, including charges of obstruction of justice and negligence in safety tests. (For further reference, *see images 9 and 10* in the "Illustrations" section.) |

| 2013 | Building upon and going beyond a first series of reforms in 2008, addressing the need to update key federal statutes regarding PEMEX in order to face the challenges of extracting resources from deep-ocean transboundary reservoirs, Mexico enacts the largest constitutional energy reform in decades. For the previous 75 years, only service contracts had been allowed between PEMEX and international companies, and contracts allocating shares or profits derived from hydrocarbon resources were not allowed at all. However, through these constitutional reforms, a provision is created to allow international investors, for the first time since 1938, to enter into licensing, production-sharing, and profit-sharing contracts with PEMEX to explore, extract, and produce oil and gas resources. PEMEX remains state-owned, but it is granted more budgetary and administrative autonomy and will need to compete with other firms for bids on new projects. The reforms expand the regulatory and oversight powers of the Ministry of Energy and the National Hydrocarbons Commission, and create a National Agency of Industrial Safety and Environmental Protection. |

Illustrations

Image 1: Boundary between the United States and the Viceroyalty of New Spain after the Transcontinental Treaty in 1819.

Source: Courtesy of Giggette on Wikimedia Creative Commons (CC BY-SA 3.0), with information from U.S. Department of Interior - United States Geological Survey and Mexico's Ministry of Public Education (SEP), https://commons.wikimedia .org/wiki/User:Giggette#/media/File:Viceroyalty_of_the_New_Spain_1819 _(without_Philippines).png.

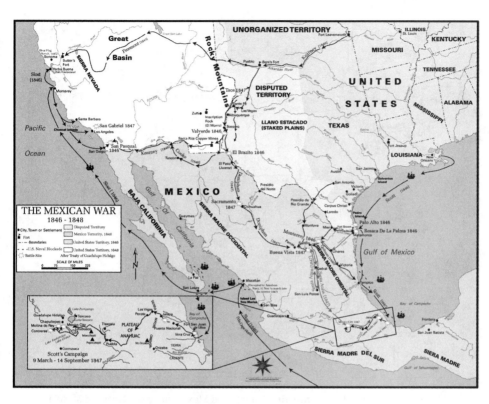

Image 2: War between the United States and Mexico in 1846–1848.
Source: U.S. Army, Combat Studies Institute.

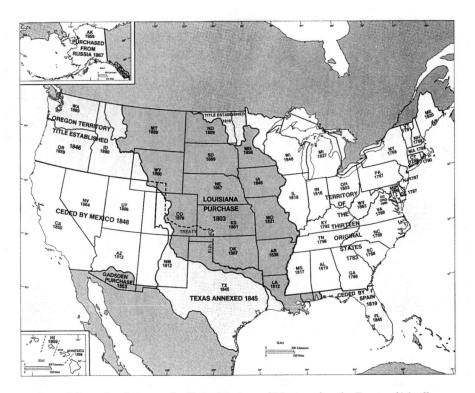

Image 3: Boundary between the United States and Mexico after the Treaty of Mesilla–Gadsen Purchase in 1853.
Source: Courtesy of the University of Texas Libraries (Perry-Castañeda), The University of Texas at Austin.

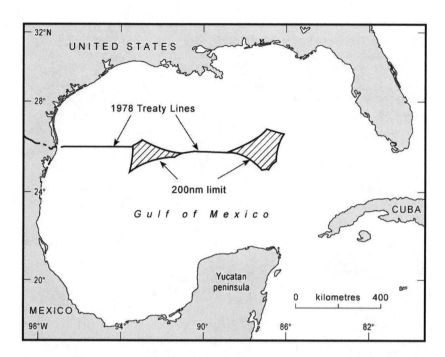

Image 4: Treaty on the Maritime Boundaries between the United States of America and Mexico, 1978.
Source: U.S. Congressional Research Service.

U.S. Extended Continental Shelf in Gulf of Mexico

The Gulf of Mexico contains two areas of submerged continental shelf that extend beyond the 200-nautical-mile exclusive economic zones (EEZ) of Mexico and the United States—the "western gap" and the "eastern gap." The U.S. and Mexico signed a treaty in June 2000 that divides the area of extended continental shelf within the "western gap" between the two nations.

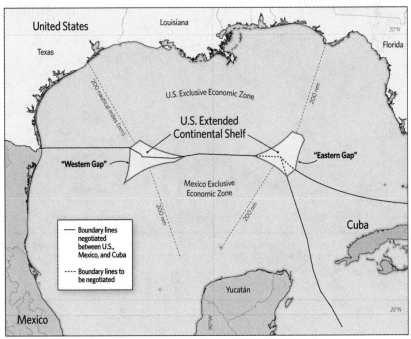

Image 5: Treaty on the Delimitation of the Continental Shelf in the Western Gulf of Mexico, 2000.
Source: U.S. Department of Interior, Bureau of Ocean Energy Management.

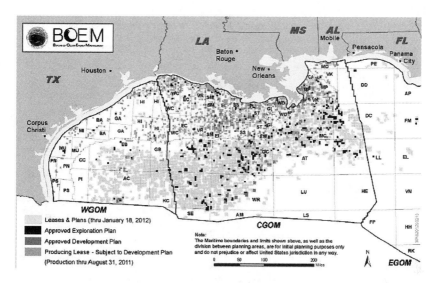

Image 6: Active offshore oil and gas leases and exploration, development, and production plans within the U.S. Exclusive Economic Zone and the U.S. Extended Continental Shelf, 2012.

Source: U.S. Department of Interior, Bureau of Ocean Energy Management.

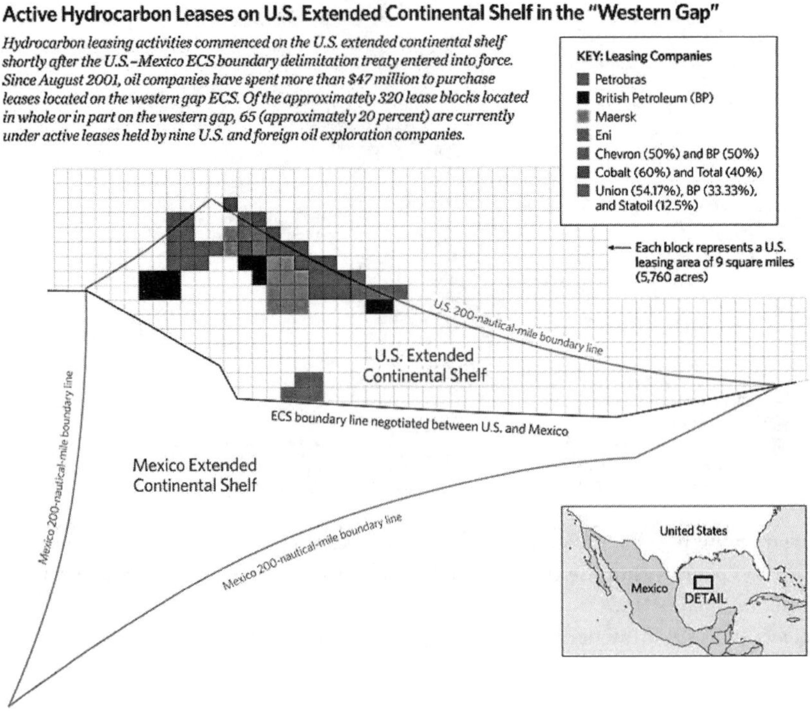

Active Hydrocarbon Leases on U.S. Extended Continental Shelf in the "Western Gap"

Hydrocarbon leasing activities commenced on the U.S. extended continental shelf shortly after the U.S.–Mexico ECS boundary delimitation treaty entered into force. Since August 2001, oil companies have spent more than $47 million to purchase leases located on the western gap ECS. Of the approximately 320 lease blocks located in whole or in part on the western gap, 65 (approximately 20 percent) are currently under active leases held by nine U.S. and foreign oil exploration companies.

KEY: Leasing Companies
- Petrobras
- British Petroleum (BP)
- Maersk
- Eni
- Chevron (50%) and BP (50%)
- Cobalt (60%) and Total (40%)
- Union (54.17%), BP (33.33%), and Statoil (12.5%)

← Each block represents a U.S. leasing area of 9 square miles (5,760 acres)

U.S. 200-nautical-mile boundary line

U.S. Extended Continental Shelf

ECS boundary line negotiated between U.S. and Mexico

Mexico 200-nautical-mile boundary line

Mexico Extended Continental Shelf

Mexico 200-nautical-mile boundary line

United States

Mexico

DETAIL

Image 7: Active hydrocarbons leases on the United States side of the Western Gap, 2012.
Source: U.S. Department of Interior, Bureau of Ocean Energy Management.

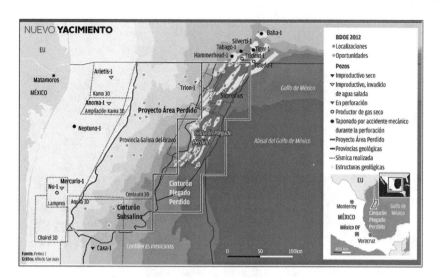

Image 8: Potential transboundary geological structures in the Gulf of Mexico maritime boundary, 2012.
Source: Courtesy of PEMEX; graphics by Alfredo San Juan.

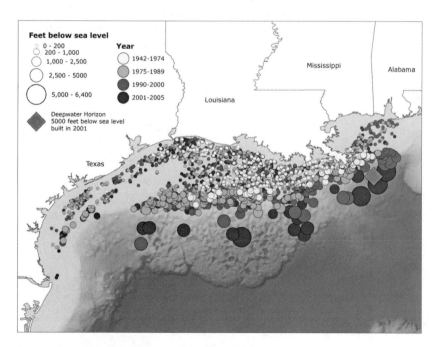

Image 9: Location of the Deepwater Horizon Oil Rig.
Source: U.S. Department of Interior, Bureau of Ocean Energy Management.

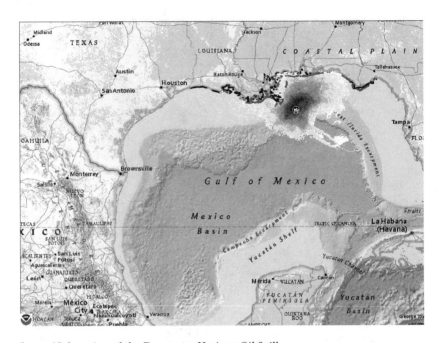

Image 10: Location of the Deepwater Horizon Oil Spill.
Source: National Oceanic and Atmospheric Administration–U.S. Environmental Protection Agency & Coastal Response Research Center, University of New Hampshire.

Appendix B: The Colorado River Case Background

Geographic and Economic Overview

The 1,450-mile Colorado River is the largest in the southwestern United States and northwestern Mexico. The river and its tributaries are managed by an extensive system of dams, reservoirs, and canals, which furnish irrigation and water to 40 million people inside and outside the watershed, 97 percent of which is in the United States. The river begins in the Poudre Pass in the southern Rocky Mountains of Colorado, two miles above sea level. After carving its way through the alpine Western Slope, it flows southwest, gaining strength from small tributaries and emerging into the Grand Valley, a major farming and ranching region.

Most of the Upper River consists of a swift whitewater stream ranging from 200 to 500 feet wide, which then arches northwest to cut across the deep gorges of bare rock and the narrow canyons of the Colorado Plateau, an expansive area of 130,000 miles of high desert within the Four Corners area of Colorado, Utah, Arizona, and New Mexico. The Colorado River continues through Ruby Canyon and Arches National Park, heading southwest to form rapids at Cataract Canyon and flowing through the folds known for their erosion-sculpted Navajo sandstones.

The Colorado River then reaches northern Arizona, where the Glen Canyon Dam forms Lake Powell, the second-largest artificial reservoir in the United States, with a storage capacity of 27 million acre-feet, a critical provider of water and electricity for the region. It continues its path to Lees Ferry, where the flows are measured for apportionment among the Upper Basin states (Colorado, New Mexico, Utah, and Wyoming), the Lower Basin states (Arizona, California, and Nevada), and Mexico (Baja California and Sonora).

Downstream, known for pools that reach 110 feet in depth, the river swings west into Granite Gorge in the Grand Canyon, where it exposes some of the oldest rocks on Earth, dating as far back as 2 billion years. At the lower end, the river widens into Lake Mead, the largest artificial reservoir in the United States, with a storage capacity of 28 million acre-feet, formed by the Hoover Dam on the border of Arizona and Nevada, southeast of metropolitan Las Vegas.

After leaving the Black Canyon, the river broadens into a waterway ranging from 500 to 1,000 feet wide through the lower Colorado River Valley, one of the most densely populated areas along the river. Here, many diversions draw from the river to provide water to distant regions, including the Salt River Valley in Arizona and the cities of southern California. The last diversion occurs at Imperial Dam, where over 90 percent of the river's flow is moved into the All-American Canal to irrigate California's Imperial Valley, the most productive winter agricultural region in the United States.

Past Yuma, Arizona, at the Morelos Dam, the remaining flow is diverted to Mexico to irrigate the Mexicali Valley, which is among the country's most fertile agricultural lands. Passing entirely into Mexico as a trickle, it defines the border between the Mexican states of Baja California and Sonora and later is joined by the Hardy River to form the Colorado River Delta, an alluvial floodplain covering 3,000 square miles, creating an estuary before emptying into the Gulf of California, also known as the Sea of Cortez.

Political, Legal, and Environmental Timeline

1848	The Treaty of Guadalupe Hidalgo sets the territorial boundary between the United States and Mexico. It upholds each country's right to navigation on the Rio Grande and the Colorado River, but it makes no mention of how to divide water resources between the two. Along the boundary's riparian reach, the Rio Grande is fed and renewed by numerous tributaries. In its overland stretch, in addition to the Colorado River, the boundary bisects hundreds of arroyos, washes, and ephemeral streams. A dozen perennial streams cross the Chihuahuan and Sonoran deserts, the lower Colorado River Valley, and the California coastal range.
1880s	Diversions in the Rio Grande headwaters diminish downstream flows. Drought accentuates water scarcity and aggravates local tensions. Mexico argues that the United States is violating the navigation clauses of the Treaty of Guadalupe Hidalgo. In reply, the United States argues that on the basis of its absolute municipal sovereignty in international law and as an upper riparian, it has no obligation to consider the impacts of its water use on Mexico.
1890	The two countries establish the International Boundary Commission (IBC) to determine the location of the U.S.-Mexico international boundary when the meandering rivers between both countries transfer tracts of land from one bank of the river to the other.
1896	The IBC attributes the problem of local water scarcity to upstream diversions on the U.S. side and supports Mexico's claim of wrongful deprivation. The IBC calls for the construction of an international dam upstream of El Paso, Texas. The purpose is to secure legal and equitable rights between the two countries, with the impounded waters to be divided equally between the two sides. The U.S. Department of State (DOS) supports the IBC ruling.
1897–1903	The Rio Grande Dam and Irrigation Company opposes the IBC ruling. It pursues the case through the courts with the goal of building instead a dam 125 miles upstream, at Elephant Butte, New Mexico. The claim is eventually struck down by the courts. However, by then, in coordination with New Mexico officials and the U.S. Department of the Interior (DOI), the company secures congressional funds to build the dam. Mexico protests, but the United States denies that it has any obligation to its downstream neighbor under international law.

1906	The two countries sign the U.S.-Mexico Convention, dividing the waters of the upper Rio Grande. Mexico acquiesces to an arrangement in which the United States claims 94 percent of an annual average flow of nearly 1 million acre-feet. Mexico is allocated 60,000 acre-feet based on the maximum known uses by Mexican settlers in the Juárez Valley. During drought conditions, the United States is allowed to unilaterally reduce the amount delivered and is not required to repay or compensate for any reduction. The Convention is seen to this day as a high-water mark of sovereign unilateralism.
1907–1920	The California Development Company and the Colorado River Land Company coordinate with U.S. interests owning 80 percent of land and water rights on the Mexican side of the border to support the use of the Alamo Canal, an overflow channel of the Colorado River located in Mexico, to irrigate U.S. agriculture in the Imperial Valley. At the time, the Imperial Valley consumes 50 percent of total Colorado River flows. Mexican authorities are shadow agents in these arrangements, facilitated by a private company, the Sociedad de Irrigación y Terrenos de Baja California.
1910–1920	Struggling with high water prices and inadequate water supply, anxious settlers, users, and developers demand public waterworks and binational accords on the use of the Lower Rio Grande and the Colorado River. The Mexican Revolution lasts the entire decade, limiting Mexico's contribution to sending troops to protect U.S. irrigation works on the Mexican side of the Colorado River.
1922	The United States proceeds unilaterally to develop the Colorado River water resources. The seven U.S. states in the Colorado River Basin, without any Mexican input, establish the Colorado River Compact. It defines a border at Lees Ferry, Arizona, between the Upper Basin (Colorado, New Mexico, Utah, and Wyoming) and the Lower Basin (Arizona, California, and Nevada). Both basins are to be managed separately by the U.S. Bureau of Reclamation. (For further reference, *see image 1* in the "Illustrations" section.) On the basis of an estimate that the river's average flow is 16.5 million acre-feet, each basin is allocated over 7.5 million acre-feet (i.e., an acre-foot is about 326,000 gallons of water, enough to cover an acre of land with 1 foot of water). Decades later, studies would show that when the Compact was signed, the period used as the basis for the average flow of the river (1905–1922) was characterized by periods of abnormally high rainfall.

1928	The United States establishes the Boulder Canyon Act. This leads to the construction of the Hoover Dam on the border between Arizona and Nevada, impounding Lake Mead and creating the largest U.S reservoir by volume. The project becomes a critical provider of irrigation water and hydroelectric power to the region. On the Rio Grande, Mexico moves to develop the Rio Conchos and other tributaries without U.S. input.
1930s	Concerned with the unilateral developments in the Rio Grande and the Colorado River, respectively, both countries try to negotiate how to divide the waters, with no success. The United States continues to assert its universal right and rule as the upstream riparian. Mexico argues that the United States is following an entirely different principle than expressed in the Boundary Waters Treaty between the United States and Great Britain (1909), regarding the Milk River, which originates in Canada. That treaty upholds that any diversion in one country that injures a party in the other country entitles the injured party to sue.
1939–1942	The United States unilaterally builds the 82-mile All-American Canal, paralleling the border with Mexico. The purpose is to end U.S. dependence on Mexico's Alamo Canal and to bolster California's claim to a larger share of Colorado River water. All major parties on the lower Colorado River understand that water seeps into the Colorado River aquifer and that the seepage follows both canals, with critical impacts on the amount of groundwater available to border communities. The All-American Canal becomes the largest irrigation canal in the world and the only source of water for intensive agriculture over 630,000 acres in the dry Imperial and Coachella valleys.
1942–1943	Once more, the United States and Mexico engage in negotiations on how to divide the waters of the Colorado River and of the Rio Grande. They consider normal expectations of availability and conditions of scarcity. The two sides discuss how to distribute the costs of the necessary works to implement a potential agreement. Both countries abandon the claim of absolute territorial sovereignty and acknowledge the international practice of reciprocal sovereignty. They try to settle their dispute on the basis of equitable apportionment, a principle that the U.S. Supreme Court has long upheld in domestic interstate river disputes.

| 1944 | The two countries sign the Treaty between the U.S. and Mexico on the Utilization of Waters of the Colorado and Tijuana Rivers, and of the Rio Grande. Also known as the Water Treaty, it apportions the waters through Mexican concessions on the middle-lower Rio Grande in exchange for U.S. concessions on the Colorado River. For the Colorado River basin, the United States is to provide Mexico with 1.5 million acre-feet of water annually. For the Rio Grande basin, the United States is to receive all the flows from the Rio Grande tributaries in the United States. Mexico is to receive two-thirds of the flows that feed into the Rio Grande from the six major tributaries on Mexico's side (Conchos, San Diego, San Rodrigo, Escondido, Salado, and Vacas). The United States is to receive one-third of flows from the Mexican tributaries. Mexico's water delivery must average at least 350,000 acre-feet on average per year, measured in five-year cycles. (For further reference, *see images 1 and 2* in the "Illustrations" section.) |

The treaty expands the functions and jurisdiction of the former IBC to include the allocation and transfer of water from one country to the other. An international body, the International Boundary Water Commission (IBWC), is created to resolve disputes arising from the execution of the treaty and to perform technical studies on flood control, hydroelectric generation, reservoir operation, and the development of infrastructure such as dams and channels. The agency is to be headed by two commissioners, who must be engineers—one from the United States (residing in El Paso, Texas), and the other from Mexico (residing in Ciudad Juárez, Chihuahua). The agreements between the commissioners are recorded in "Minutes," akin to bilateral agreements, approved by the DOI and Mexico's Ministry of Foreign Affairs. The Minutes are legally enforceable and essentially amend the Water Treaty. The executive branches of the federal governments in both countries have the authority to approve or disapprove the proposed Minutes arising from the treaty. If either government disapproves of a Minute, the matter is removed from IBWC control, and the two countries must negotiate the issue through other means.

In many ways, the Water Treaty is the first time that the two countries recognize the need to address the political, economic, social, and management asymmetries that had characterized the border region since the mid-nineteenth century. It proposes cooperation instead of confrontation and establishes the following hierarchy of uses for the water: (1) domestic and municipal uses; (2) agriculture and stock-raising; (3) electric power; (4) other industrial uses; (5) navigation; (6) fishing and hunting; and (7) any other beneficial uses as determined by the IBWC. However, besides proposing to subsidize the development of binational sanitation and sewage facilities, the Water Treaty does not include provisions to resolve a number of transboundary water problems highlighted at the time, principally water quality, aquifers, environmental impacts, and the division of water from nontributary rivers and streams crossing the border.

1950s	By securing the water rights of each country, the Water Treaty triggers a surge of water development on both sides of the border. U.S. and Mexican irrigation districts spread along the lower Colorado River and the Rio Grande.
1961–1963	The Wellton-Mohawk irrigation district in southwestern Arizona, acting to reduce saline groundwater accumulation in district soils in coordination with the U.S. Bureau of Reclamation, conducts a pumping program to discharge brackish water via the Gila River into the Colorado River. The discharges occur at a point below Laguna Dam, the last U.S. reservoir on the Colorado River. The result is an immediate increase in the salinity of Mexican treaty water and a drop in the agricultural productivity of the Mexicali Valley. The decision to dump brackish water into Mexico's treaty allotment and to count it as covering 75 percent of Mexico's entitlement causes an uproar. The United States responds by indicating that Articles 10 and 11 of the Water Treaty specify that the waters that the United States are to deliver to Mexico shall be made up of the waters of the Colorado River "whatever their origin, from any and all sources." Contentious diplomacy ensues. United States officials argue that the Water Treaty has been fairly and mutually agreed upon, that the agreement cannot possibly be read to disallow return flows, and that it provides a license to meet the Mexican quota with all available flows to the Colorado River. Mexico argues that the phrase "whatever their origin, and from any and all sources," cannot imply patently unusable water, that the assumption is that the treaty will ensure sufficient water quality, and that in the spirit of the agreement, under international law, the purpose is to provide water that effectively sustains irrigated agriculture and domestic uses. Mexico declares that the salinity issue is the greatest diplomatic conflict confronting the two countries.
1964	The sharp deterioration of agriculture in the Mexicali Valley leads to louder protests, attracting regional and national press from both sides. The production of cotton diminishes dramatically, with yields less than half of what they once were. Mexico decides not to use the water from the Wellton-Mohawk district and to dispose of it in the ocean. U.S. diplomats, led by Secretary of State Henry Kissinger and Attorney General Herbert Brownwell, recognize the weakness of the U.S. position and try to work out a solution. They face strong opposition within their own country by the congressional delegations and officials from the Colorado River Basin states, as well as by the Bureau of Reclamation. These interests oppose any agreement that would only benefit Mexico and demand federally funded salinity control programs and desalination plants on the U.S. side.

1965	The IBWC and the DOS, concerned with the consequences should Mexico pursue the case through the international courts, try to find a way around their back-table conundrum by shaping and signing Minute 218. They put forth an interim five-year solution, by which the United States agrees to build, at its own expense, a bypass drain below the Morelos Dam (Mexico's diversion dam for Colorado River water). The objective is to prevent further contamination of Mexican treaty waters.
1966–1972	Despite the new bypass drain, which diverts the worst of the brine from the Colorado River, the salinity from upstream return flows continues to undermine Mexican agriculture. Mexico places a salinity deal at the top of the binational agenda and hints at taking the question to the international courts on the basis of equity in downstream obligations. A review of U.S. internal interagency correspondence indicates that most U.S. officials consider that to argue that there is no assumption about irrigation water quality standards in the Water Treaty is untenable. The DOS chief legal advisor, in a confidential memorandum, highlights that, based on the discussions that shaped the treaty negotiations, if a substantial part of the water delivered to Mexico is of unusable quality, Mexico will win the case to terminate and withdraw from the Water Treaty under international law.
1973	The DOS successfully convinces Mexico not to take the case to the international courts, while mounting enough pressure for U.S. internal interests to acquiesce to an equitable solution. The Bureau of Reclamation cooperates, worrying about the domestic implications of the National Environmental Policy Act (1969), as nongovernmental organizations (NGOs) threaten to sue the bureau for the pollution of a national waterway. In this context, the two countries sign Minute 242, through which the United States commits to deliver to Mexico water of equivalent quality to that impounded at Imperial Dam, the lowest U.S. storage dam on the Colorado River, and to build an extended bypass drain for the Wellton-Mohawk brine. Simultaneously, for the first time, the two countries try to address groundwater issues, though with little success. They only succeed at limiting pumping on the San Luis Mesa and establishing a binational consultation mechanism in advance of any domestic action that may affect groundwater use on the other side of the border.

1977–1978	At locations like Nogales and Tijuana, sewage contamination plagues Mexican communities, undermining the sanitation of the urban settlements at the border with spillage threatening U.S. cities. The issue worsens as spillage from copper-tailing ponds at Cananea (Sonora) enters the San Pedro River east of Arizona's Huachuca Mountains, polluting the irrigation water of farms and ranches along Sierra Vista and the Gila River. DOS officials believe the matter falls under the scope of the IBWC, but the U.S. commissioner is hesitant about venturing into issues related to environmental regulation.
	U.S. activists respond by asking the Environmental Protection Agency (EPA) to get involved. The problem is discussed in a presidential summit between the United States and Mexico, resulting on a formal promise by Mexico to deal with San Pedro through the first-ever joint memorandum between the EPA and its Mexican counterpart. The IBWC quickly moves to amplify its jurisdiction, through Minute 261, to incorporate border sanitation conditions that affect the use of all waters crossing the international boundary. This marks the first time the IBWC achieves partial jurisdiction over transboundary flows.
1983	The two countries sign the U.S.-Mexico Border Cooperation Agreement, also known as the La Paz Agreement, broadening the IBWC's administrative responsibilities to include ecological concerns regarding water pollution. The agreement proposes an emerging perspective that sees water as embedded in watersheds and ecosystems, in a broader spatial frame, with natural and social impacts through chosen use, quantity, and quality. For the first time, states, municipalities, and NGOs are granted official standing; however, this does not offer anything more than a forum to voice concerns in binational deliberations.
1990–1994	Commercial and investment interests shape the negotiations on the North American Free Trade Agreement (NAFTA). Concerned with border prospects of increased water demand, rights transfers, and pollution, a series of institutions are established through the Integrated Border Environmental Plan (IBEP). The Border Environment Cooperation Commission (BECC), the North American Development Bank (NADB), and the Commission for Environmental Cooperation (CEC) are asked to support the IBWC's water planning efforts by addressing issues of economic development, public health, administrative decentralization, local capacity building, and public participation in policy design and implementation.

1994–2000s	The NAFTA institutions try to enhance public relations and citizen outreach, promoting joint participatory mechanisms between environmental agencies in the two countries and fostering regional and watershed advisory bodies. Whereas IBWC projects are funded by government subsidies, local communities must shoulder the operation and maintenance costs of BECC-NADB projects. The objective is to achieve a gradual transition into projects financed by user fees and other revenues, providing local communities with more control over whether a project remains functional over its life cycle.

The BECC certifies a proposed water infrastructure on the basis of sustainable development criteria such as local and regional resource conservation plans and ecosystems-based planning, but since the NADB is restricted to lending at market rates, the demand for NADB's funds remains low. Most of the progress comes from an emphasis on public health, not the legal system of apportionment and rights or the market. Severe social and environmental disruptions remain. However, some control over setting the terms of the debate is yielded to local government, NGOs, and citizens.

1997–2005	Under conditions of severe drought (1993–2004), on the southeastern Rio Grande, Mexico fails to deliver the full amount of water to the United States in two consecutive five-year cycles (1992–2002). Mexico had fully met its deliveries to the United States without exception since the Water Treaty (1944), but this had been accomplished through wet weather flows rather than purposeful planning. Mexico's Rio Conchos is the most significant tributary to the southeastern Rio Grande basin, originally providing 70 percent of the flow, whereas U.S. tributaries provide 30 percent. The two countries are allotted 50 percent of the middle and lower basins' water. Significant irrigation infrastructure developed by Mexico in the early 1990s, coupled with an increase in transnational manufacturing facilities, the failure to develop adequate conservation plans, and inadequate agriculture insurance programs, reduce the Conchos' contribution.

Tensions over the water debt rise between both countries and within the states, with parties in Texas calling for retaliation on the Colorado River Basin, to no avail, as Mexico accumulates a debt of over 1.5 million acre-feet for the two cycles. The conflict is eventually resolved through presidential intervention; a series of IBWC Minutes; investments in water efficiency, including buybacks in water rights; and culminating in a clearing of the debt in 2005, under hurricane-induced wet conditions. Studies show, however, that the Rio Grande basin is heavily overallocated on both sides of the border, that the five-year cycle complicates forecasts on water storage and management plans, and that urban population growth, economic development, and drought are likely to trigger further conflict in the coming years.

2000s	Prior to expansion of the basin's water consumption, the Colorado River Delta covered 2 million acres in the United States and Mexico. A large part on the Mexican side contains woodlands and desert areas, is home to many endangered species, and is designated as a United Nations Biosphere Reserve and Ramsar Wetland. Environmental interests on both sides of the border argue that insufficient water flowing into the delta has decimated 90 percent of the wetlands. They suggest that increased annual flows, accompanied by larger pulses of water every four years, would restore them. Water users, concerned about the potential of reduced allocations, oppose these arguments.
2001–2003	Conservation concerns in California draw attention to the desirability of recapturing an estimated 80,000 acre-feet of seepage lost to Mexico from the All-American Canal by lining it with concrete. The U.S. Bureau of Reclamation brokers a conservation agreement among the seven Colorado River Basin states. Among the mitigation actions, in order to bring California into compliance with the Law of the River, the lining project of the All-American Canal is approved. The Imperial Irrigation District agrees to transfer water to other southern California users, provided that the canal is lined to recapture the water seeping into Mexico. The U.S. Congress passes legislation funding the canal's lining. The environmental impact assessment is done with minimal consultation with Mexico, without consultation with users in the Mexicali Valley who rely on this seepage through drainage and pumps, and without evaluating transboundary biota and ecological resources affected by lining the canal.
2004–2009	A coalition of U.S. and Mexican business and nonprofit representatives sue the DOI in U.S. federal court in Las Vegas. They point to administrative irregularities in the original environmental impact assessment of the All-American Canal lining, a violation of U.S. environmental standards as it pertains to seepage's effects on the nearby Andrade Mesa Wetlands, and disregard for Mexico's high reliance on groundwater in the Mexicali Valley. However, the unusual binational lawsuit, supported by Mexican president Vicente Fox, is rendered moot when a rider in the Tax Relief and Health Care Act of 2006 demands the immediate conclusion of the lining. The lining is successfully finished in 2009.

2005–2010	At a 22-mile stretch where the Colorado River runs at a virtual trickle downstream of the Morelos Dam, unchecked nonnative plant growth complicates the landscape, rendering a staging ground for unauthorized crossings and for the criminal gangs that prey on migrants. Regional environmentalists, in partnership with the U.S. Border Patrol, the Mexican NGO Pronatura, and the Yuma Crossing National Heritage Corporation, begin a reclamation effort to clear nonnative species from the riverbed, plant native grasses and cottonwoods, and enhance public safety in the overrun area. Through a grant by the Bureau of Reclamation, they secure the funds to irrigate a section called Hunter's Hole, in an effort to recreate the ecological conditions for sustainable-species growth.
2010–2013	Under conditions of drought, with heavier impacts on the U.S. side, Mexico accumulates a water debt of roughly 290,000 acre-feet during the first three years of the current five-year cycle (2010–2015) of water deliveries in the Rio Grande. As tensions escalate between state officials, the two countries engage in bilateral negotiations to find a solution. (For further reference, *see image 3a* in the "Illustrations" section.)
2011–2014	With continued drought as the harbinger of a drier era, Colorado River Basin stakehodlers continue their efforts to re-iamgine and re-assess how to slake the thirst of the region, as inflows, storage, percent capacity, and water elevation levels fall. (For further reference, *see images 3b, 4, 5, and 6* in the "Illustrations" section.)
2014	More than 105,000 acre-feet of water are released in one large pulse flow between March and May. Less than one percent of what would naturally flow into the delta without upstream diversions, it significantly impacts the ecosystem throughout the streamside area and well beyond the restoration sites. The river channel and floodplain are inundated, connecting the Colorado River with California for the first time in decades.

Illustrations

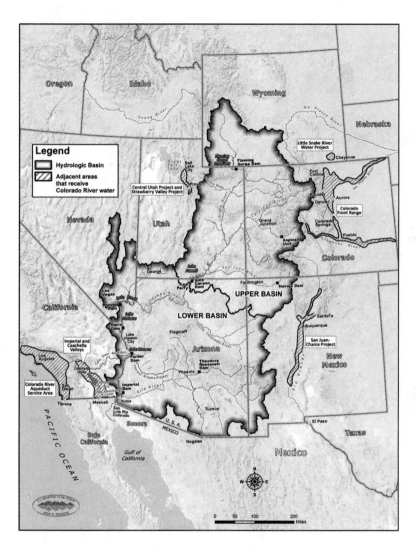

Image 1: The Colorado River Upper and Lower Basin.
Source: U.S. Department of Interior, Bureau of Reclamation.

Image 2: The Rio Grande Basin.
Source: U.S. Geological Survey, Shuttle Radar Topography Mission.

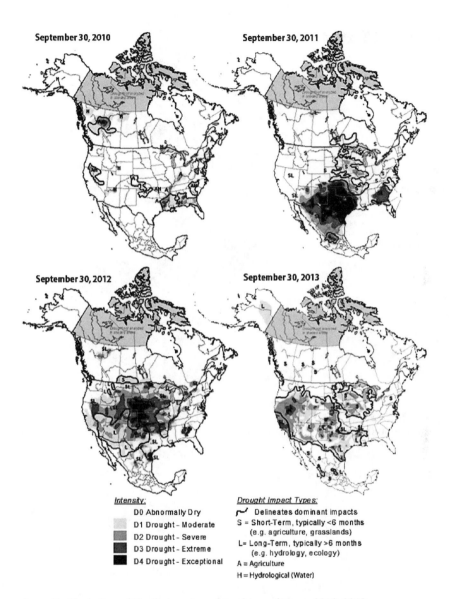

Image 3a: Evolution of North American drought conditions, 2010–2013.
Source: North American Drought Monitor, U.S. Department of Commerce, National Oceanic and Atmospheric Administration.

September 30, 2014

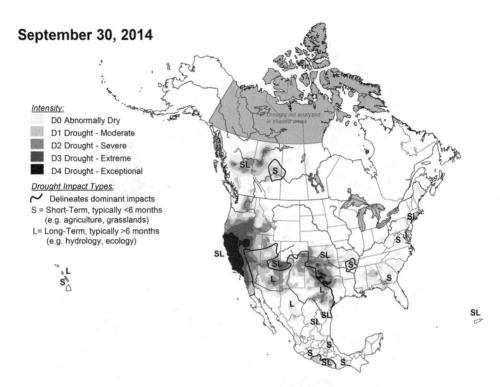

Image 3b: North American drought conditions, 2014.
Source: North American Drought Monitor, U.S. Department of Commerce, National Oceanic and Atmospheric Administration.

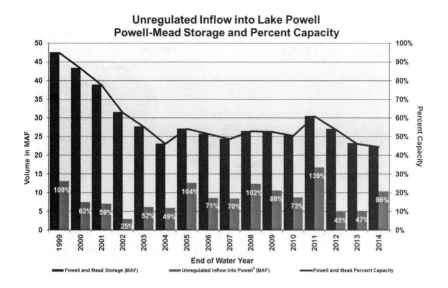

¹Percentages at the top of the light blue bars represent percent of average unregulated inflow into Lake Powell for a given water year. Water years 1999-2011 are based on the 30-year average from 1971 to 2000. Water years 2012-2014 are based on the 30-year average from 1981-2010.

Image 4: State of the water system, storage and percent capacity, 1999–2014.
Source: U.S. Department of Interior, Bureau of Reclamation.

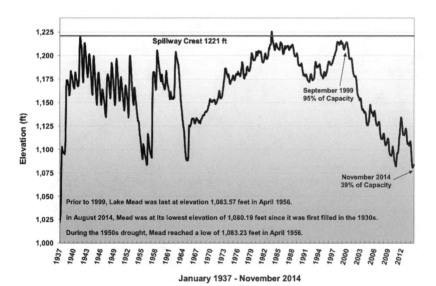

Image 5: Lake Mead water level end-of-month elevations, 1937–2014.
Source: U.S. Department of Interior, Bureau of Reclamation.

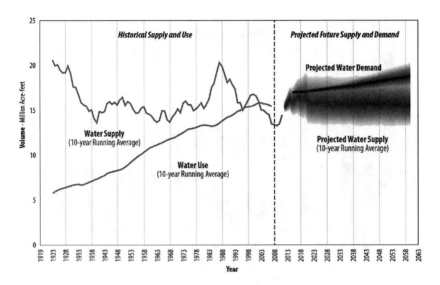

Image 6: Colorado River Basin historical water supply and use and projected future water supply and demand.
Source: U.S. Department of Interior, Bureau of Reclamation.

Appendix C: List of Interviewees

The interviews for this book were scheduled with the parties who directly negotiated the agreements between the United States and Mexico. The process provided the opportunity to have a conversation and learn from the people responsible for the decisions made at the negotiating table, both on a political level and on a substantive level. The interview with each negotiator lasted on average 60 minutes. I am deeply grateful to the negotiators of the many agencies and organizations involved, who were generous with their time and inspiring with their expertise.

More than 70 interviewees are listed here, in the following format:

Country
Organization
Name
Date of interview
Position at time of interview
Position during the negotiations

Gulf of Mexico Negotiations—Transboundary Hydrocarbons Agreement

United States
U.S. Department of State
1. The Honorable David L. Goldwyn
January 12, 2015
At time of interview:
   President, Goldwyn Global Strategies, International Energy Advisors
   Senior Fellow, Energy Security Initiative, Brookings Institution
During the negotiations:
   Special Envoy and Coordinator for International Energy Affairs (2009–2011)
   U.S. Department of State

2.   Ambassador Richard Morningstar

December 11, 2014

At time of interview:

　　Head, Energy Initiative

　　Atlantic Council

During the negotiations:

　　Special Envoy for Eurasian Energy (2009–2012)

　　U.S. Department of State

3.   David Sullivan

January 15, 2015

At time of interview:

　　Assistant Legal Adviser

　　European and Eurasian Affairs

　　U.S. Department of State

During the negotiations:

　　Assistant Legal Adviser

　　Oceans and International Environmental and Scientific Affairs

　　U.S. Department of State

4.   Michael P. Stewart

February 18, 2015

At time of interview:

　　Economic Counselor

　　U.S. Embassy, Romania

During the negotiations:

　　Desk Officer, International Energy and Commodity Policy

　　U.S. Department of State

5.   Michael P. Taylor

March 13, 2015

At time of interview:

　　Economic Counselor

　　U.S. Embassy, Honduras

　　U.S. Department of State

During the negotiations:

　　Desk Officer, Mexico

　　U.S. Department of State

U.S. Embassy, Mexico City

6. Ambassador Carlos Pascual

January 28, 2015

During the negotiations:

Special Envoy and Coordinator for International Energy Affairs (2011–2012)

U.S. Ambassador to Mexico (2009–2011)

U.S. Department of State

7. Sigrid Emrich

January 23, 2015

At time of interview:

Deputy Director

Office of Central European Affairs

U.S. Department of State

During the negotiations:

Deputy Economic Counselor (2008–2010)

U.S. Embassy, Mexico

U.S. Department of State

U.S. Department of Interior
Bureau of Ocean Energy Management

8. The Honorable Michael R. Bromwich

March 3, 2015

At time of interview:

Founder, Managing Principal

The Bromwich Group

During the negotiations:

Director, Head of the Agency (2010–2011)

U.S. Bureau of Ocean Energy Management

U.S. Department of Interior

9. Renee Orr

March 12, 2015

At time of interview and during the negotiations:

Chief

Office of Strategic Resources

Bureau of Ocean Energy Management

U.S. Department of Interior

10. Kevin Karl

February 12, 2015

At time of interview:

    Senior Adviser to the Regional Director

    Gulf of Mexico Outer Continental Shelf Region

    U.S. Bureau of Safety and Environmental Enforcement

    U.S. Department of Interior

During the negotiations:

    Regional Supervisor

    Office of Production and Development, Gulf of Mexico Region

    U.S. Minerals Management Service

    U.S. Department of Interior

11. Mark Hanan

March 10, 2015

At time of interview and during the negotiations:

    Chief

    Development and Unitization Section

    Gulf of Mexico Region

    U.S. Bureau of Safety and Environmental Enforcement

    U.S. Department of Interior

Outer Continental Shelf Advisory Board

The Outer Continental Shelf (OCS) Advisory Board is an organization that focuses on outer continental shelf issues related to oil and gas exploration, development, and production. It is the largest oil and gas advisory board in the United States. It works in close coordination with the U.S. Department of Interior, the Bureau of Ocean Energy Management, and the Bureau of Safety and Environmental Enforcement. Board members include BP, Chevron, ConocoPhilips, ExxonMobil, Petrobras, Royal Dutch Shell, Statoil, Deep Gulf Energy, Energy XXI, Ankor Energy, Calypso Exploration, Hess Corporation, Venari Resources, Cobalt International Energy, Apache Corporation, and Stone Energy Corporation.

12. J. Keith Couvillion

March 4, 2015

At time of interview and during the negotiations:

    Member and Former Chairman of the OCS Advisory Board

    Deepwater Land Manager

    Exploration and Production Business Unit

    Chevron

Mexico
Office of the Presidency

1. The Honorable Felipe Calderón

December 2, 2013

During the negotiations:

President of Mexico (2006–2012)

Ministry of Foreign Affairs

2. Ambassador Arturo Dager

February 19, 2015

At time of interview:

    Director General of Legal Affairs

    Mexican Federal Government Trade and Investment Strategy

    ProMéxico

During the negotiations:

    Head of Delegation (2011–2012)

    Chief Legal Adviser

    Ministry of Foreign Affairs

3. Ambassador Joel Hernández

October 28, 2014

At time of interview:

    President

    Commission Overseeing the Members of the Mexican Foreign Service

    Ministry of Foreign Affairs

During the negotiations:

    Head of Delegation (2008–2011)

    Chief Legal Adviser

    Ministry of Foreign Affairs

4. Víctor M. Uribe

January 14, 2015

At time of interview and during the negotiations:

    Minister, Legal Affairs

    Mexican Embassy, Washington, D.C.

5.   Antonio Ortiz-Mena

January 12, 2015

At time of interview and during the negotiations:

   Minister, Economic Affairs

   Mexican Embassy, Washington, D.C.

Ministry of Energy
Office of the Deputy Secretary for Hydrocarbons
6.   Mario G. Budebo

January 8, 2015

At time of interview:

   Director General

   Mexico Infrastructure Partners

During the negotiations:

   Deputy Secretary for Hydrocarbons (2006–2012), Ministry of Energy

   Board of Directors (2006–2012), PEMEX

7.   David Madero

January 9, 2015

At time of interview:

   Head

   National Center for the Control of Natural Gas

During the negotiations:

   Director General (2007–2011)

   Exploration and Production of Hydrocarbons

   Ministry of Energy

Ministry of Energy
Legal Affairs Unit
8.   Guillermo Zúñiga

January 8, 2015

At time of interview:

   Commissioner

   Energy Regulatory Commission

During the negotiations:

   Legal Director for Petroleum Operations (2008–2011)

   Ministry of Energy

   Legal Affairs Unit

9.   Iván A. Alemán

March 4, 2015

At time of interview:

Vice President

National Banking and Securities Commission

During the negotiations:

Chief Attorney

Legal Affairs Units

Ministry of Energy

10.   Viviana M. Santiago

March 4, 2015

At time of interview:

Deputy Director General

Preventive Operations

National Banking and Securities Commission

During the negotiations:

Attorney

Legal Affairs Unit

Ministry of Energy

Ministry of Energy
Office for International Affairs

11.   Leonardo Beltrán

December 22, 2014

At time of interview:

Deputy Secretary for Energy Transition and Planning

Ministry of Energy

During the negotiations:

Director of International Negotiations

Ministry of Energy

12.   Aldo Flores

December 17, 2014

At time of interview:

Secretary General

International Energy Forum

During the negotiations:

Director General for International Affairs (2007–2012)

Ministry of Energy

13.   Leydi Barceló

December 22, 2014

At time of interview:

    Deputy Director-General

    Office for Energy Planning and Technological Development

    Ministry of Energy

During the negotiations:

    Deputy Director of International Negotiations

    Ministry of Energy

PEMEX

14.   Luis Macías

November 12, 2014

At time of interview:

    Advisor

    Strategic International Affairs

    Exploration and Production

    PEMEX

During the negotiations:

    Manager

    New Business Ventures

    Exploration and Production

    PEMEX

15.   Sergio Guaso

January 22, 2015

At time of interview and during the negotiations:

    Vice President

    New Ventures

    Upstream Business Unit

    PEMEX

16.   Xavier A. de la Garza

January 19, 2015

At time of interview and during the negotiations:

    General Manager

    International Legal Affairs

    PEMEX

17.   José L. Herrera

January 9, 2015

At time of interview:

  Senior Associate

  Hogan Lovells BSTL

During the negotiations:

  Deputy General Manager (2006–2013)

  International Legal Affairs Office

  PEMEX

18.   Elizabeth Ceballos

January 19, 2015

At time of interview:

  Legal Counsel

  International Legal Affairs Office

  PEMEX

During the negotiations:

  Senior Legal Adviser

  Director General's Office

  PEMEX

19.   Fernando Rosenzweig

January 19, 2015

At time of interview and during the negotiations:

  Senior Legal Specialist

  International Legal Affairs

  PEMEX

20.   Daniel A. Cárdenas

January 19, 2015

At time of interview and during the negotiations:

  Senior Legal Specialist

  Exploration and Production

  PEMEX

Colorado River Negotiations—Minute 319

United States
U.S. Department of Interior
1.   The Honorable Michael L. Connor
January 14, 2015
At time of interview:
    Deputy Secretary of the Interior
    U.S. Department of Interior
During the negotiations:
    Commissioner (2009–2014)
    U.S. Bureau of Reclamation
    U.S. Department of Interior

2.   Robert Snow
November 17, 2014
At time of interview and during the negotiations:
    Attorney, Solicitor's Office
    U.S. Department of Interior

3.   Lorri Gray-Lee
November 17, 2014
At time of interview:
    Regional Director
    Pacific Northwest
    U.S. Bureau of Reclamation
    U.S. Department of Interior
During the negotiations:
    Regional Director (2007–2011)
    Lower Colorado Region
    U.S. Bureau of Reclamation
    U.S. Department of Interior

4.   Terrance Fulp
November 6, 2014
At time of interview:
    Regional Director
    Lower Colorado Region
    U.S. Bureau of Reclamation
    U.S. Department of Interior

During the negotiations:

    Deputy Regional Director (2008–2011)

    Lower Colorado Region

    U.S. Bureau of Reclamation

    U.S. Department of Interior

5.   Jennifer McCloskey

October 30, 2014

At time of interview and during the negotiations:

    Deputy Regional Director

    Lower Colorado Region

    U.S. Bureau of Reclamation

    U.S. Department of Interior

International Boundary and Water Commission, U.S. Section

6.   The Honorable Edward Drusina

February 4, 2015

At time of interview and during the negotiations:

    Commissioner

    International Boundary and Water Commission, U.S. Section

7.   Sally E. Spener

January 9, 2015

At time of interview and during the negotiations:

    Foreign Affairs Secretary

    International Boundary and Water Commission, U.S. Section

8.   Carlos Peña Jr.

December 11, 2014

At time of interview and during the negotiations:

    Principal Engineer, Operations Department

    International Boundary and Water Commission, U.S. Section

9.   Alfredo J. Riera

November 6 and December 15, 2014

During the negotiations:

    Acting Commissioner

    International Boundary and Water Commission, U.S. Section

U.S. Environmental Protection Agency
10. Peter Silva

November 25, 2014

During the negotiations:

Assistant Administrator (2009–2011)

Office of Water

U.S. Environmental Protection Agency

Lower Colorado River Basin States
Nevada
11. Patricia Mulroy

December 12, 2014

At time of interview:

Senior Fellow for Climate Adaptation and Environmental Policy

Brookings Mountain West

During the negotiations:

President

U.S. Association of Metropolitan Water Agencies

General Manager

Southern Nevada Water Authority and Las Vegas Valley Water District

12. John Entsminger

December 12, 2014

At time of interview:

General Manager

Southern Nevada Water Authority and Las Vegas Valley Water District

During the negotiations:

Senior Deputy General Manager

Director for Environmental and Water Resource Law

Southern Nevada Water Authority and Las Vegas Valley Water District

Arizona
13. Perri Benemelis

October 27, 2014

At time of interview and during the negotiations:

Manager, Colorado River Section

Arizona Department of Water Resources

14.   Charles Cullom

January 26, 2015

At time of interview and during the negotiations:

    Manager, Colorado River Programs

    Central Arizona Water Project

California

15.   Gerald R. Zimmerman

January 21, 2015

During the negotiations:

    Executive Director

    Colorado River Board of California

16.   William Hasencamp

January 9, 2015

At time of interview and during the negotiations:

    Manager, Colorado River Resources

    Metropolitan Water District of Southern California

Upper Colorado River Basin States

Representing Utah, Wyoming, and New Mexico

17.   Don Ostler

October 2, 2014

At time of interview and during the negotiations:

    Executive Director and Secretary

    Upper Colorado River Commission

18.   Patrick Tyrrell

January 5, 2015

At time of interview and during the negotiations:

    State Engineer

    Wyoming State Engineer's Office

Colorado

19.   Jennifer Gimbel

December 19, 2014

At time of interview:

    Deputy Commissioner

    External and Intergovernmental Affairs

    U.S. Bureau of Reclamation

    U.S. Department of Interior

During the negotiations:

    Director

    Colorado Water Conservation Board

20.   Karen Kwon

November 21, 2014

At time of interview and during the negotiations:

    First Assistant Attorney General

    State of Colorado

21.   Ted Kowalski

November 26, 2014

At time of interview and during the negotiations:

    Chief Intestate and Federal Section

    Colorado Water Conservation Board

Environmental Stakeholders

Environmental Defense Fund

22.   Jennifer Pitt

November 7, 2014

At time of interview and during the negotiations:

    Director

    Colorado River Project

    Environmental Defense Fund

The Nature Conservancy

23.   Taylor Hawes

October 15 and 16, 2014

At time of interview and during the negotiations:

    Director

    Colorado River Program

    The Nature Conservancy

Sonoran Institute

24.   Peter Culp

November 10, 2014

At time of interview and during the negotiations:

    Chief Attorney, Sonoran Institute

    Partner, Squire Patton Boggs (U.S.) LLP

Mexico
Office of the Presidency
1. The Honorable Felipe Calderón

December 2, 2013

During the negotiations:

President of Mexico (2006–2012)

Mexican Embassy, Washington, D.C.
2. Ambassador Arturo Sarukhán

January 20, 2015

During the negotiations:

Mexican Ambassador to the United States (2006–2012)

Mexican Embassy, Washington, D.C.

3. Víctor M. Uribe

February 10, 2015

At time of interview and during the negotiations:

Minister, Legal Affairs

Mexican Embassy, Washington, D.C.

4. Antonio Ortiz-Mena

January 12, 2015

At time of interview and during the negotiations:

Minister, Economic Affairs

Mexican Embassy, Washington, D.C.

International Boundary and Water Commission, Mexican Section
5. Roberto F. Salmón

December 11, 2014

At time of interview and during the negotiations:

Commissioner

International Boundary and Water Commission, Mexican Section

6. José de Jesús Luévano

October 24, 2014

At time of interview and during the negotiations:

Secretary

International Boundary and Water Commission, Mexican Section

7. L. Antonio Rascón

January 20, 2015

At time of interview and during the negotiations:

Principal Engineer

International Boundary and Water Commission, Mexican Section

8. Francisco A. Bernal

January 9, 2015

At time of interview and during the negotiations:

Regional Director, Mexicali—Baja California State Office,

International Boundary and Water Commission, Mexican Section

9. Adriana B. Reséndez

January 28, 2015

At time of interview and during the negotiations:

Deputy Director, Colorado River Program

International Boundary and Water Commission, Mexican Section

CONAGUA—National Water Commission

10. Mario López

December 1, 2014

At time of interview and during the negotiations:

General Manager

Binational Projects

CONAGUA

11. Oscar Ibáñez

January 30, 2015

During the negotiations:

Chief of Staff for the Director General

CONAGUA

12. José D. Gutiérrez

January 30, 2015

At time of interview and during the negotiations:

Deputy General Manager

Binational Projects

CONAGUA

13.   Efraín Muñoz

January 20, 2015

During the negotiations:

    Director General

    Baja California Water Commission

Environmental Stakeholders

Pronatura

14.   Osvel Hinojosa

October 13, 2014

At time of interview and during the negotiations:

    Director

    Water and Wetlands Program

    Pronatura

15.   Carlos A. de la Parra

November 20, 2014

At time of interview and during the negotiations:

    Environmental Consultant

    International Boundary Water Commission, Mexican Section

    Professor, Urban Studies and Environment

    Colegio de la Frontera Norte

16.   Gastón Luken-Aguilar

November 18, 2014

At time of interview and during the negotiations:

    President,

    Pronatura, Sea of Cortez

    Former CEO, General Electric—Mexico

Appendix D: Interview Conversation Topics

During the spring of 2014, I had the opportunity to attend the faculty roundtables held at the Harvard Business School in preparation for that year's distinguished Great Negotiator Award by the Program on Negotiation at Harvard Law School. Chaired by Professor James K. Sebenius (Gordon Donaldson Professor of Business Administration at Harvard Business School, Vice Chair of the Program on Negotiation at Harvard Law School) and Alex Green (Senior Research Associate at Harvard University), the roundtables were very interesting. They featured faculty discussions that focused on how to best structure a conversation with Ambassador Tommy Koh, the recipient later that spring of the Great Negotiator Award. The goal was to explore how to best learn from Ambassador Koh's illustrious negotiation career at the United Nations, and on behalf of his country, Singapore.

The roundtables were shaped by the insights of several attending negotiation experts. These included Professor Robert H. Mnookin (Samuel Williston Professor of Law, Director of the Harvard Negotiation Research Project, and Chair of the Program on Negotiation at Harvard Law School), Professor Michael Wheeler (MBA Class of 1952 Professor of Management Practice at Harvard Business School), and Professor Daniel Shapiro (Associate Professor in Psychology at Harvard Medical School/McLean Hospital, and Associate Director of the Harvard Negotiation Project at Harvard Law School), among many other faculty, practitioners, and executive committee members affiliated with the interuniversity Program on Negotiation.

In turn, the observations derived from the roundtables, combined with the generous mentorship of Professor Lawrence E. Susskind (Ford Professor of Urban and Environmental Planning at MIT, Co-Founder and Vice-Chair of Pedagogy of the Program on Negotiation at Harvard Law School), Professor Melissa Nobles (Kenan Sahin Dean of the School of Humanities, Arts, and Social Sciences at MIT, former Department Head of MIT's Political Science Department), and Steve Jarding (Presidential, Gubernatorial, and Senatorial Campaign Manager, Leadership and Media Expert, Lecturer in Public Policy at the Shorenstein Center on Media, Politics, and Public Policy at the Harvard Kennedy School of Government), helped to shape the list of conversation topics that I developed as a template for the discussions with the negotiators responsible for the Colorado River and Gulf of Mexico agreements.

Examples of the questions that underpinned the conversations with the negotiators follow:

• Could you very briefly contextualize the origins of the negotiations, the main issues the stakeholders faced, and the key challenges?

• Were you seeking a comprehensive agreement from the beginning, or did you opt for an incremental approach, in which each stage builds on the previous one?

• Resource management stakeholders can vary widely in their priorities and expertise. How important was the sequence in which you approached and focused your efforts on different stakeholders during the negotiations? That is, who was first, who was next, and why?

• How about the sequence in which you dealt with issues? Some argue that you "deal with the easy issues first to establish that you can make progress and to build momentum." Others argue instead that you "deal with the hard issues first so everything else is easy and you don't end up with a deal-breaker at the very end." What was your experience?

• During the negotiations, did a group of core stakeholders take the lead? If so, was it helpful? What impact do you think this had on the negotiation process?

• Did some of your interests evolve over time through your interactions with other stakeholders? Was this a function of acquiring more information, developing trust in one another, and/or responding to new circumstances?

• At some point, were the negotiations divided into working groups charged with handling different issues? If so, did the parties try to foster linkage across these issues or to keep them separate? Were trades ever made across these working groups?

• How many scenarios did you work with? What kind of scenarios did you use?

• How important were prior and concurrent domestic developments to the evolution and results of the transboundary negotiations?

• What were your alternatives to a negotiated agreement?

• To what extent and how often did you improvise during the negotiations?

• Did the stakeholders on the other side of the table, or even on your own side, hold particular preconceptions that you found hard to overcome? If so, how did you turn this around?

• Apart from the "across-the-table" challenges, significant barriers to reaching a successful agreement tend to involve each side's "behind-the-table" issues. What did you do to address these challenges on your side? To what extent and how did you try to help the other stakeholders with challenges from their own constituents?

- How did you or your negotiation team define a policy on what to say to the press? How can handling the media help or hurt a negotiation?

- Briefly describe one of the most challenging moments during the negotiations. How did you and the other stakeholders handle it?

- How did you deal with the challenge of numbers, balancing the role of involving a broader set of stakeholders with a concern for political sensibility and efficiency? Can the two be reconciled?

- Was there a nightmare scenario—a coalition that could have derailed a fair agreement? What steps did you take to forestall the formation of a blocking entity? How did you identify potential allies?

- How important were specific personalities during the negotiations? Were there leadership tactics that you would particularly highlight (or consider instead that needed to be improved upon)?

- What did you find the most difficult in bringing these negotiations to closure?

- Did the parties agree on a follow-through mechanism? If so, how did you choose the monitoring references, metrics, and experts?

- This agreement is unprecedented in its scope and impact for the binational resource management sector. What is most important moving forward?

- Reflecting back, is there anything that could have been done better that was at least arguably within the limits of political possibility?

- Are there distinctive characteristics of negotiating between the United States and Mexico that call for a different approach to negotiation than might be the case with other countries? If so, what are they?

- What would you suggest or highlight as an interesting strategy or decision to explore further in my conversations with your colleagues and counterparts?

- If you were advising stakeholders on future transboundary negotiations, what specific steps would you urge them to take to maximize the chances of reaching a mutually beneficial outcome?

Notes

Part 1

1. Lawrence E. Susskind, *Good for You, Great for Me: Finding the Trading Zone and Winning at Win-Win Negotiation* (New York: Public Affairs), 2014; Michael A. Wheeler, *The Art of Negotiation: How to Improvise Agreement on a Chaotic World* (New York: Simon and Schuster), 2013; David Lax and James Sebenius, *3-D Negotiation: Powerful Tools to Change the Game in Your Most Important Deals* (Cambridge, MA: Harvard Business Press), 2006; Kenneth Arrow, Robert H. Mnookin, Lee Ross, Amos Tversky, and Robert Wilson, ed. *Barriers to Conflict Resolution* (New York: W. W. Norton Company) 1995.

2. Dean Williams, *Leadership for a Fractured World* (Oakland, CA: Berrett-Koehler), 2015; Ronald Heifetz, Martin Linsky, and Alexander Grashow, *The Practice of Adaptive Leadership: Tools and Tactics for Changing Your Organization and the World* (Boston: Harvard Business Review Press), 2009; Barbara Kellerman, *Followership: How Followers are Creating Change and Changing Leaders* (Boston: Harvard Business Press), 2008.

3. Richard Margerum, *Beyond Consensus: Improving Collaborative Planning and Management* (Cambridge, MA: MIT Press), 2011; Judith Innes and David Booher, *Planning with Complexity: An Introduction to Collaborative Rationality for Public Policy* (New York: Routledge), 2010; Xavier De Souza Briggs, *Democracy as Problem-Solving: Civic Capacity in Communities across the Globe* (Cambridge, MA: MIT Press), 2008.

4. Marshall Ganz, "Public Narrative, Collective Action, and Power," in *Accountability through Public Opinion: From Inertia to Public Action*, ed. Sina Odugbemi and Taeku Lee (Washington, DC: The World Bank), 2011; George, Lakoff, *The Political Mind: Why You Can't Understand 21st Century Politics with an 18th Century Brain* (New York: Viking), 2008; Drew Westen, *The Political Brain: The Role of Emotion in Deciding the Fate of the Nation* (New York: Public Affairs), 2007.

5. Paul Steinberg, *Who Rules the Earth? How Social Rules Shape Our Planet and Our Lives* (New York: Oxford University Press), 2015; Elinor Ostrom, *The Future of the*

Commons: Beyond Market Failure and Government Regulations (London: Institute of Economic Affairs), 2012.

6. Shafiqul Islam and Lawrence E. Susskind, *Water Diplomacy: A Negotiated Approach to Managing Complex Water Networks* (New York: Resources for the Future Press), 2013.

7. Lawrence E. Susskind, Danya Rumore, Carri Hulet, and Patrick Field, *Managing Climate Risks in Coastal Communities: Strategies for Engagement, Readiness, and Adaptation* (London: Anthem Press), 2015.

8. Robert H. Mnookin, *Bargaining with the Devil: When to Negotiate, When to Fight* (New York: Simon & Schuster), 2010; Howard Raiffa, John Richardson, and David Metcalfe, *Negotiation Analysis: The Science and Art of Collaborative Decision-Making* (Cambridge: Harvard University Press), 2002.

9. Deepak Malhotra, *Negotiating the Impossible: How to Break Deadlock and Resolve Ugly Conflicts (Without Money or Muscle)*, (Oakland, CA: Berret-Koehler), 2016; Roger Fisher, William Ury, and Bruce Patton, *Getting to Yes: Negotiating Agreement Without Giving In* (New York: Penguin Books), 1991.

10. Susskind, 2014; Guhan Subramanian, *Dealmaking: The New Strategy of Negotiauctions* (New York: W. W. Norton Company), 2010.

11. Wheeler, 2013; Jeswald Salacuse, *Negotiating Life: Secrets for Everyday Diplomacy and Dealmaking* (New York: Palgrave Macmillan), 2013.

12. Susan Podziba, *Civic Fusion: Mediating Polarized Public Disputes* (Chicago, IL: American Bar Association), 2012; John Forester, *Dealing with Differences: Dramas of Mediating Public Disputes* (New York: Oxford University Press), 2009.

13. William Ury, *Getting to Yes with Yourself (and Other Worthy Opponents)*, (New York: Harper Collins), 2015; Lawrence E. Susskind and Patrick Field, *Dealing with an Angry Public: The Mutual Gains Approach* (New York: The Free Press), 1997.

14. Deborah Kolb and Jessica Porter, *Negotiating at Work: Turn Small Wins into Big Gains* (San Francisco, CA: Jossey-Bass), 2015; Douglas Stone, Bruce Patton, and Sheila Heen, *Difficult Conversations: How to Discuss What Matters Most* (New York: Penguin Books), 2000.

15. Dan Shapiro, *Negotiating the Nonnegotiable: How to Resolve Your Most Emotionally Charged Conflicts* (New York: Viking), 2016; Brian Mandell, "Unnecessary Toughness," in *Negotiating on Behalf of Others*, ed. Robert H. Mnookin, Lawrence E. Susskind, and Pacey C. Foster (Thousand Oaks, CA: Sage Publications), 1999.

16. Deepak Malhotra and Max Bazerman, *Negotiation Genius: How to Overcome Obstacles and Achieve Brilliant Results at the Bargaining Table and Beyond* (New York: Bantam Books), 2008; Roger Fisher and Daniel Shapiro, *Beyond Reason: Using Emotions as You Negotiate* (New York: Penguin Books), 2006.

17. William Ury, *The Power of a Positive No: Save the Deal, Save the Relationship, and Still Say No* (New York: Bantam Books), 2007; Robert H. Mnookin, Scott R. Peppet, and Andrew S. Tulumello, *Beyond Winning: Negotiating to Create Value in Deals and Disputes* (Cambridge, MA: Belknap Press), 2004.

18. Scott Derue, Jennifer Nahrang, Ned Wellman, and Stephen Humphrey, "Trait and Behavioral Theories of Leadership: An Integration and Meta-Analytic Test of Their Validity," *Personnel Psychology* 64 (Spring), 7–52, 2011; Richard Samuels, "Why Leaders Matter? Creation Stories," in *Machiavelli's Children: Leaders and Their Legacies in Italy and Japan* (Ithaca, NY: Cornell University Press), 2003.

19. Williams, 2015; Heifetz, Linsky, and Grashow, 2009; Linda A. Hill, Maurizio Travaglini, Greg Brandeau, and Emily Stecker, "Unlocking the Slices of Genius in Your Organization: Leading for Innovation," in *Handbook of Leadership Theory and Practice*, ed. Nitin Nohria and Rakesh Khurana (Boston: Harvard Business Press), 2010; Mark Gerzon, *Leading Through Conflict: How Successful Leaders Transform Differences into Opportunities* (Boston: Harvard Business Review Press), 2006.

20. Max Bazerman, *The Power of Noticing: What the Best Leaders See* (New York: Simon & Schuster), 2014; Barbara Kellerman, *Bad Leadership: What It Is, How It Happens, Why It Matters* (Boston: Harvard Business Press), 2004; Ronald Heifetz and Martin Linsky, *Leadership on the Line: Staying Alive through the Dangers of Leading* (Boston: Harvard Business Review Press), 2002.

21. John S. Hammond, Ralph L. Keeney, and Howard Raiffa, *Smart Choices: A Practical Guide To Making Better Decisions* (Boston: Harvard Business Review Press), 2015; Max Bazerman and Ann Tenbrunsel, *Blind Spots: Why We Fail to Do What's Right and What to Do about It* (Princeton: Princeton University Press), 2011.

22. Douglas Stone and Sheila Heen, *Thanks for the Feedback: The Science and Art of Receiving Feedback Well* (New York: Penguin Books), 2014; Marshall Ganz, "Leading Change: Leadership, Organization, and Social Movements," in *Handbook of Leadership Theory and Practice*, ed. Nitin Nohria and Rakesh Khuran (Boston: Harvard Business Press), 2010; John Forester, "Dealing with Deep Value Differences," in *The Consensus Building Handbook*, ed. Lawrence E. Susskind, Sarah McKearnan, and Jennifer Thomas-Larmer (Thousand Oaks, CA: Sage Publications), 1999.

23. Francesca Gino, *Sidetracked: Why Our Decisions Get Derailed, and How We Can Stick to the Plan* (Cambridge, MA: Harvard Business Review), 2013; George A. Akerlof and Robert J. Shiller, *Animal Spirits: How Human Psychology Drives the Economy and Why It Matters for Global Capitalism* (Princeton, NJ: Princeton University Press), 2009; Daniel Kahneman and Amos Tversky, "Conflict Resolution: A Cognitive Perspective," in *Barriers to Conflict Resolution*, ed. Kenneth Arrow, Robert H. Mnookin, Lee Ross, Amos Tversky, and Robert Wilson (New York: W. W. Norton Company), 1995.

24. Innes and Booher, 2010; Julia M. Wondolleck and Steven L. Yaffee, *Making Collaboration Work: Lessons from Innovation in Natural Resource Management* (Washington, DC: Island Press), 2000.

25. Xavier De Souza Briggs, 2008; Archon Fung, "Democratic Theory and Political Science: A Pragmatic Method of Constructive Engagement," *American Political Science Review* 101:3 (August 2007): 443–458.

26. Jason Corburn, *Street Science: Community Knowledge and Environmental Health Justice* (Cambridge, MA: MIT Press), 2005; Karen Bäckstrand, "Civic Science for Sustainability: Reframing the Role of Experts, Policy-makers and Citizens in Environmental Governance," *Global Environmental Politics* 3:4 (2003), 24–41.

27. Kathryn S. Quick and Martha S. Feldman, "Boundaries as Junctures: Collaborative Boundary Work for Building Efficient Resilience," *Journal of Public Administration Research and Theory* 24:1 (2014), 1–23; Lynn Mandarano, "Evaluating Collaborative Environmental Planning Outputs and Outcomes." *Journal of Planning Education and Research* 27:4 (2008), 456–468.

28. Margerum, 2011; Andrea K. Gerlak, "Today's Pragmatic Water Policy: Restoration, Collaboration, and Adaptive Management along U.S. Rivers," *Society & Natural Resources* 21:6 (2008): 538–545; Leen Hordijk and Markus Amman, "How Science and Policy Combined to Combat Air Pollution Problems," *Environmental Policy and Law* 37:4 (2007), 336–340.

29. Gary Klein, *Streetlights and Shadows: Searching for the Keys to Adaptive Decision-Making* (Cambridge, MA: MIT Press), 2009; Jody Freeman, "Collaborative Governance in the Administrative State," *UCLA Law Review* 45:1 (1997), 1–77.

30. Joshua Greene, *Moral Tribes: Emotion, Reason, and the Gap Between Us and Them* (New York: Penguin Books), 2013; Anthony Damasio, *Descartes' Error: Emotion, Reason, and the Human Brain* (New York: Penguin Books), 2005.

31. Westen, 2007; George E. Marcus, *The Sentimental Citizen* (University Park: Pennsylvania State University Press), 2002.

32. Ganz, 2011; Steven Jarding and Dave "Mudcat" Saunders, *Foxes in the Henhouse: How the Republicans Stole the South and the Heartland and What the Democrats Must Do To Run'em Out* (New York: Touchstone), 2006.

33. Andrew J. Hoffman, *How Culture Shapes the Climate Change Debate* (Stanford, CA: Stanford University Press), 2015; William R. Moomaw and Mihaela Papa, "Creating a Mutual Gains Climate Regime through Universal Clean Energy Services," *Sustainable Development Diplomacy and Governance Program-Tufts Center for International Environment and Resource Policy* 6 (May 2012), 1–27.

34. Frank Luntz, *Words that Work: It's Not What You Say, It's What People Hear* (New York: Hyperion), 2007; Craig Crawford, *Attack the Messenger: How Politicians Turn You Against the Media* (New York: Rowman & Littlefield Publishers), 2006.

35. Melissa Nobles, *The Politics of Official Apologies* (New York: Cambridge University Press), 2008; Anthony G. Amsterdam and Jerome Bruner, *Minding the Law: How the Courts Rely on Storytelling and How Their Stories Change the Ways We Understand the Law —and Ourselves* (Cambridge, MA: Harvard University Press), 2002.

36. Raul Lejano, Mrill Ingram, and Helen Ingram, *The Power of Narrative in Environmental Networks* (Cambridge, MA: MIT Press), 2013; Richard Kearney, "Narrative Matters," in *On Stories: Thinking in Action* (New York: Routledge), 2006; Dan P. McAdams, "Life Stories," in *The Redemptive Self: Stories Americans Live By* (New York: Oxford University Press), 2006.

Chapter 1

1. More details about the geographic and economic context of the case; a political, environmental, and legal timeline; and several illustrations can be found in appendix A.

2. U.S. Department of State (DOS), *Agreement between the United States of America and the United Mexican States Concerning Transboundary Hydrocarbon Reservoirs in the Gulf of Mexico,* Los Cabos, Mexico, February 20, 2012.

3. U.S. Congressional Research Service, "U.S.-Mexico Transboundary Hydrocarbons Agreement: Background Issues for Congress," Report for Members and Committees of Congress, Washington, DC, August 2013.

4. White House, "Joint Statement from President Barack Obama and President Felipe Calderón," Office of the Press Secretary, Washington, DC, May 19, 2010.

5. Ibid.

6. Hillary Clinton, "Remarks at the Signing of the U.S.-Mexico Transboundary Agreement," U.S. Department of State, Los Cabos, Mexico, February 20, 2012.

7. Ibid.

8. Ibid.

Chapter 2

Note: Detailed information on all the interviews is listed in appendix C, including the interviewees' positions at the time of the conversation. These notes indicate their professional positions during the time of the negotiations.

1. José Luis Herrera, Deputy General Manager for International Legal Affairs at PEMEX, personal conversation, January 9, 2015.

2. Leydi Barceló, Deputy Director for International Negotiations at Mexico's Ministry of Energy, personal conversation, December 22, 2014.

3. Joel Hernández, Ambassador and Chief Legal Adviser at Mexico's Ministry of Foreign Affairs, personal conversation, October 28, 2014.

4. Guillermo Zúñiga, Legal Director for Petroleum Operations at Mexico's Ministry of Energy, personal conversation, January 8, 2015.

5. U.S. Congressional Research Service, "Mexico's Oil and Gas Sector: Reform Efforts and Implications for the United States," Report prepared for Members and Committees of Congress, Washington, D.C., August 2015.

6. Felipe Calderón, President of Mexico, personal conversation, December 2, 2013.

7. Hernández, 2014.

8. Calderón, 2013.

9. Sigrid Emrich, Deputy Economic Counselor at the U.S. Embassy in Mexico, personal conversation, January 23, 2015.

10. Renee Orr, Chief, Office of Strategic Resources at the U.S. Bureau of Ocean Energy Management, personal conversation, March 12, 2015.

11. Carlos Pascual, U.S. Ambassador to Mexico, personal conversation, January 28, 2015.

12. Emrich, 2015.

13. Hernández, 2014.

14. Luis Macías, Manager, New Business Ventures for Exploration and Production at PEMEX, personal conversation, November 12, 2014.

15. Richard Morningstar, Ambassador, Special Envoy for Eurasian Energy at the U.S. Department of State, personal conversation, December 11, 2014.

16. Zúñiga, 2015.

17. Daniel Cárdenas, Senior Legal Specialist in Exploration and Production at PEMEX, personal conversation, January 19, 2015.

18. Elizabeth Ceballos, Senior Legal Adviser to PEMEX's Director-General, personal conversation, January 19, 2015.

19. Mario Budebo, Deputy Secretary for Hydrocarbons at Mexico's Ministry of Energy and member of the Board of Directors at PEMEX, personal conversation, January 8, 2015.

20. Herrera, 2015.

21. David Madero, Director-General for Exploration and Production of Hydrocarbons at Mexico's Ministry of Energy, personal conversation, January 9, 2015.

22. Aldo Flores, Director-General for International Affairs at Mexico's Ministry of Energy, personal conversation, December 17, 2014.

23. Leonardo Beltrán, Director for International Negotiations at Mexico's Ministry of Energy, personal conversation, December 22, 2014.

24. Sergio Guaso, Vice President, New Ventures, Upstream Business Unit at PEMEX, personal conversation, January 22, 2015.

25. Xavier Antonio de la Garza, General Manager for International Legal Affairs at PEMEX, personal conversation, January 19, 2015.

26. Macías, 2014.

27. Budebo, 2015.

28. Calderón, 2013.

29. White House, "Joint Statement from President Barack Obama and President Felipe Calderón," Office of the Press Secretary, Washington, D.C., May 19, 2010.

30. U.S. State Department, "U.S.-Mexico Intention to Negotiate Transboundary Hydrocarbon Reservoirs Agreement," Office of the Spokesman, June 23, 2010.

31. Arturo Dager, Ambassador, Head of Delegation, and Chief Legal Adviser at Mexico's Ministry of Foreign Affairs, personal conversation, February 19, 2015.

32. Michael Taylor, Desk Officer, Mexico, U.S. Department of State, personal conversation, March 13, 2015.

33. Pascual, 2015.

34. David L. Goldwyn, Special Envoy for International Energy Affairs at the U.S. Department of State, personal conversation, January 12, 2015.

35. Ibid.

36. Michael Bromwich, Director of the U.S. Bureau of Ocean Energy Management, personal conversation, March 3, 2015.

37. Kevin Karl, Regional Supervisor, Office of Production and Development, Gulf of Mexico Region, U.S. Minerals Management Service, personal conversation, February 12, 2015.

38. Goldwyn, 2015.

39. Karl, 2015.

40. Goldwyn, 2015.

41. Ibid.

42. Bromwich, 2015.

43. Taylor, 2015.

44. Morningstar, 2015.

45. Mark Hanan, Chief, Development and Unitization Section for the Gulf of Mexico Region at the U.S. Bureau of Safety and Environmental Enforcement, personal conversation, March 10, 2015.

Chapter 3

1. Elizabeth Ceballos and Fernando Rosenzweig, Legal Counsels at PEMEX, personal conversation, January 19, 2015.

2. Guaso, 2015.

3. Zúñiga, 2015.

4. Macías, 2014.

5. De la Garza, 2015.

6. Flores, 2014.

7. Dager, 2014.

8. Macías, 2014.

9. Flores, 2014.

10. Budebo, 2015.

11. Barceló, 2014.

12. Beltrán, 2014.

13. Zúñiga, 2015.

14. Beltrán, 2014.

15. Emrich, 2015.

16. Madero, 2015.

17. Goldwyn, 2015.

18. Beltrán, 2014.

19. Karl, 2015.

20. Bromwich, 2015.

21. Goldwyn, 2015.

22. Zúñiga, 2015.

23. Budebo, 2015.

24. Madero, 2015.

25. Budebo, 2015.

26. Ceballos and Rosenzweig, 2015.

27. Cárdenas, 2015.

28. Flores, 2014.

29. Zúñiga, 2015.

30. Hernández, 2014.

31. Víctor Manuel Uribe, Minister for Legal Affairs at the Mexican Embassy in Washington, D.C., personal conversation, February 10, 2015.

32. Dager, 2015.

33. Beltrán, 2014.

34. Madero, 2015.

35. Budebo, 2015.

36. Orr, 2015.

37. Cárdenas, 2015.

38. David Sullivan, Assistant Legal Adviser for Oceans and International Environmental and Scientific Affairs at the U.S. State Department, personal conversation, January 15, 2015.

39. Guaso, 2015.

40. J. Keith Couvillion, Deepwater Land Manager at Chevron and Chair of the Outer Continental Shelf Advisory Board, personal conversation, March 4, 2015.

41. Dager, 2015; De la Garza, 2015; Flores, 2014; Hanan, 2015; Hernández, 2014; Karl, 2015; Macías, 2014; Orr, 2015; Taylor, 2015.

42. Sullivan, 2015.

43. Goldwyn, 2015.

44. Sullivan, 2015.

45. Bromwich, 2015.

46. Zúñiga, 2015.

47. Hanan, 2015.

48. Orr, 2015.

49. Hanan, 2015.

50. Sullivan, 2015.

51. Bromwich, 2015.

52. Sullivan, 2015.

53. Karl, 2015.

54. Taylor, 2015.

55. Sullivan, 2015.

56. Dager, 2015; Flores, 2014; Madero, 2015.

57. Hanan, 2015.

58. Sullivan, 2015.

59. Karl, 2015.

60. De la Garza, 2015.

61. Taylor, 2015.

62. Orr, 2015.

63. Taylor, 2015.

64. Sullivan, 2015.

65. Michael P. Stewart, Desk Officer, International Energy and Commodity Policy at U.S. Department of State, personal conversation, February 18, 2015.

66. Morningstar, 2015.

67. Hanan, 2015.

Chapter 4

1. Hernández, 2014.

2. Macías, 2014.

3. Guaso, 2015.

4. De la Garza, 2015.

5. Beltrán, 2014.

6. Budebo, 2015.

7. Hernández, 2014.

8. Sullivan, 2015.

9. Budebo, 2015.

10. Herrera, 2015.

11. Morningstar, 2014.

12. Dager, 2015.

13. Madero, 2015.

14. Flores, 2014.

15. Dager, 2015.

16. Hernández, 2014.

17. Flores, 2014.

18. Sullivan, 2015.

19. Herrera, 2015.

20. Ceballos, 2015; De la Garza, 2015; Rosenzweig, 2015.

21. Bromwich, 2015.

22. Sullivan, 2015.

23. Stewart, 2015.

24. Taylor, 2015.

25. Morningstar, 2014.

26. Sullivan, 2015.

27. Uribe, 2015.

28. Sullivan, 2015.

29. Bromwich, 2015.

Chapter 5

1. Orr, 2015.

2. Goldwyn, 2015.

3. Taylor, 2015.

4. Goldwyn, 2015.

5. Stewart, 2015.

6. Bromwich, 2015.

7. Ibid.

8. Couvillion,. 2015.

9. Karl, 2015.

10. Couvillion, 2015.

11. Sullivan, 2015.

12. Morningstar, 2015.

13. Browmich, 2015.

14. Couvillion, 2015.

15. Ibid.

16. Karol García, "PEMEX, la Petrolera Que Paga Más Impuestos en el Mundo," *El Economista*, February 29, 2012.

17. Couvillion, 2015.

18. Budebo, 2015.

19. Sullivan, 2015.

20. Couvillion, 2015.

21. Hanan, 2015.

22. Uribe, 2015.

23. Sullivan, 2015.

24. Morningstar, 2015.

25. Stewart, 2015.

26. Macías, 2014.

27. Hanan, 2015.

28. Herrera, 2015.

29. Goldwyn, 2015.

30. Zúñiga, 2015.

31. Sullivan, 2015.

32. Hernández, 2014.

33. Madero, 2015.

34. Dager, 2015.

35. Sullivan, 2015.

36. Herrera, 2015.

37. Sullivan, 2015.

38. Hanan, 2015.

39. Budebo, 2015.

40. Bromwich, 2015; Couvillion, 2015; Guaso, 2015; Macías, 2014.

41. Sullivan, 2015.

42. Beltrán, 2014.

43. Flores, 2014.

44. Sullivan, 2015.

45. Dager, 2015.

46. Sullivan, 2015.

Chapter 6

1. More details on the geographic and economic context of the case; a political, environmental, and legal timeline; and a number of illustrations can be found in appendix B.

2. International Boundary and Water Commission (IBWC), *Minute 319: Interim International Cooperative Measures in the Colorado River Basin through 2017*, Coronado, California, November 20, 2012.

3. U.S. Senate, *Treaty between the United States of America and Mexico: Utilization of Waters of the Colorado and Tijuana Rivers, and of the Rio Grande*, Washington, DC, February 3, 1944.

4. Great resources for studying several of these episodes in the binational relationship in depth are listed in the bibliography, including, among others: Stephen Mumme, "The Liquid Frontier: Water and Sustainable Development on the U.S.-Mexico Border," *Journal of the West* 48(4): 104-112, 2009; Evan Ward, *Border Oasis: Water and the Political Ecology of the Colorado River Delta 1940–1975* (Tucson: University of Arizona Press), 2003; Helen Ingram, Nancy K. Laney, and David M. Gillilan, *Divided Waters: Bridging the U.S.-Mexico Border* (Tucson: University of Arizona Press), 1995; Albert Utton, "Problems and Successes of International Water Agreements: The Example of the United States and Mexico," in *International Environmental Diplomacy*, ed. John E. Carroll (Cambridge: Cambridge University Press), 1988; Ernesto

Enriquez-Coyro, *El Tratado entre México y los Estados Unidos de América sobre Ríos Internacionales: Una Lucha de Noventa Años* (Ciudad de México: Universidad Nacional Autónoma de México), 1976; Norris Hundley, *Dividing the Waters: A Century of Controversy between the United States and Mexico* (Berkeley: University of California Press), 1966.

5. An acre-foot is about 326,000 gallons of water, enough to cover an acre of land with one foot of water.

6. Julie A. Vano, Bradley Udall, Daniel R. Cayan, Jonathan T. Overpeck, Levi D. Brekke, Tapash Das, Holly C. Hartmann, Hugo G. Hidalgo, Martin Hoerling, Gregory J. McCabe, Kiyomi Morino, Robert S. Webb, Kevin Werner, and Dennis P. Lettenmaier, "Understanding Uncertainties in Future Colorado River Streamflow," *Bulletin of the American Meteorological Society* 95: 59–78, 2014.

7. José L. Luege, "Acta 319," *El Universal*, Mexico City, March 31, 2014.

8. Back in 2000, on the heels of a set conferences and workshops organized by a consortium of NGOs, and through the binational signing of Minute 306 (Conceptual Framework for U.S.-Mexico Studies for Future Recommendations Concerning the Riparian and Estuarine Ecology of the Limitrophe Section of the Colorado River and its Associated Delta), the aim of working together to restore the delta had gained prominence with the establishment of a binational task force to assess its ecological needs; the All-American Canal conflict, however, had stalled the political drive towards progress.

9. Ken Salazar, "Remarks at the Signing of Minute 319 to the Mexican Water Treaty," U.S. Bureau of Reclamation, San Diego, CA, November 20, 2012.

10. Michael Connor, "Remarks at the Signing of Minute 319 to the Mexican Water Treaty," U.S. Bureau of Reclamation, San Diego, CA, November 20, 2012.

11. Ibid.

12. Roberto Salmón, "Remarks at the Signing of Minute 319 to the Mexican Water Treaty," Mexican section of the IBWC, San Diego, CA, November 20, 2012.

13. Arturo Sarukhán, Mexican ambassador to the United States (2006–2012), personal conversation, January 20, 2015.

Chapter 7

Note: Detailed information on all the interviews is listed in Appendix C, including the interviewees' positions at the time of the conversation. The footnotes indicate their professional appointment during the time of the negotiations.

1. Osvel Hinojosa, Director of the Water and Wetlands Program at Pronatura, personal conversation, October 13, 2014.

2. William Hasencamp, Manager of Colorado River Resources for the Metropolitan Water District of Southern California, personal conversation, January 9, 2015.

3. Gerald Zimmerman, Executive Director of the Colorado River Board of California, personal conversation, January 21, 2015.

4. José de Jesús Luévano, Secretary of the Mexican Section of the International Boundary and Water Commission, personal conversation, October 24, 2014.

5. Zimmerman, 2015.

6. Tony Perry, "A Fresh Battle between Southern California Water Adversaries," *Los Angeles Times*, October 18, 2010; Bettina Boxall, "Colorado River Water Deal Overturned," *Los Angeles Times*, January 15, 2010; Tony Perry, "Imperial Farmers Should Get Less Water," *Los Angeles Times*, July 4, 2003; Tony Perry, "Battle Lines Drawn Over Water Rights," *Los Angeles Times*, January 13, 1999.

7. John Keys, "Water Dust-Up: District Must Look at Waste," *Los Angeles Times*, July 27, 2003.

8. Hasencamp, 2015.

9. Peter Silva, Assistant Administrator of the Office of Water at the U.S. Environmental Protection Agency, personal conversation, November 25, 2014.

10. Carlos de la Parra, Environmental Consultant for the International Boundary and Water Commission's Mexican Section, personal conversation, November 20, 2014.

11. Hinojosa, 2014.

12. Luévano, 2014.

13. Silva, 2014.

14. Sarukhán, 2015.

15. Víctor Uribe, Minister for Legal Affairs at the Mexican Embassy in Washington, DC, personal conversation, February 10, 2015.

16. Sarukhán, 2015.

17. U.S. Department of Interior, "U.S. and Mexico Agree to Discuss Joint Cooperative Actions Related to the Colorado River," Washington, DC, August 13, 2007.

18. Sally Spener, Foreign Affairs Secretary of the International Boundary Waters Commission, personal conversation, January 9, 2015.

19. Sarukhán, 2015.

20. Uribe, 2015.

21. Sarukhán, 2015.

22. Ibid.

23. Michael Connor, Commissioner of the U.S. Bureau of Reclamation, personal conversation, January 14, 2015.

24. Robert Snow, Attorney, Solicitor's Office of the U.S. Department of Interior, personal conversation, November 17, 2014.

25. Antonio Ortiz-Mena, Minister for Economic Affairs at the Mexican Embassy in Washington, DC, personal conversation, January 12, 2015.

26. Carlos Peña, Principal Engineer of the U.S. Section of the International Boundary and Water Commission, personal conversation, December 11, 2014.

27. Felipe Calderón, President of Mexico (2006–2012), personal conversation, December 2, 2013.

28. Greg Moran, "U.S.-Mexico Boost Collaboration on Colorado River," *San Diego Union Tribune*, March 12, 2015; José L. Luege, "Acta 319," *El Universal*, March 31, 2014; U.S. Geological Survey, "Tectonic Summary," U.S. Department of the Interior, April 5, 2010.

29. Óscar Ibáñez, Chief of Staff for the Director General of Mexico's National Water Commission, personal conversation, January 30, 2015.

30. Efraín Muñoz, Director General, Baja California Water Commission, personal conversation, January 20, 2015.

31. Ibáñez, 2015.

32. Luévano, 2014.

33. Connor, 2015.

34. Antonio Rascón, Principal Engineer of the Mexican Section of the International Boundary and Water Commission, personal conversation, January 20, 2015.

35. Calderón, 2013.

36. Muñoz, 2015.

37. Roberto Salmón, Commissioner of the Mexican Section of the International Boundary and Water Commission, personal conversation, December 11, 2014.

38. Sarukhán, 2015.

39. Connor, 2015.

40. Ibáñez, 2015.

41. Karen Kwon, First Assistant Attorney General for the State of Colorado, personal conversation, November 21, 2014.

42. Don Ostler, Executive Director and Secretary of the Upper Colorado River Commission, personal conversation, October 2, 2014.

43. John Entsminger, Senior Deputy General Manager and Director for Environmental and Water Resource Law, Southern Nevada Water Authority, personal conversation, December 12, 2014.

44. Ward, 2003; Ingram, Laney, and Gillilan, 1995; Enriquez-Coyro, 1976; Hundley, 1966.

45. Patrick Tyrrell, Head of the State Engineer's Office of Wyoming, personal conversation, January 5, 2015.

46. Kwon, 2014.

47. Entsminger, 2014.

48. Ted Kowalski, Chief of the Interstate and Federal Section of the Colorado Conservation Board of the State of Colorado, personal conversation, November 26, 2014.

49. Mulroy, 2014.

50. Spener, 2015.

51. Peña, 2014.

52. Jennifer Gimbel, Director of the Colorado Water Conservation Board of the State of Colorado, personal conversation, December 19, 2014.

53. Connor, 2015.

54. Terrance Fulp, Director of the Lower Colorado Region at the U.S. Bureau of Reclamation, personal conversation, November 6, 2014.

55. Lorri Gray-Lee, Director of the Lower Colorado Region at the U.S. Bureau of Reclamation (2007–2011), personal conversation, November 17, 2014.

56. Rascón, 2015.

57. Francisco Bernal, Regional Director, Baja California State Office of the International Boundary and Water Commission, personal conversation, January 9, 2015.

58. Charles Cullom, Manager of the Colorado River Programs of the Central Arizona Water Project, personal conversation, January 26, 2015.

59. Hinojosa, 2014.

60. Ibáñez, 2015.

61. Kwon, 2014.

62. Luévano, 2014.

63. Rascón, 2015.

64. Entsminger, 2014.

65. Gray-Lee, 2014.

Chapter 8

1. U.S. Bureau of Reclamation, "Final Environmental Impact Statement: Colorado River Interim Guidelines," October 2007.

2. Tyrrell, 2015.

3. Kwon, 2014.

4. Kowalski, 2014.

5. U.S. Department of Interior, "Colorado River Interim Guidelines for Lower Basin Shortages and Coordinated Operations for Lake Powell and Lake Mead," December 2007.

6. Hasencamp, 2015.

7. Zimmerman, 2015.

8. Kwon, 2014.

9. Entsminger, 2014.

10. Ostler, 2014.

11. Spener, 2015.

12. Cullom, 2015.

13. Rascón, 2015.

14. Zimmerman, 2015.

15. Luévano, 2014.

16. Fulp, 2014.

17. Ibid.

18. Rascón, 2015.

19. Tyrrell, 2015.

20. Hinojosa, 2014.

21. Peña, 2014.

22. Silva, 2014.

23. Edward Drusina, Commissioner of the U.S. Section of the International Boundary and Water Commission, personal conversation, February 4, 2015.

24. Gray-Lee, 2014.

25. Peter Culp, Chief Attorney at the Sonoran Institute, personal conversation, November 10, 2014.

26. De la Parra, 2014.

27. Cullom, 2015.

28. Bernal, 2015.

29. Cullom, 2015.

30. Rascón, 2015.

31. Gray-Lee, 2014.

32. Adriana Reséndez, Technical Director, Colorado River Program of the Mexican Section of the International Boundary Waters Commission, personal conversation, January 28, 2015.

33. Pitt, Director of the Colorado River Project at the Environmental Defense Fund, personal conversation, November 7, 2014.

34. Mario López, General Manager of Binational Projects at Mexico's National Water Commission, personal conversation, December 1, 2014.

35. Pitt, 2014.

36. López, 2014.

37. Reséndez, 2015.

38. Rascón, 2015.

39. Patricia Mulroy, General Manager of the Southern Nevada Water Authority and Former President of the U.S. Association of Metropolitan Water Agencies, personal conversation, December 12, 2014.

40. José Gutiérrez, Deputy General Manager of Binational Projects at Mexico's National Water Commission, personal conversation, January 30, 2015.

41. Ibáñez, 2015.

42. Calderón, 2013.

43. De la Parra, 2014.

44. Ibáñez, 2015.

45. López, 2014.

46. Rascón, 2015.

47. Salmón, 2014.

48. Gutiérrez, 2015.

49. Ostler, 2014.

50. Peña, 2014.

51. Kwon, 2014.

52. Drusina, 2015.

53. Ibáñez, 2014.

54. De la Parra, 2014.

55. Fulp, 2014.

56. Entsminger, 2014.

57. López, 2014.

58. Hasencamp, 2015.

59. Zimmerman, 2015.

60. Peña, 2014.

61. Ostler, 2014.

62. Cullom, 2015.

63. Rascón, 2015.

64. Entsminger, 2014.

65. Fulp, 2014.

66. Snow, 2014.

67. Connor, 2015.

68. Culp, 2014.

69. Entsminger, 2014.

Chapter 9

1. Taylor Hawes, Director of the Colorado River Program at the Nature Conservancy, personal conversation, October 15, 2014.

2. Hinojosa, 2014.

3. Pitt, 2014.

4. Gastón Luken-Aguilar, President of Pronatura—Sea of Cortez, personal conversation, November 18, 2014.

5. Perri Benemelis, Manager, Colorado River Section, Arizona Department of Water Resources, personal conversation, October 27, 2014.

6. Culp, 2014.

7. Consortium of Environmental NGOs, *Conservation before Shortage II: Proposal for Colorado River Operations*, Letter submitted to the Honorable Dirk Kempthorne, Secretary U.S. Department of Interior, by Defenders of Wildlife, Environmental Defense, National Wildlife Federation, Pacific Institute, Sierra Club, Nature Conservancy, Rivers Foundation of the Americas, and Sonoran Institute, Washington, DC, July 7, 2006; Francisco Zamora-Arroyo, Jennifer Pitt, Steve Cornelius, Edward Glenn, Osvel Hinojosa-Huerta, Marcia Moreno, Jaqueline García, Pamela Nagler, Meredith de la Garza, and Iván Parra, *Conservation Priorities in the Colorado River Delta, Mexico and the United States,* Workshop Report prepared by the Sonoran Institute, Environmental Defense, University of Arizona, Pronatura Noroeste Dirección de Conservación Sonora, Centro de Investigación en Alimentación y Desarrollo, and World Wildlife Fund—Gulf of California Program, available online at www.sonoran.org, 2005.

8. de la Parra, 2014.

9. Snow, 2014.

10. Pitt, 2014.

11. Connor, 2015.

12. Ibáñez, 2015.

13. Hinojosa, 2014.

14. López, 2014.

15. Luken-Aguilar, 2015.

16. Hinojosa, 2014.

17. Ibáñez, 2015.

18. Hinojosa, 2014.

19. Gutiérrez, 2015.

20. De la Parra, 2014.

21. Salmón, 2014.

22. Ibáñez, 2015.

23. Kowalski, 2014.

24. Benemelis, 2014.

25. De la Parra, 2014.

26. Kwon, 2014.

27. Mulroy, 2014.

28. Tyrrell, 2015.

29. Cullom, 2015.

30. Benemelis, 2014.

31. Gimbel, 2014.

32. De la Parra, 2014.

33. Hawes, 2014.

34. Kwon, 2014.

35. Pitt, 2014.

36. Peña, 2014.

37. Entsminger, 2014.

38. De la Parra, 2014.

39. Pitt, 2014.

40. Hinojosa, 2014.

41. Culp, 2014.

42. Luévano, 2014.

43. Hinojosa, 2014.

44. Hawes, 2014.

45. Luken-Aguilar, 2014.

46. Benemelis, 2014.

47. Fulp, 2014.

48. Hawes, 2014.

49. Pitt, 2014.

50. Ibid.

51. Hinojosa, 2014.

52. De la Parra, 2014.

53. Kwon, 2014.

54. Pitt, 2014.

55. Entsminger, 2014.

56. Peña, 2014.

57. Salmón, 2014.

58. López, 2014.

59. Mulroy, 2014.

60. Hawes, 2014.

61. De la Parra, 2014.

62. Culp, 2014.

63. Drusina, 2015.

64. López, 2014.

65. Salmón, 2014.

66. Zimmerman, 2015.

67. Luken-Aguilar, 2014.

Chapter 10

1. Zimmerman, 2015.

2. Peña, 2014.

3. Tyrrell, 2015.

4. Gray-Lee, 2014.

5. Kwon, 2014.

6. Cullom, 2015.

7. Benemelis, 2014.

8. Entsminger, 2014.

9. Ibid.

10. Mulroy, 2014.

11. Ibid.

12. U.S. Congressional Research Service, *U.S.-Mexico Water Sharing: Background and Recent Developments,* Report prepared by Nicole R. Carter, Clare R. Seelke, and Daniel T. Shedd for members and committees of Congress, Washington, DC, January 2015.

13. John Cornyn (U.S. Senator) and Filemon Vela (U.S. Representative), *Letter to Commissioner Drusina,* U.S. Congress, November 13, 2014; Marta Wesimann, "Texas Legislators Hint at Possible Funding Cuts for Minute 319," *Journal of Water,* December 10, 2013.

14. Mulroy, 2014.

15. U.S. Congressional Research Service, *U.S.-Mexico Water Sharing: Background and Recent Developments,* Report prepared by Nicole R. Carter, Clare R. Seelke, and Daniel T. Shedd for members and committees of Congress, Washington, DC, January 2015.

16. De la Parra, 2014.

17. Luévano, 2014.

18. Entsminger, 2014.

19. Ibáñez, 2015.

20. Hinojosa, 2014.

21. Salmón, 2014.

22. De La Parra, 2014.

23. Gutiérrez, 2015.

24. López, 2014.

25. Muñoz, 2015.

26. Ostler, 2014.

27. Silva, 2014.

28. Calderón, 2013.

29. Cullom, 2015.

30. Culp, 2014.

31. Benemelis, 2014.

32. Ortiz-Mena, 2015.

33. Mulroy, 2014.

34. Pitt, 2014.

35. Luken-Aguilar, 2014.

36. Jennifer McCloskey, Deputy Director of the Lower Colorado Region at the U.S. Bureau of Reclamation, personal conversation, October 30, 2014.

37. Fulp, 2014.

38. Gray-Lee, 2014.

39. Connor, 2015.

40. Ibid.

41. Snow, 2014.

42. Fulp, 2014.

43. Rascón, 2015.

44. Luévano, 2014.

45. Gray-Lee, 2014.

46. Drusina, 2015.

47. Peña, 2014.

48. Spener, 2015.

49. Connor, 2015.

50. Salmón, 2014.

51. Hasencamp, 2015.

52. Zimmerman, 2015.

53. López, 2014.

54. Mulroy, 2014.

55. Drusina, 2015.

56. Culp, 2014.

57. Gimbel, 2014.

58. Peña, 2014.

59. Luévano, 2014.

60. McCloskey, 2014.

61. Connor, 2015.

62. Salmón, 2014.

63. Connor, 2015.

64. Salmón, 2014.

65. Connor, 2015.

66. Salmón, 2014.

67. Connor, 2015.

68. McCloskey, 2014.

69. Rascón, 2015.

70. Luévano, 2014.

71. De la Parra, 2014.

72. Kowalski, 2014.

73. Mulroy, 2014.

74. Gutiérrez, 2015.

75. Entsminger, 2014.

76. Spener, 2015.

77. Fulp, 2014.

78. Pitt, 2014.

79. Drusina, 2015.

80. Peña, 2014.

81. Salmón, 2014.

82. Gray-Lee, 2014.

83. Snow, 2014.

84. Hinojosa, 2014.

85. Luévano, 2014.

86. Gutiérrez, 2015.

87. Snow, 2014.

88. Drusina, 2015.

89. Ostler, 2014.

90. Kwon, 2014.

Chapter 11

1. Deepak Malhotra, *Negotiating the Impossible: How to Break Deadlock and Resolve Ugly Conflicts (Without Money or Muscle)* (Oakland, CA: Berret-Koehler), 2016; Robert C. Bordone, Nancy H. Rogers, Frank E. A. Sander, Craig A. McEwen, *Designing Systems and Processes for Managing Disputes* (New York: Aspen Publishers), 2013; Robert H. Mnookin, Scott R. Peppet, and Andrew S. Tulumello, *Beyond Winning: Negotiating to Create Value in Deals and Disputes* (Cambridge, MA: Belknap Press), 2004.

2. Susan Podziba, *Civic Fusion: Mediating Polarized Public Disputes* (Chicago, IL: American Bar Association), 2012; John Forester, *Dealing with Differences: Dramas of Mediating Public Disputes* (New York: Oxford University Press), 2009; Brian Mandell, "Unnecessary Toughness: Hard-Bargaining as an Extreme Sport," in *Negotiating on Behalf of Others*, ed. Robert H. Mnookin, Lawrence E. Susskind, and Pacey C. Foster (Thousand Oaks, CA: Sage Publications), 1999.

3. For further reference, see the respective timeline sections of appendices A and B.

4. Dan Shapiro, *Negotiating the Nonnegotiable: How To Resolve Your Most Emotionally Charged Conflicts* (New York: Viking), 2016; Guhan Subramanian, *Dealmaking: The New Strategy of Negotiauctions* (New York: W. W. Norton Company), 2010; Roger Fisher, William Ury, and Bruce Patton, *Getting to Yes: Negotiating Agreement Without Giving In* (New York: Penguin Books), 1991.

5. Michael A. Wheeler, *The Art of Negotiation: How to Improvise Agreement on a Chaotic World* (New York: Simon and Schuster), 2013; David Lax and James Sebenius, *3-D Negotiation: Powerful Tools to Change the Game in Your Most Important Deals* (Boston, MA: Harvard Business Review Press), 2006; Howard Raiffa, John Richardson, and David Metcalfe, *Negotiation Analysis: The Science and Art of Collaborative Decision-Making* (Cambridge, MA: Harvard University Press), 2002.

6. Benjamin Pohl and Ashok Swain, "Leveraging Diplomacy for Resolving Transboundary Water Problems," In *Water Diplomacy in Action: Contingent Approaches to Managing Complex Water Problems*, ed. Shafiqul Islam and Kaveh Madani (London: Anthem Press), 2017; Lawrence E. Susskind, Danya Rumore, Carri Hulet, and Patrick Field, *Managing Climate Risks in Coastal Communities: Strategies for Engagement, Readiness, and Adaptation* (London: Anthem Press), 2015; Shafiqul Islam and Lawrence E. Susskind, *Water Diplomacy: A Negotiated Approach to Managing Complex Water Networks* (New York: Resources for the Future Press), 2013.

7. William Ury, *Getting to Yes with Yourself (and Other Worthy Opponents)* (New York: Harper Collins), 2015; Douglas Stone and Sheila Heen, *Thanks for the Feedback: The Science and Art of Receiving Feedback Well* (New York: Penguin Books), 2014; Max Bazerman and Ann Tenbrunsel, *Blind Spots: Why We Fail to Do What's Right and What to Do About It* (Princeton, NJ: Princeton University Press), 2011.

8. Francesca Gino, *Sidetracked: Why Our Decisions Get Derailed, and How We Can Stick to the Plan* (Cambridge, MA: Harvard Business Review), 2013; George A. Akerlof and Robert J. Shiller, *Animal Spirits: How Human Psychology Drives the Economy and Why It Matters for Global Capitalism* (Princeton, NJ: Princeton University Press), 2009; Daniel Kahneman and Amos Tversky, "Conflict Resolution: A Cognitive Perspective," in *Barriers to Conflict Resolution*, ed. Kenneth Arrow, Robert H. Mnookin, Lee Ross, Amos Tversky, and Robert Wilson (New York: W. W. Norton Company), 1995.

9. Ronald Heifetz, Martin Linsky, and Alexander Grashow, *The Practice of Adaptive Leadership: Tools and Tactics for Changing Your Organization and the World* (Boston, MA: Harvard Business Press), 2009; Mark Gerzon, *Leading Through Conflict: How Successful Leaders Transform Differences into Opportunities* (Boston, MA: Harvard Business Review Press), 2006.

10. John S. Hammond, Ralph L. Keeney, and Howard Raiffa, *Smart Choices: A Practical Guide To Making Better Decisions* (Boston, MA: Harvard Business Review Press), 2015; Barbara Kellerman, *Bad Leadership: What It Is, How It Happens, Why It Matters* (Boston, MA: Harvard Business Press), 2004.

11. Max Bazerman, *The Power of Noticing: What the Best Leaders See* (New York: Simon & Schuster), 2014; Barry Schwartz and Kenneth Sharpe, *Practical Wisdom: The Right Way to Do the Right Thing* (New York: Riverhead Books), 2010; Mark Young, "Sharks, Saints, and Samurai: The Power of Ethics in Negotiation," *Negotiation Journal* 24:2 (April 2008): 145–155.

12. Dean Williams, *Leadership for a Fractured World* (Oakland, CA: Berrett-Koehler), 2015; Lawrence E. Susskind and Jeffrey Cruikshank, *Breaking Robert's Rules* (New York: Oxford University Press), 2006; Hannah Riley Bowles, "What Could a Leader Learn from a Mediator? Dispute Resolution Strategies for Organizational Leadership," in *Handbook of Dispute Resolution*, ed. Michael L. Moffit and Robert C. Bordone (San Francisco, CA: Jossey-Bass), 2005.

13. Richard Margerum, *Beyond Consensus: Improving Collaborative Planning and Management* (Cambridge, MA: MIT Press), 2011; Xavier De Souza Briggs, *Democracy as Problem-Solving: Civic Capacity in Communities across the Globe* (Cambridge, MA: MIT Press), 2008; Archon Fung, "Democratic Theory and Political Science: A Pragmatic Method of Constructive Engagement," *American Political Science Review* 101:3 (August 2007): 443–458.

14. Judith Innes and David Booher, *Planning with Complexity: An Introduction to Collaborative Rationality for Public Policy* (New York: Routledge), 2010; Julia M. Wondolleck and Steven L. Yaffee, *Making Collaboration Work: Lessons from Innovation in Natural Resource Management* (Washington, DC: Island Press), 2000.

15. Kathryn S. Quick and Martha S. Feldman, "Boundaries as Junctures: Collaborative Boundary Work for Building Efficient Resilience," *Journal of Public Administration Research and Theory* 24:1 (January 2014): 1–23; Lynn Mandarano, "Evaluating

Collaborative Environmental Planning Outputs and Outcomes," *Journal of Planning Education and Research* 27:4 (2008): 456–468; Leen Hordijk and Markus Amman, "How Science and Policy Combined to Combat Air Pollution Problems," *Environmental Policy and Law* 37:4 (2007): 336–340.

16. Margaret Wilder and Helen Ingram, "Knowing Equity When We See It: Water Equity in Contemporary Global Contexts," in *Oxford Handbook of Water Politics and Policy*, ed. Ken Conca and Erika Weinthal (Oxford: Oxford University Press), 2016; Stephen Mumme, "From Equitable Utilization to Sustainable Development: Advancing Equity in U.S.-Mexico Border Water Management," in *Water, Place, and Equity*, ed. John M. Whiteley, Helen Ingram, and Richard Perry (Cambridge, MA: MIT Press), 2008; Paul F. Steinberg, *Environmental Leadership in Developing Countries* (Cambridge, MA: MIT Press), 2001.

17. Gary Klein, *Streetlights and Shadows: Searching for the Keys to Adaptive Decision-Making* (Cambridge, MA: MIT Press), 2009; Mark Sagoff, *The Economy of the Earth: Philosophy, Law, and the Environment* (Cambridge, UK: Cambridge University Press), 2007; Jody Freeman, "Collaborative Governance in the Administrative State," *UCLA Law Review* 45 (1997): 1–77.

18. Andrea K. Gerlak, "Today's Pragmatic Water Policy: Restoration, Collaboration, and Adaptive Management along U.S. Rivers," *Society & Natural Resources* 21:6 (July 2008): 538–545; Jason Corburn, *Street Science: Community Knowledge and Environmental Health Justice* (Cambridge, MA: MIT Press), 2005; Karen Bäckstrand, "Civic Science for Sustainability: Reframing the Role of Experts, Policy-makers and Citizens in Environmental Governance," *Global Environmental Politics* 3:4 (2003): 24–41.

19. George Lakoff, *The Political Mind: Why You Can't Understand 21st Century Politics with an 18th Century Brain* (New York: Viking), 2008; Ted Brader, *Campaigning for Hearts and Minds: How Emotional Appeals in Political Ads Work* (Chicago, IL: Chicago University Press), 2006; Craig Crawford, *Attack the Messenger: How Politicians Turn You Against the Media* (New York: Rowman & Littlefield Publishers), 2006.

20. Raul Lejano, Mrill Ingram, and Helen Ingram, *The Power of Narrative in Environmental Networks* (Cambridge, MA: MIT Press), 2013; Melissa Nobles, *The Politics of Official Apologies* (Cambridge, MA: Cambridge University Press), 2008; Anthony G. Amsterdam and Jerome Bruner, "On Narrative," in *Minding the Law* (Cambridge, MA: Harvard University Press), 2002.

21. Joshua Greene, *Moral Tribes: Emotion, Reason, and the Gap Between US and Them* (New York: Penguin Books), 2013; Drew Westen, *The Political Brain: The Role of Emotion in Deciding the Fate of the Nation* (New York: Public Affairs), 2007.

22. Marshall Ganz, "Public Narrative, Collective Action, and Power," in *Accountability through Public Opinion: From Inertia to Public Action*, eds. Sina Odugbemi and Taeku Lee (Washington, DC: The World Bank), 2011; Dan P. McAdams, "Life Stories," in *The Redemptive Self: Stories Americans Live By* (New York: Oxford University Press),

2006; George E. Marcus, *The Sentimental Citizen* (University Park, PA: Pennsylvania State University Press), 2002.

23. Andrew J. Hoffman, "Climate Science as Culture War," *Stanford Social Innovation Review* (Fall 2012): 1–9; Jeff Ansell and Jeffrey Leeson, *When the Headline Is You: An Insider's Guide to Handling the Media* (San Francisco, CA: Jossey-Bass), 2010; Lawrence E. Susskind and Patrick Field, *Dealing with an Angry Public: The Mutual Gains Approach* (New York: Free Press), 1997.

24. William R. Moomaw and Mihaela Papa, "Creating a Mutual Gains Climate Regime through Universal Clean Energy Services," *Sustainable Development Diplomacy and Governance Program-Tufts Center for International Environment and Resource Policy* 6 (May 2012): 1–27; Frank Luntz, *Words that Work: It's Not What You Say, It's What People Hear* (New York: Hyperion), 2007; Steven Jarding and Dave "Mudcat" Saunders, *Foxes in the Henhouse* (New York: Touchstone), 2006.

Bibliography

Negotiation, Mediation, and Dispute Resolution

Arrow, Kenneth. 1995. Information Acquisition and the Resolution of Conflict. In *Barriers to Conflict Resolution*, ed. Kenneth Arrow, Robert H. Mnookin, Lee Ross, Amos Tversky, and Robert Wilson, 258–272. New York: W. W. Norton.

Bordone, Robert C., Nancy H. Rogers, Frank E. A. Sander, and Craig A. McEwen. 2013. *Designing Systems and Processes for Managing Disputes*. New York: Aspen Publishers.

Breslin, J. William, and Jeffrey Z. Rubin. 2010. *Negotiation Theory and Practice*. Cambridge, MA: Program on Negotiation at Harvard Law School.

Elster, John. 1995. Strategic Uses of Argument. In *Barriers to Conflict Resolution*, ed. Kenneth Arrow, Robert H. Mnookin, Lee Ross, Amos Tversky, and Robert Wilson, 236–256. New York: W. W. Norton.

Fisher, Roger. 1983. Negotiating Power: Getting and Using Influence. *American Behavioral Scientist* 27 (November-December):150–166.

Fisher, Roger, and Daniel Shapiro. 2006. *Beyond Reason: Using Emotions as You Negotiate*. New York: Penguin Books.

Fisher, Roger, Elizabeth Kopelman, and Andrea Kupfer Schneider. 1996. *Beyond Machiavelli: Tools for Coping with Conflict*. New York: Penguin Books.

Fisher, Roger, William Ury, and Bruce Patton. 1991. *Getting to Yes: Negotiating Agreement without Giving In*. New York: Penguin Books.

Forester, John. 2009. *Dealing with Differences: Dramas of Mediating Public Disputes*. New York: Oxford University Press.

Forester, John, and David Stitzel. 1989. Beyond Neutrality: The Possibilities of Activist Mediation in Public Sector Conflicts. *Negotiation Journal* 5:3 (July): 251–264.

Gilson, Ronald J., and Robert H. Mnookin. 1995. Cooperation and Competition in Litigation: Can Lawyers Dampen Conflict? In *Barriers to Conflict Resolution*, ed. Kenneth Arrow, Robert H. Mnookin, Lee Ross, Amos Tversky, and Robert Wilson, 184–210. New York: W. W. Norton.

Kolb, Deborah. 2004. Staying in the Game or Changing It: An Analysis of Moves and Turns in a Negotiation. *Negotiation Journal* 20:2 (April): 253–268.

Kolb, Deborah, and Jessica Porter. 2015. *Negotiating at Work: Turn Small Wins into Big Gains*. San Francisco: Jossey-Bass.

Lax, David, and James Sebenius. 2006. *3-D Negotiation: Powerful Tools to Change the Game in Your Most Important Deals*. Boston, MA: Harvard Business Review Press.

Lax, David, and James Sebenius. 1986. *The Manager as Negotiator*. New York: The Free Press.

Lewicki, Roy J., and Joseph A. Litterer. 1987. Strategy and Tactics of Distributive Bargaining. In *Negotiation, Readings, Exercises and Cases, 48-79*. Homewood, IL: R. D. Irwin.

Lewicki, Roy J., and Robert J. Robinson. 1998. Ethical and Unethical Bargaining Tactics: An Empirical Study. *Journal of Business Ethics* 17:665–682.

Malhotra, Deepak. 2016. *Negotiating the Impossible: How to Break Deadlock and Resolve Ugly Conflicts (without Money or Muscle)*. Oakland, CA: Berret-Koehler.

Malhotra, Deepak, and Max Bazerman. 2008. *Negotiation Genius: How to Overcome Obstacles and Achieve Brilliant Results at the Bargaining Table and Beyond*. New York: Bantam Books.

Mandell, Brian. 1999. Unnecessary Toughness: Hard-Bargaining as an Extreme Sport. In *Negotiating on Behalf of Others*, ed. Robert H. Mnookin, Lawrence E. Susskind, and Pacey C. Foster, 263–273. Thousand Oaks, CA: Sage Publications.

Martinez, Janet, and Lawrence E. Susskind. 2000. Parallel Informal Negotiation: An Alternative to Second Track Diplomacy. *International Negotiation* 5 (3):1–18.

Mnookin, Robert H. 2010. *Bargaining with the Devil: When to Negotiate, When to Fight*. New York: Simon & Schuster.

Mnookin, Robert H., Scott R. Peppet, and Andrew S. Tulumello. 2004. *Beyond Winning: Negotiating to Create Value in Deals and Disputes*. Cambridge, MA: Belknap Press.

Mnookin, Robert H., and Lee Ross. 1995. Introduction. In *Barriers to Conflict Resolution*, ed. Kenneth Arrow, Robert H. Mnookin, Lee Ross, Amos Tversky, and Robert Wilson, 2–24. New York: W. W. Norton.

Moore, Christopher. 2003. *The Mediation Process: Practical Strategies for Resolving Conflict*. San Francisco: Jossey Bass.

Parson, Edward, and Richard J. Zeckhauser. 1995. Cooperation in the Unbalanced Commons. In *Barriers to Conflict Resolution*, ed. Kenneth Arrow, Robert H. Mnookin, Lee Ross, Amos Tversky, and Robert Wilson, 212-234. New York: W. W. Norton.

Podziba, Susan. 2012. *Civic Fusion: Mediating Polarized Public Disputes*. Chicago, IL: American Bar Association.

Presman, Gavin. 2017. *Negotiation: How to Craft Agreements that Give Everyone More*. London: Icon.

Putnam, Robert. 1988. Diplomacy and Domestic Politics: The Logic of Two-Level Games. *International Organization* 42:427–460.

Raiffa, Howard. 1995. Analytical Barriers. In *Barriers to Conflict Resolution*, ed. Kenneth Arrow, Robert H. Mnookin, Lee Ross, Amos Tversky, and Robert Wilson, 132-148. New York: W. W. Norton.

Raiffa, Howard. 1985. *The Art and Science of Negotiation: How to Resolve Conflicts and Get the Best Out of Bargaining*. Cambridge, MA: Harvard University Press.

Raiffa, Howard, John Richardson, and David Metcalfe. 2002. *Negotiation Analysis: The Science and Art of Collaborative Decision-Making*. Cambridge, MA: Harvard University Press.

Salacuse, Jeswald. 2013. *Negotiating Life: Secrets for Everyday Diplomacy and Dealmaking*. New York: Palgrave Macmillan.

Salacuse, Jeswald. 2003. *The Global Negotiator: Making, Managing, and Mending Deals around the World in the Twenty-First Century*. New York: Palgrave Macmillan.

Sebenius, James. 1996. Sequencing to Build Coalitions: With Whom Should I Talk First? In *Wise Choices: Decisions, Games, and Negotiations*, ed. Richard J. Zeckhauser, Ralph L. Keeney, and James K. Sebenius, 301–322. Cambridge, MA: Harvard Business School Press.

Sebenius, James. 1995. Dealing with Blocking Coalitions and Related Barriers to Agreement: Lessons from Negotiations on the Oceans, the Ozone, and the Climate. In *Barriers to Conflict Resolution*, ed. Kenneth Arrow, Robert H. Mnookin, Lee Ross, Amos Tversky, and Robert Wilson, 150–182. New York: W. W. Norton.

Shapiro, Dan. 2016. *Negotiating the Nonnegotiable: How to Resolve Your Most Emotionally Charged Conflicts*. New York: Viking.

Stone, Douglas, and Sheila Heen. 2014. *Thanks for the Feedback: The Science and Art of Receiving Feedback Well*. New York: Penguin Books.

Stone, Douglas, Bruce Patton, and Sheila Heen. 2000. *Difficult Conversations: How to Discuss What Matters Most*. New York: Penguin Books.

Subramanian, Guhan. 2010. *Dealmaking: The New Strategy of Negotiauctions*. New York: W. W. Norton.

Susskind, Lawrence E. 2014. *Good for You, Great for Me: Finding the Trading Zone and Winning at Win-Win Negotiation*. New York: Public Affairs.

Susskind, Lawrence E., and Jeffrey Cruikshank. 2006. *Breaking Robert's Rules*. New York: Oxford University Press.

Susskind, Lawrence E., and Jeffrey Cruikshank. 1987. *Breaking the Impasse: Consensual Approaches to Resolving Public Disputes*. New York: Basic Books.

Susskind, Lawrence E., and Patrick Field. 1997. *Dealing with an Angry Public: The Mutual Gains Approach*. New York: Free Press.

Susskind, Lawrence E., and Sarah McKearnan. 1999. The Evolution of Public Policy Dispute Resolution. *Journal of Architectural and Planning Research* 16:2 (Summer): 97–115.

Ury, William. 2015. *Getting to Yes with Yourself (and Other Worthy Opponents)*. New York: HarperCollins.

Ury, William. 2007. *The Power of a Positive No: Save the Deal, Save the Relationship, and Still Say No*. New York: Bantam Books.

Ury, William. 1993. *Getting Past No: Negotiating in Difficult Situations*. New York: Bantam Books.

Ury, William L., Jeanne M. Brett, and Stephen B. Goldberg. 1988. *Getting Disputes Resolved: Designing Systems to Cut the Costs of Conflict*. San Francisco: Jossey-Bass.

Wheeler, Michael A. 2013. *The Art of Negotiation: How to Improvise Agreement in a Chaotic World*. New York: Simon and Schuster.

Wheeler, Michael A. 2004. Anxious Moments: Openings in Negotiation. *Negotiation Journal* 20:2 (April), 153–169.

Wheeler, Michael A. 2004. Swimming with Saints/Praying with Sharks. In *What's Fair: Ethics for Negotiators*, ed. Carrie Menkel-Meadow and Michael Wheeler. San Francisco: Jossey-Bass.

Wheeler, Michael A. 2003. *Negotiation*. Boston: Harvard Business School Publishing.

Wheeler, Michael A. 1999. First, Let's Kill All the Agents! In *Negotiating on Behalf of Others*, ed. Robert H. Mnookin, Lawrence E. Susskind, and Pacey C. Foster, 235–261. Thousand Oaks, CA: Sage Publications.

Wu, George. 1999. Sources of Joint Gains in Negotiations. *Harvard Business School 9–396–241* (October): 1–8.

Young, Mark. 2008. Sharks, Saints, and Samurai: The Power of Ethics in Negotiation. *Negotiation Journal* 24:2 (April): 145–155.

Leadership and Judgment

Akerlof, George A., and Robert J. Shiller. 2009. *Animal Spirits: How Human Psychology Drives the Economy and Why It Matters for Global Capitalism*. Princeton, NJ: Princeton University Press.

Baumgartner, Frank, and Bryan D. Jones. 1991. Agenda Dynamics and Policy Subsystems. *Journal of Politics* 53:1044–1074.

Bazerman, Max. 2014. *The Power of Noticing: What the Best Leaders See*. New York: Simon & Schuster.

Bazerman, Max, and Ann Tenbrunsel. 2011. *Blind Spots: Why We Fail to Do What's Right and What to Do about It*. Princeton, NJ: Princeton University Press.

Bazerman, Max, and Michael Watkins. 2008. *Predictable Surprises: The Disasters You Should Have Seen Coming and How to Prevent Them*. Boston: Harvard Business School Press.

Bazerman, Max, and Don Moore. 2013. *Judgment in Managerial Decision-Making*. Hoboken, NJ: John Wiley and Sons.

Bazerman, Max, and Margaret Neale. 1995. The Role of Fairness Considerations and Relationships in a Judgmental Perspective of Negotiation. In *Barriers to Conflict Resolution*, ed. Kenneth Arrow, Robert H. Mnookin, Lee Ross, Amos Tversky, and Robert Wilson, 86–104. New York: W. W. Norton.

Bowles, Hannah Riley. 2005. What Could a Leader Learn from a Mediator? Dispute Resolution Strategies for Organizational Leadership. In *Handbook of Dispute Resolution*, ed. Michael L. Moffit and Robert C. Bordone, 409–424. San Francisco: Jossey-Bass.

Cohen, Michael, James March, and Johan Olsen. 1972. A Garbage Can Model of Organizational Choice. *Administrative Science Quarterly* 17 (March): 1–25.

Derue, Scott, Jennifer Nahrang, Ned Wellman, and Stephen Humphrey. 2011. Trait and Behavioral Theories of Leadership: An Integration and Meta-Analytic Test of Their Validity. *Personnel Psychology* 64:7–52.

Doyle, Michael, and David Straus. 2003. *How to Make Meetings Work*. New York: Jove Books.

Fisher, Roger, and Alan Sharp. 1999. *Getting It Done: How to Lead When You Are Not in Charge*. New York: Harper Business.

Forester, John. 1999. Dealing with Deep Value Differences. In *The Consensus Building Handbook*, ed. Lawrence E. Susskind, Sarah McKearnan, and Jennifer Thomas-Larmer, 463–494. Thousand Oaks, CA: Sage Publications.

Ganz, Marshall. 2010. Leading Change: Leadership, Organization, and Social Movements. In *Handbook of Leadership Theory and Practice*, ed. Nitin Nohria and Rakesh Khurana, 527–567. Boston: Harvard Business School Press.

Gerzon, Mark. 2006. *Leading Through Conflict: How Successful Leaders Transform Differences into Opportunities*. Boston: Harvard Business Review Press.

Gino, Francesca. 2013. *Sidetracked: Why Our Decisions Get Derailed, and How We Can Stick to the Plan*. Cambridge, MA: Harvard Business Review.

Hammond, John S., Ralph L. Keeney, and Howard Raiffa. 2015. *Smart Choices: A Practical Guide to Making Better Decisions*. Boston: Harvard Business Review Press.

Heifetz, Ronald. 1998. *Leadership without Easy Answers*. Cambridge, MA: Harvard University Press.

Heifetz, Ronald, and Martin Linsky. 2002. *Leadership on the Line: Staying Alive through the Dangers of Leading*. Boston: Harvard Business Review Press.

Heifetz, Ronald, Martin Linsky, and Alexander Grashow. 2009. *The Practice of Adaptive Leadership: Tools and Tactics for Changing Your Organization and the World*. Boston: Harvard Business Review Press.

Hermann, Margaret, Thomas Preston, Baghat Korany, and Timothy Shaw. 2001. Who Leads Matters: The Effects of Powerful Individuals. *International Studies Review* 3 (2): 83–131.

Hill, Linda A., Maurizio Travaglini, Greg Brandeau, and Emily Stecker. 2010. Unlocking the Slices of Genius in Your Organization: Leading for Innovation. In *Handbook of Leadership Theory and Practice*, ed. Nitin Nohria and Rakesh Khurana, 611–653. Boston: Harvard Business Press.

Jones, Bryan, Frank Baumgartner, and Jeffrey Talbert. 1993. The Destruction of Issue Monopolies in Congress. *American Political Science Review* 87:657–671.

Kahneman, Daniel. 2011. *Thinking, Fast and Slow*. New York: Farrar, Straus, and Giroux.

Kahneman, Daniel, and Amos Tversky. 2000. *Choices, Values, and Frames*. Cambridge, MA: Cambridge University Press.

Kahneman, Daniel, and Amos Tversky. 1995. Conflict Resolution: A Cognitive Perspective. In *Barriers to Conflict Resolution*, ed. Kenneth Arrow, Robert H. Mnookin, Lee Ross, Amos Tversky, and Robert Wilson, 44-59. New York: W. W. Norton.

Kellerman, Barbara. 2012. *The End of Leadership*. New York: HarperCollins.

Kellerman, Barbara. 2008. *Followership: How Followers Are Creating Change and Changing Leaders*. Boston: Harvard Business Press.

Kellerman, Barbara. 2004. *Bad Leadership: What It Is, How It Happens, Why It Matters*. Boston: Harvard Business Press.

Kingdon, John W. 1995. *Agendas, Alternatives, and Public Policies*. Michigan, MI: Harper Collins College Publishers.

Krasner, Stephen D. 2009. The Garbage Can Framework for Locating Policy Planning. In *Avoiding Trivia: The Role of Strategic Planning in American Foreign Policy*. Washington, DC: Brookings Press.

Mintrom, Michael, and Sandra Vergari. 1996. Advocacy Coalitions, Policy Entrepreneurs, and Policy Change. *Policy Studies Journal: The Journal of the Policy Studies Organization* 24:420–434.

Miroff, Bruce. 2003. Entrepreneurship and Leadership. *Studies in American Political Development* 17:204–211.

Moffit, Michael L. 2005. Disputes as Opportunities to Create Value. In *Handbook of Dispute Resolution*, ed. Michael L. Moffit and Robert C. Bordone, 173-186. San Francisco: Jossey-Bass.

Movius, Hallam, and Lawrence E. Susskind. 2009. *Built to Win: Creating a World Class Organization*. Boston: Harvard Business Press.

Reid, Thomas R. 1980. *Congressional Odyssey: The Saga of a Senate Bill*. San Francisco: W. H. Freeman and Company.

Russo, J. Edward, and Paul J. H. Schoemaker. 1989. *Decision Traps. The Ten Barriers to Brilliant Decision-Making and How to Overcome Them*. New York: Fireside.

Sabatier, Paul A. 1988. An Advocacy Coalition Model of Policy Change and the Role of Policy Oriented Learning Therein. *Policy Sciences* 21:129–168.

Samuels, Richard. 2003. Why Leaders Matter? Creation Stories. In *Machiavelli's Children: Leaders and Their Legacies in Italy and Japan*. Ithaca, NY: Cornell University Press.

Schwartz, Barry, and Kenneth Sharpe. 2010. *Practical Wisdom: The Right Way to Do the Right Thing*. New York: Riverhead Books.

Schwartz, Barry, and Kenneth Sharpe. 2004. *The Paradox of Choice*. New York: HarperCollins.

Sheingate, Adam D. 2003. Political Entrepreneurship, Institutional Change, and American Political Development. *Studies in American Political Development* 17:185–203.

Straus, David. 1999. Managing Meetings to Build Consensus. In *The Consensus Building Handbook*, ed. Lawrence E. Susskind, Sarah McKearnan, and Jennifer Thomas-Larmer, 287–322. Thousand Oaks, CA: Sage.

Tversky, Amos, and Daniel Kahneman. 1981. The Framing of Decisions and the Psychology of Choice. *Science* 211 (4481): 453–458.

Williams, Dean. 2015. *Leadership for a Fractured World*. Oakland, CA: Berrett-Koehler.

Williams, Dean. 2005. *Real Leadership: Helping People and Organizations Face Their Toughest Challenges*. San Francisco: Berrett-Koehler Publishers.

Collaborative Decision-Making

Bäckstrand, Karen. 2003. Civic Science for Sustainability: Reframing the Role of Experts, Policy-makers, and Citizens in Environmental Governance. *Global Environmental Politics* 3 (4): 24–41.

Corburn, Jason. 2005. *Street Science: Community Knowledge and Environmental Health Justice*. Cambridge, MA: MIT Press.

Daly, Herman. 1996. The Shape of Current Thought on Sustainable Development. In *Beyond Growth: The Economics of Sustainable Development*. Boston: Beacon Press.

De Souza Briggs, Xavier. 2008. *Democracy as Problem-Solving: Civic Capacity in Communities across the Globe*. Cambridge, MA: MIT Press

Freeman, Jody. 1997. Collaborative Governance in the Administrative State. *UCLA Law Review* 45:1–77.

Fung, Archon. 2007. Democratic Theory and Political Science: A Pragmatic Method of Constructive Engagement. *American Political Science Review* 101:3 (August), 443–458.

Hordijk, Leen, and Markus Amman. 2007. How Science and Policy Combined to Combat Air Pollution Problems. *Environmental Policy and Law* 37 (4): 336–340.

Innes, Judith, and David Booher. 2010. *Planning with Complexity: An Introduction to Collaborative Rationality for Public Policy*. New York: Routledge.

Innes, Judith, and David Booher. 1999. Consensus Building and Complex Adaptive Systems: A Framework for Evaluating Collaborative Planning. *APA Journal* 65:4 (Autumn), 412–423.

Islam, Shafiqul, and Kaveh Madani. 2017. *Water Diplomacy in Action: Contingent Approaches to Managing Complex Water Problems*. London: Anthem Press.

Islam, Shafiqul, and Lawrence E. Susskind. 2013. *Water Diplomacy: A Negotiated Approach to Managing Complex Water Networks*. New York: Resources for the Future Press.

Forester, John. 1999. *The Deliberative Practitioner: Encouraging Participatory Planning Processes*. Cambridge, MA: MIT Press.

Klein, Gary. 2009. *Streetlights and Shadows: Searching for the Keys to Adaptive Decision-Making*. Cambridge, MA: MIT Press.

Mandarano, Lynn. 2008. Evaluating Collaborative Environmental Planning Outputs and Outcomes. *Journal of Planning Education and Research* 27 (4): 456–468.

Margerum, Richard. 2011. *Beyond Consensus: Improving Collaborative Planning and Management*. Cambridge, MA: MIT Press.

Moomaw, William R., Kilparti Ramakrishna, Kevin Gallagher, and Tobin Freid. 1999. The Kyoto Protocol: A Blueprint for Sustainable Development. *Journal of Environment & Development* 8 (1): 82–90.

Najam, Adil. 2005. Developing Countries and Global Environmental Governance: From Contestation to Participation to Engagement. *International Environmental Agreement: Politics, Law, and Economics* 5:303–321.

Najam, Adil, Ioli Christopolou, and William R. Moomaw. 2004. The Emergent System of Global Environmental Governance. *Global Environmental Politics* 4 (4): 23–35.

Ostrom, Elinor. 2012. *The Future of the Commons: Beyond Market Failure and Government Regulations*. London, UK: Institute of Economic Affairs.

Pohl, Benjamin, and Ashok Swain. 2017. Leveraging Diplomacy for Resolving Transboundary Water Problems. In *Water Diplomacy in Action: Contingent Approaches to Managing Complex Water Problems*, ed. Shafiqul Islam and Kaveh Madani, 19–34. London: Anthem Press.

Quick, Kathryn S., and Martha S. Feldman. 2014. Boundaries as Junctures: Collaborative Boundary Work for Building Efficient Resilience. *Journal of Public Administration Research and Theory* 24:1 (January): 1–23.

Sagoff, Mark. 2007. *The Economy of the Earth: Philosophy, Law, and the Environment*. Cambridge: Cambridge University Press.

Sebenius, James K. 1990. The Computer as Mediator: Law of the Sea and Beyond. *Journal of Policy Analysis and Management* 1 (1): 77–95.

Steinberg, Paul. 2015. *Who Rules the Earth? How Social Rules Shape Our Planet and Our Lives*. New York: Oxford University Press.

Steinberg, Paul F. 2001. *Environmental Leadership in Developing Countries*. Cambridge, MA: MIT Press.

Susskind, Lawrence E. 2013. Water and Democracy: New Roles for Civil Society in Water Governance. *International Journal of Water Resources Development* 29:4 (May): 666–677.

Susskind, Lawrence E., and Saleem Ali. 2014. *Environmental Diplomacy: Negotiating More Effective Global Agreements*. New York: Oxford University Press.

Susskind, Lawrence E., Boyd W. Fuller, Michèle Ferenz, and David Fairman. 2003. Multistakeholder Dialogue at the Global Scale. *International Negotiation* 8:235–266.

Susskind, Lawrence E., Ravi K. Jain, and Andrew O. Martyniuk. 2001. How Environmental Policy Studies Can Be Used Effectively. In *Better Environmental Policy Studies*. Washington, DC: Island Press.

Susskind, Lawrence E., Danya Rumore, Carri Hulet, and Patrick Field. 2015. *Managing Climate Risks in Coastal Communities: Strategies for Engagement, Readiness, and Adaptation*. London: Anthem Press.

Wondolleck, Julia M., and Steven L. Yaffee. 2000. *Making Collaboration Work: Lessons from Innovation in Natural Resource Management*. Washington, DC: Island Press.

Young, Oran. 2013. *On Environmental Governance: Sustainability, Efficiency, and Equity*. New York: Taylor and Francis.

Young, Oran. 2010. *Institutional Dynamics: Emergent Patterns in International Environmental Governance*. Cambridge, MA: MIT Press.

Political Communication

Amsterdam, Anthony G., and Jerome Bruner. 2002. *Minding the Law: How the Courts Rely on Storytelling and How Their Stories Change the Ways We Understand the Law – and Ourselves*. Cambridge, MA: Harvard University Press.

Ansell, Jeff, and Jeffrey Leeson. 2010. *When the Headline Is You: An Insider's Guide to Handling the Media*. San Francisco: Jossey-Bass.

Brader, Ted. 2006. *Campaigning for Hearts and Minds: How Emotional Appeals in Political Ads Work*. Chicago, IL: Chicago University Press.

Brown, Andrew D. 2006. A Narrative Approach to Collective Identities. *Journal of Management Studies* 43 (4): 731–753.

Bruner, Jerome. 2002. *Making Stories: Law, Literature, Life*. Cambridge, MA: Harvard University Press.

Bruner, Jerome. 1991. The Narrative Construction of Reality. *Critical Inquiry* 18:1 (Autumn), 1–21.

Bruner, Jerome. 1986. Two Modes of Thought. In *Actual Minds, Possible Worlds.* Cambridge, MA: Harvard University Press.

Crawford, Craig. 2006. *Attack the Messenger: How Politicians Turn You Against the Media.* New York: Rowman & Littlefield Publishers.

Couto, Richard A. 1993. Narrative, Free Space, and Political Leadership in Social Movements. *Journal of Politics* 55 (1): 57–79.

Damasio, Anthony R. 2005. *Descartes' Error: Emotion, Reason, and the Human Brain.* New York: Penguin Books.

Ganz, Marshall. 2011. Public Narrative, Collective Action, and Power. In *Accountability through Public Opinion: From Inertia to Public Action*, ed. Sina Odugbemi and Taeku Lee, 273-289. Washington, DC: World Bank.

Greene, Joshua. 2013. *Moral Tribes: Emotion, Reason, and the Gap Between Us and Them.* New York: Penguin Books.

Hoffman, Andrew J. 2015. *How Culture Shapes the Climate Change Debate.* Stanford, CA: Stanford University Press.

Iyengar, Sheena. 2010. *The Art of Choosing.* New York: Twelve Hachette Publishing Group.

Jarding, Steven, and Dave Saunders. 2006. *Foxes in the Henhouse: How the Republicans Stole the South and the Heartland and What the Democrats Must Do to Run 'Em Out.* New York: Touchstone.

Kearney, Richard. 2006. Narrative Matters. In *On Stories: Thinking in Action.* New York: Routledge.

Lakoff, George. 2008. *The Political Mind: Why You Can't Understand 21st-Century Politics with an 18th-Century Brain.* New York: Viking.

Luntz, Frank. 2007. *Words That Work: It's Not What You Say, It's What People Hear.* New York: Hyperion.

Marcus, George E. 2002. *The Sentimental Citizen.* University Park, PA: Pennsylvania State University Press.

McAdams, Dan P. 2006. *The Redemptive Self: Stories Americans Live By.* New York: Oxford University Press.

Moomaw, William R., and Mihaela Papa. 2012. Creating a Mutual Gains Climate Regime through Universal Clean Energy Services. *Sustainable Development Diplomacy and Governance Program-Tufts Center for International Environment and Resource Policy* 6 (May): 1–27.

Navarro, Joe, and Marvin Karlins. 2008. *What Every BODY Is Saying*. New York: HarperCollins Publishers.

Nobles, Melissa. 2008. *The Politics of Official Apologies*. Cambridge, MA: Cambridge University Press.

Scott, James C. 1990. *Domination and the Arts of Resistance: Hidden Transcripts*. New Haven, CT: Yale University Press.

Shamir, Boas, and Galit Eliam. 2006. What's Your Story? A Life-Stories Approach to Authentic Leadership Development. *Leadership Quarterly* 16:395–417.

Westen, Drew. 2007. *The Political Brain: The Role of Emotion in Deciding the Fate of the Nation*. New York: Public Affairs.

White, James B. 1989. The Judicial Opinion and the Poem: Ways of Reading, Ways of Life. In *Heracles' Bow: Essays in the Rhetoric and Poetics of the Law*. Madison: University of Wisconsin Press.

White, James B. 1985. Law as Rhetoric, Rhetoric as Law: The Arts of Cultural and Communal Life. *University of Chicago Law Review. University of Chicago. Law School* 52:684–702.

Transboundary Energy Resources: Gulf of Mexico

Baker, Timothy H., and Aloise Bozell Vansant. 2014. United States and Mexico Open Offshore Transboundary Hydrocarbons to Development. *Natural Resources and Environment* 29:1 (Summer): 1–5.

Clinton, Hillary Rodham. 2012. *Remarks at the Signing of the U.S.-Mexico Transboundary Agreement*. February 20. Los Cabos, Mexico: U.S. Department of State.

Congressional Record. 2013. Extensions of Remarks. In *Outer Continental Shelf Transboundary Hydrocarbons Agreement Authorization Act* (E1006), June 28. Washington, DC: U.S. House of Representatives.

Congressional Record. 2013. Extensions of Remarks. In *Outer Continental Shelf Transboundary Hydrocarbons Agreement Authorization Act* (H4094), June 27. Washington, DC: U.S. House of Representatives.

Congressional Record. 2013. *Outer Continental Shelf Transboundary Hydrocarbons Agreement Authorization Act* (H4097), June 27. Washington, DC: U.S. House of Representatives.

Congressional Record. 2013. Report Together with Dissenting Views. In *Outer Continental Shelf Transboundary Hydrocarbons Agreement Authorization Act* (HR 1613), June 27. Washington, DC: U.S. House of Representatives.

Couvillion, J. Keith. 2012. The Offshore Energy Industry Challenges and Opportunities. *Presentation at the 29th Conference of the National Association of Lease and Title Analysts* (September 25). Nashville.

García, Guillermo. 2009. *La Expltoación de Recursos Transfronterizos en el Golfo de México: Una Solución de Derecho Internacional. Tesis de Licenciatura en Derecho.* Mexico City: Instituto Tecnológico Autónomo de México.

García, Karol. 2012. PEMEX, la Petrolera Que Paga Más Impuestos en el Mundo. *El Economista,* Mexico City (February 29).

Goldwyn, David L. 2013. *Mexico Rising: Comprehensive Energy Reform at Last?* Washington, DC: Atlantic Council, Adrienne Arsht Latin America Center.

Goldwyn, David L. 2008. *Drilling Down: The Civil Society Guide to Extractive Industry Revenues and the Extractive Industries Transparency Initiative.* New York: Revenue Watch Institute.

Goldwyn, David L., Neil R. Brown, and Megan R. Cayten. 2014. *Mexico's Energy Reform: Ready to Launch.* Washington, DC: Atlantic Council, Adrienne Arsht Latin America Center.

Goldwyn, David L., Neil R. Brown, and Cory R. Gill. 2013. *Time to Implement the U.S.-Mexico Transboundary Hydrocarbons Agreement—Congress: Drop the Poison Pill.* Washington, DC: Brookings.

Grunstein, Miriam. 2014. Coordinated Regulatory Agencies: New Governance for Mexico's Energy Sector. *Rice University Baker Institute for Public Policy Issue Brief* (June 10).

Herrera, José Luis. 2013. *Yacimientos Compartidos de Hidrocarburos entre México y los Estados Unidos de América: Status de la Cuestión y Propuestas de Diálogo entre Sistemas Jurídicos Disímbolos. Tesis de Maestría en Derecho.* Mexico City: Universidad Panamericana.

Herrera, José Luis. 2012. The New Legal Framework for Oil and Gas Activities near the Maritime Boundaries between Mexico and the U.S. *Journal of World Energy Law and Business* 5 (3): 235–247.

Smith, Peter H., and Andrew Seele. 2013. *Mexico and the United States: The Politics of Partnership.* Boulder, CO: Lynne Rienner.

Sullivan, David. 2014. Mexico–United States: Agreement between the U.S.A. and Mexico Concerning Transboundary Hydrocarbon Reservoirs in the Gulf of Mexico. *International Maritime Boundaries.* Report Number 1–5 (3). American Society of International Law, 1–33.

Trauzzi, Monica. 2013. OnPoint Interview to David L. Goldwyn: The Impact of Mexico's Energy Deal on U.S. Companies. *Environment and Energy Television*. December 19. Washington, DC.

U.S. Congress. 2014. *An Act to Authorize the Secretary of the Interior to Take Actions to Implement the Agreement between the United States of America and the United Mexican States Concerning Transboundary Hydrocarbon Reservoirs in the Gulf of Mexico*. Washington, DC (October 12): 113th Congress, 1st Session, S.812.

U.S. Congress. 1997. *U.S.-Mexico Treaty on Maritime Boundaries*. Washington, DC (October 22): 105th Congress, 1st Session, Executive Report 105-04.

U.S. Congressional Research Service. 2015. *Mexico's Oil and Gas Sector: Reform Efforts and Implications for the United States*. Report prepared by Clare R. Seelke, A. Villareal, M. Ratner, and P. Brown for members and committees of Congress. January. Washington, DC.

U.S. Congressional Research Service. 2014. *Mexico: Background and U.S. Relations*. Report prepared by Clare Seelke for members and committees of Congress. January. Washington, DC.

U.S. Congressional Research Service. 2013. *Proposed U.S.-Mexico Transboundary Hydrocarbons Agreement: Background Issues for Congress*. Report prepared by Curry L. Hagerty and James C. Uzel for members and committees of Congress. September. Washington, DC.

U.S. Department of Interior. 2013. *Passage of U.S.-Mexico Transboundary Hydrocarbons Agreement*. Press release by Office of the Secretary of the Interior Sally Jewel. December 23. Washington, DC.

U.S. Department of State. 2012. *Agreement between the United States of America and the United Mexican States Concerning Transboundary Hydrocarbon Reservoirs in the Gulf of Mexico*. Los Cabos, Mexico: Bureau of Western Hemisphere Affairs.

U.S. Energy Information Administration. 2014. *Analysis Brief: Mexico*. April. Washington, DC: U.S. Department of Energy.

Vargas, Jorge A. 2012. The 2012 U.S.-Mexico Agreement on Transboundary Hydrocarbons Reservoirs in the Gulf of Mexico: A Blueprint for Progress or a Recipe for Conflict? *San Diego International Law Journal* 14 (Fall): 1–76.

Villareal, Angeles. 2012. *U.S.-Mexico Economic Relations: Trends, Issues, and Implications*. Report prepared for members and committees of Congress by the Congressional Research Service. August. Washington, DC.

White House. 2010. *Joint Statement from President Barack Obama and President Felipe Calderón*. May 19. Washington, DC: Office of the Press Secretary.

Wilson Center Mexico Institute. 2012. *A New Beginning for Mexican Oil: Principles and Recommendations for a Reform in Mexico's National Interest.* Report prepared under Chatham House rules, with contributions by Ernesto Marcos, David Shields, David Enríquez, Miriam Grunstein, Lourdes Melgar, Juan Eibenschutz, Javier Estrada, Marcelo Mereles, Enrique Hidalgo, Fluvio Ruiz, Carlos Berdeja, Juan Pardinas, Josefina Cortés, Tania Ortiz, Isidro Morales, Eduardo Andrade, John Padilla, and Duncan Wood. Ernesto Marcos, David Shields, David Enríquez, Miriam Grunstein, Lourdes Melgar, Juan Eibenschutz, Javier Estrada, Marcelo Mereles, Enrique Hidalgo, Fluvio Ruiz, Carlos Berdeja, Juan Pardinas, Josefina Cortés, Tania Ortiz, Isidro Morales, Eduardo Andrade, John Padilla, and Duncan Wood. Washington, DC: Instituto Tecnológico Autónomo de México and Woodrow Wilson Center for International Scholars.

Wood, Duncan. 2012. U.S.-Mexico Cross Border Energy Cooperation: A New Era in the Gulf of Mexico. Monthly *Report on PEMEX and U.S.–Mexico Cooperation* (March). Washington, DC: Woodrow Wilson International Center for Scholars.

Wood Mackenzie. 2014. Executive Summary: Secondary Legislation Sets the New Rules of the Energy Sector in Mexico. *Client Insight* (May 14).

Yergin, Daniel. 2012. *The Quest: Energy, Security, and the Remaking of the Modern World.* New York: Penguin Books.

Yergin, Daniel. 2008. *The Prize: The Epic Quest for Oil, Money, and Power.* New York: Free Press.

Transboundary Water Resources: Colorado River

Blatter, Joachim, Helen Ingram, and Suzanne Lorton Levesque. 2001. Expanding Perspectives on Transboundary Water. In *Reflections on Water: New Approaches to Transboundary Conflicts and Cooperation,* ed. Joachim Blatter and Helen Ingram. Cambridge, MA: MIT Press.

Border Governors Conference. 2009. *Strategic Guidelines for the Competitive and Sustainable Development of the U.S.–Mexico Transborder Region.* Monterrey, Mexico: Woodrow Wilson International Center for Scholars—Colegio de la Frontera Norte.

Bouno, Regina, and Gabriel Eckstein. 2014. Minute 319: A Cooperative Approach to Mexico-U.S. Hydro-Relations on the Colorado River. *Water International* 39:3 (January): 263–276.

Boxall, Bettina. 2010. Colorado River Water Deal Overturned. *Los Angeles Times,* January 15.

Brownell, Herbert, and Samuel Eaton. 1975. The Colorado River Salinity Problem with Mexico. *American Journal of International Law* 69:2 (April): 255–271.

Bustamante, Joaquin. 1999. *La Comisión Internacional de Límites y Agua entre México y los Estados Unidos.* Ciudad Juárez, Mexico: Universidad Autónoma de Ciudad Juárez.

Consortium of Environmental NGOs. 2006. *Conservation before Shortage II: Proposal for Colorado River Operations.* Defenders of Wildlife, Environmental Defense, National Wildlife Federation, Pacific Institute, Sierra Club, Nature Conservancy, Rivers Foundation of the Americas, and Sonoran Institute. July. Washington, DC: Submitted to the Honorable Dirk Kempthorne, Secretary, U.S. Department of Interior.

Cornyn, John (U.S. Senator) and Filemon Vela (U.S. Representative). 2014. *Letter to Commissioner Drusina. U.S. Congress.* Washington, DC. November 13.

Cortez-Lara, Alfonso A. 2014. *Transboundary Water Conflicts in the Lower Colorado River Basin: Mexicali and the Salinity and the All-American Lining Crises.* Tijuana, BC: El Colegio de la Frontera Norte.

De la Parra, Carlos A., and Carlos Heredia. 2015. Lessons from the Development of Binational and Civil Society Cooperation on Water Management at the U.S.-Mexico Border. In *The Anatomy of a Relationship: A Collection of Essays on the Evolution of U.S.-Mexico Cooperation on Border Management.* Washington, DC: Woodrow Wilson Center for International Scholars.

Dibble, Sandra. 2007. Calderón Stands Firm against Lining the Canal: Leader Voices Worry about Water Rights. *Union-Tribune San Diego* (May 5).

Donnelly, Robert. 2012. *Our Shared Border: Success Stories in U.S.-Mexico Collaboration.* Washington, DC: Border Research Partnership by the Woodrow Wilson International Center for Scholars—Arizona State University North American Center for Transborder Studies.

Doughman, Pamela. 2001. Discourses and Water in the U.S.-Mexico Border Region. In *Reflections on Water: New Approaches to Transboundary Conflicts and Cooperation,* ed. Joachim Blatter and Helen Ingram, 189–210. Cambridge, MA: MIT Press.

Enriquez-Coyro, Ernesto. 1976. *El Tratado entre México y los Estados Unidos de América sobre Ríos Internacionales.* Ciudad de México: Universidad Nacional Autónoma de México.

Festa, David, and John Entsminger. 2014. A Historic Course Change in the Colorado River. *Las Vegas Review Journal* (May 29).

Fischhendler, Itay, Eran Feitelson, and David Eaton. 2004. The Short-Term and Long-Term Ramifications of Linkages Involving Natural Resources: The U.S.-Mexico Transboundary Water Case. *Environment and Planning. C, Government & Policy* 22:633–650.

Flessa, Karl, Eloise Kendy, and Karen Schlatter. 2014. *Minute 319 Colorado River Delta Environmental Flows Monitoring.* Joint Report for International Boundary Water

Commission. December 4. U.S. and Mexico Sections, International Boundary Water Commission.

Fulp, Terry. 2014. In the Heat of the Drought: Sustaining Our Basin Supplies. *Colorado River Water Users Association Annual Meeting*, December 11. U.S. Department of Interior, Bureau of Reclamation.

Fulp, Terry. 2005. How Low Can It Go? *Southwest Hydrology* 4:2 (March/April): 16-18.

García-Acevedo, María Rosa. 2001. The Confluence of Water, Patterns of Settlement, and Constructions of the Border in the Imperial and Mexicali Valleys (1900–1999). In *Reflections on Water: New Approaches to Transboundary Conflicts and Cooperation*, ed. Joachim Blatter and Helen Ingram, 57–85. Cambridge, MA: MIT Press.

Gerlak, Andrea K. 2015. Resistance and Reform: Transboundary Water Governance in the Colorado River Delta. *Review of Policy Research* 32:1 (January): 100–123.

Gerlak, Andrea K. 2008. Today's Pragmatic Water Policy: Restoration, Collaboration, and Adaptive Management along U.S. Rivers. *Society & Natural Resources* 21:6 (July): 538–545.

Haefner, Andrea. 2016. *Negotiating for Water Resources: Bridging Transboundary River Basins*. NewYork: Routledge.

Hinojosa-Huerta, Osvel, and Yamilett Carrillo-Guerrero. 2004. Restoring the Colorado River Delta. *Southwest Hydrology* 3:1 (January/February): 20–21.

Hundley, Norris. 1966. *Dividing the Waters: A Century of Controversy between the United States and Mexico*. Berkeley: University of California Press.

Ingram, Helen, David Feldman, and John M. Whiteley. 2008. Water and Equity in a Changing Climate. In *Water, Place, and Equity*, ed. John M. Whiteley, Helen Ingram and Richard Perry, 271-308. Cambridge, MA: MIT Press.

Ingram, Helen, Nancy K. Laney, and David M. Gillilan. 1995. *Divided Waters: Bridging the U.S.-Mexico Border*. Tucson: University of Arizona Press.

International Boundary and Water Commission (IBWC). 2012. *Minute 319: Interim International Cooperative Measures in the Colorado River Basin through 2017*. November 20. Coronado, CA.

International Boundary and Water Commission (IBWC). 2010. *Minute 318: Adjustment of Delivery Schedules for Water Allotted to Mexico for the Years 2010 through 2013 as a Result of Infrastructure Damage in Irrigation District*. December 17. El Paso, TX.

International Boundary and Water Commission (IBWC). 2010. *Minute 317: Conceptual Framework for U.S.-Mexico Discussions on Colorado River Cooperative Actions*. June 17. Ciudad Juarez, Mexico.

Ketcham, Christopher. 2014. Razing Arizona: Will Drought Destroy the Southwest? *Harper's Magazine* (April): 53–63.

Keys, John. 2003. Water Dust-up: District Must Look at Waste. *Los Angeles Times,* July 27.

King, Jonathan S., Peter W. Culp, and Carlos de la Parra. 2015. Minute 319: Lessons for International Water Management. *University of Denver Water Law Review* 18:2.

Lauer, Susan. 2013. *Minute 319: Building on the Past to Provide for the Future.* Sacramento, CA (Winter): Colorado River Project–Water Education Foundation.

Lejano, Raul, Mrill Ingram, and Helen Ingram. 2013. *The Power of Narrative in Environmental Networks.* Cambridge, MA: MIT Press.

Levesque, Suzanne Lorton. 2001. The Yellowstone to Yukon Conservation Initiative: Reconstructing Boundaries, Biodiversity, and Beliefs. In *Reflections on Water: New Approaches to Transboundary Conflicts and Cooperation*, ed. Joachim Blatter and Helen Ingram, 123–160. Cambridge, MA: MIT Press.

Liverman, Diana, Robert Varady, Octavio Chávez, and Roberto Sánchez. 1999. Environmental Issues along the United States–Mexico Border: Drivers of Change and Responses of Citizens and Institutions. *Annual Review of Energy and the Environment* 24 (November): 607–643.

López, Mario. 2012. National Adaptation Planning and Practices on Water Resources from Mexican Perspective. *UNFCCC Technical Workshop on Water and Climate Change Impacts* (July): National Water Commission.

López, Mario. 2011. *Inicios, Evolución, Desarrollo y Situación Actual en la Zona Fronteriza. Cumbre Binacional de Saneamiento Fronterizo Y Calidad del Agua (San Antonio, TX). March 17*. National Water Commission.

Luege, José L. 2014. Acta 319. *El Universal,* Mexico City (March 31).

Moran, Greg. 2015. U.S.-Mexico Boost Collaboration on Colorado River. *San Diego Union Tribune.* March 12.

Mumme, Stephen. 2016. Enhancing the U.S.-Mexico Treaty Regime on Transboundary Rivers: Minutes 317–319 and the Elusive Environmental Minute. *Journal of Water and Law* 25:1 (January/February): 27–37.

Mumme, Stephen. 2009. The Liquid Frontier: Water and Sustainable Development on the U.S.-Mexico Border. *Journal of the West* 48 (4): 104–112.

Mumme, Stephen. 2008. From Equitable Utilization to Sustainable Development: Advancing Equity in U.S.-Mexico Border Water Management. In *Water, Place, and Equity*, ed. John M. Whiteley, Helen Ingram and Richard Perry, 117-146. Cambridge, MA: MIT Press.

Mumme, Stephen. 2000. Minute 242 and Beyond: Challenges and Opportunities for Managing Transboundary Groundwater on the Mexico–United States Border. *Natural Resources Journal* 40:2 (Spring): 341–378.

Mumme, Stephen, and Oscar Ibáñez. 2013. Power and Cooperation in Mexico–United States Water Management since NAFTA. In *Theorizing Borders through Analyses of Power Relationships*, ed. Peter Gilles, Harlan Koff, Carmen Maganda, and Christian Schulz, 151-175. Brussels: Peter Lang.

Mumme, Stephen, and Oscar Ibáñez. 2009. U.S.-Mexico Environmental Treaty Impediments to Tactical Security Infrastructure along the International Boundary. *Natural Resources Journal* 49:3/4 (Summer/Fall): 801–824.

Mumme, Stephen, and Donna Lybecker. 2005. The All-American Canal: Perspectives on the Possibilities of Reaching a Bilateral Agreement. In *The Lining of the All American Canal: Competition or Cooperation for the Waters at the U.S.-Mexican Border*, ed. Vicente Sánchez, 175-196. San Diego: San Diego State University Press.

Mumme, Stephen, Oscar Ibáñez, and Suzanne Till. 2012. Multilevel Governance of Water on the U.S.-Mexico Border. *Regions and Cohesion* 2:2 (Summer): 6–29.

National Research Council. 2007. *Colorado River Basin Water Management: Evaluating and Adjusting to Hydroclimatic Variability*. Washington, DC: National Academies Press.

Nava, Luzma, and Samuel Sandoval. 2014. Multi-Tiered Governance of the Rio Grande/Bravo Basin: The Fragmented Water Resources Management Model of the United States and Mexico. *International Journal of Water Governance* 2:85–106.

Nava, Luzma, et al. 2016. Existing Opportunities to Adapt the Rio Grande/Bravo Basin Water Resources Allocation Framework. *Journal Water* 8:291.

Perry, Tony. 2012. The All-American Canal May Deliver across the Border. *Los Angeles Times* (November 27).

Perry, Tony. 2010. A Fresh Battle between Southern California Water Adversaries. *Los Angeles Times* (October 18).

Perry, Tony. 2003. Imperial Farmers Should Get Less Water. *Los Angeles Times* (July 4).

Perry, Tony. 1999. Battle Lines Drawn over Water Rights. *Los Angeles Times*, January 13.

Ries, Nicole. 2008. The (Almost) All-American Canal: The Pursuit of Environmental Justice in Transboundary Resources Management. *Ecology Law Quarterly* 35 (3): 491–530.

Sánchez, Vicente, and Alfonso Cortes. 2015. Minute 319 of the International Boundary and Water Commission between the United States and Mexico: Colorado River Binational Water Management Implications. *International Journal of Water Resources Development* 31 (March): 17–27.

Samaniego, Marco. 2006. *Ríos Internacionales entre México y los Estados Unidos: Los Tratados de 1906 y 1944.* Ciudad de México, Mexico: Colegio de México.

Saravanan, V. S., Geoffrey T. McDonald, and Peter Mollinga. 2009. Critical Review of Integrated Water Resources Management: Moving beyond Polarized Discourse. *Natural Resources Forum* 33:1 (February) 76–86.

Secretaría de Medio Ambiente y Recursos Naturales. 2007. *Programa de Conservación y Manejo Reserva de la Biosfera Alto Golfo de California Y Delta del Río Colorado.* Mexico City, D.F.: Consejo Nacional de Áreas Protegidas.

Scott, Christopher, and Jeff M. Banister. 2008. The Dilemma of Water Management Regionalization in Mexico under Centralized Resource Allocation. *Water Resources Development* 24:61–74.

Silva, Peter. 2013. *Binational Cooperation with Mexico on Colorado River Issues. Presentation at the* Urban Water Institute/Metropolitan Water District of Southern California (August 15).

Sprouse, Terry. 2005. Water Issues on the Arizona-Mexico Border: The Santa Cruz, San Pedro, and Colorado Rivers. *Issue Paper Udall Center* (February): 1–33.

Stanger, William F. 2014. The Colorado River Delta and Minute 319: A Transboundary Water Law Analysis. *Environmental Law and Policy Journal* 37:1 (January 31): 77–104.

Szekely, Alberto. 1992. Establishing a Region for Ecological Cooperation in North America. *Natural Resources Journal* 32 (Summer): 563–622.

Tarlock, Dan. 2014. Mexico and the United States Assume a Legal Duty to Provide Colorado River Delta Restoration Flows: An Important International and Water Law Precedent. *Review of European, Comparative, and International Environmental Law* 23:1 (April): 76–87.

United States Senate. 1944. *Treaty between the United States of America and Mexico: Utilization of Waters of the Colorado and Tijuana Rivers, and of the Rio Grande.* Washington, DC: Treaty Series 994.

U.S. Congressional Research Service. 2015. *U.S.-Mexico Water Sharing: Background and Recent Developments.* Report prepared by Nicole R. Carter, Clare R. Seelke, and Daniel T. Shedd for members and committees of Congress. January. Washington, DC.

U.S. Department of Interior. 2007. *Record of Decision: Colorado River Interim Guidelines for Lower Basin Shortages and the Coordinated Operations for Lake Powell and Lake Mead.* December. Washington, DC: The Honorable Dirk Kempthorne, Secretary, U.S. Department of Interior.

U.S. Department of Interior. 2007. *U.S. and Mexico Agree to Discuss Joint Cooperative Actions Related to the Colorado River.* Press release (August 13). Washington, DC.

U.S. Department of Interior. 2001. *Record of Decision: Colorado River Interim Surplus Guidelines, Final Environmental Impact Assessment.* December. Washington, DC: The Honorable Bruce E. Babbitt, Secretary, U.S. Department of Interior.

U.S. Department of Interior and Mexican Embassy in Washington, DC. 2009. *Joint Declaration on Colorado River Issues.* January 13. Washington, DC.

Utton, Albert. 1991. The Transfer of Water from an International Border Region: A Tale of Six Cities and the All-American Canal. *North Carolina Journal of International Law and Commercial Regulation* 16:1 (Fall): 477–495.

Utton, Albert. 1988. Problems and Successes of International Water Agreements: The Example of the United States and Mexico. In *International Environmental Diplomacy*, ed. John E. Carroll, 67–84. Cambridge: Cambridge University Press.

Utton, Albert. 1982. An Assessment of the Management of U.S.-Mexican Water Resources: Anticipating the Year 2000. *Natural Resources Journal* 22:4 (October): 1093–1118.

Vano, Julie A., Bradley Udall, Daniel R. Cayan, Jonathan T. Overpeck, Levi D. Brekke, Tapash Das, Holly C. Hartmann, Hugo G. Hidalgo, Martin Hoerling, Gregory J. McCabe, Kiyomi Morino, Robert S. Webb, Kevin Werner, and Dennis P. Lettenmaier. 2014. Understanding Uncertainties in Future Colorado River Streamflow. *Bulletin of the American Meteorological Society* 95:59–78.

Ward, Evan. 2003. *Border Oasis: Water and the Political Ecology of the Colorado River Delta 1940–1975.* Tucson: University of Arizona Press.

Weismann, Marta. 2013. Texas Legislators Hint at Possible Funding Cuts for Minute 319. *Journal of Water* (December 10).

Wescoat, James L, and Gilbert F. White. 2003. *Water for Life: Water Management and Environmental Policy.* Cambridge: Cambridge University Press.

Wilder, Margaret. 2008. Equity and Water in Mexico's Changing Institutional Landscape. In *Water, Place, and Equity*, ed. John M. Whiteley, Helen Ingram and Richard Perry, 95–113. Cambridge, MA: MIT Press.

Wilder, Margaret, and Helen Ingram. 2016. Knowing Equity When We See It: Water Equity in Contemporary Global Contexts. In *Oxford Handbook of Water Politics and Policy*, ed. Ken Conca and Erika Weinthal. Oxford: Oxford University Press.

Zamora-Arroyo, Francisco, Jennifer Pitt, Steve Cornelius, Edward Glenn, Osvel Hinojosa-Huerta, Marcia Moreno, Jaqueline García, Pamela Nagler, Meredith de la Garza, and Iván Parra. 2005. *Conservation Priorities in the Colorado River Delta, Mexico and the United States*. Workshop report prepared by the Sonoran Institute, Environmental Defense, University of Arizona, Pronatura Noroeste Dirección de Conservación Sonora, Centro de Investigación en Alimentación y Desarrollo, and World Wildlife Fund—Gulf of California Program. Available online at www.sonoran.org.

Acknowledgments

The reason we are here

This book would not be in your hands without the vision from the wonderful team at MIT Press. Beth Clevenger, whose brilliance, drive, and creativity are off the charts, singlehandedly made this opportunity happen. Susan McClung, Emily Gutheinz, Mary Reilly, Jay McNair, Sheila Bodell, and Anthony Zanino generously shared their talent and expertise. Marcy Ross is the kindest, most interesting, and caring colleague I could dream of having. Thank you, from the bottom of my heart, for this unforgettable opportunity!

With joy, in deep gratitude, to my mentors

Some years back, I got a phone call from Professor Larry Susskind. It was a blazing hot summer afternoon, and as I paced the lawn of my MIT dorm, I listened intently to each and every word he said. Larry was calling to say that he believed that we could pursue a dream I had shared with him, no matter how much it seemed that the odds were stacked against it. You could not find a steadier and more caring voice. His message was that no challenge was insurmountable and that we would turn every stone to find a way to accomplish what at first sight might seem impossible. I could barely contain my joy. It would not be the last time I experienced, through his support, that dreams come true, a hundred times more meaningfully than I could have envisioned. That is the experience with Professor Susskind; that is what he does, tirelessly. He brings light and inspiration to every person who crosses his path. Larry, you have been committed to mentoring, protecting, and expanding a professional path, in which I can continuously discover, practice, and grow by exploring the subjects I am passionate about. You always see 10 steps ahead and multiple permutations in the flash of an eye. I am moved by the boldness and courage with which you have guided me from one step to the next, with kindness and hope. There is not a more imaginative and noble coach I could dream of working with. I am profoundly happy to continue to learn so much more from you every day.

I met Dean Melissa Nobles in 2010, after I had recently arrived at MIT as a graduate student. Dean Nobles' seminar on political thought was held on the upper floor of a building overlooking the Charles River. I can close my eyes and still see in wonder, that stunning sunset over the Boston skyline, so new to me then and equally unforgettable today. Melissa's class was deeply inspiring because the ideas she asked us to consider, and the reasons why it was important to contemplate them, were absolutely compelling. There was an unbreakable moral backbone to the structure of the lessons she was guiding us to discover, and a great sense of responsibility about what we could do with them if we worked hard to understand their implications about how people structure power and the many ways they can choose to wield it. Those teachings have stayed with me ever since. I am forever thankful to you, Professor Nobles, because throughout my professional journey, you have believed in me with a great sense of joy and against all odds. Your guidance and support have had the most profound impact on my life. Words can't fully describe it. I am so thankful to count on your mentorship moving forward.

Many autumns ago, it was the beginning of the term at the Harvard Kennedy School. I forgot the syllabus at home, which had the building and the room number, so by the time I finally figured out where Professor Steve Jarding's class was, I was 10 minutes late. I peeked through the door's window: the auditorium was packed. I could not see Professor Jarding, I could only hear his voice. Its power could not be mistaken. I did not want to interrupt, so I took a chair from a nearby office, and sat outside the auditorium for over 60 minutes next to an entrance door. The sound that came through the walls was an impassioned speech about what politics can and should be, about what campaigns hinge on, about what leaders should stand for. It embodied that connection between heart and soul that gives you goose bumps. The kind of experience you get when you know you are in the presence of a force of nature. I was hooked right from the start. And I made sure to get to that packed auditorium way ahead of time from the next class onward! I am so thankful, Professor Jarding, for how inspiring you have been from that very first class and for your wisdom at every step. To be able to continue to learn from you in the years to come is a blessing.

In recognition to the negotiators

I am deeply thankful to the negotiators for their candid and straightforward conversations, for their enlightening anecdotes, and for their commitment to knock on every door, send the e-mails, make the calls, and convince their colleagues to also share their stories. Many of you went out of your way to explore key insights and were extremely generous with your time and expertise. By sharing your hard work, vision, and commitment to the communities you serve, you have set in motion a stream of opportunities that have brought immense happiness to my life. You are the reason why this research has been possible. Thank you so much!

With admiration

Leonardo Beltrán, there is an unflappable sense of generosity, boldness, and courage to your vision for Mexico, the path to which it should aim, and the capacities the country needs to continue to build and develop. My professional track is forever anchored by your strong, steady, and inspiring talent and support. You have absolutely changed my life with your mentorship. I thank you with all my soul. In the same vein, I deeply cherish the guidance and grace that you have brought to my life, dear Leydi Barceló. Carlos Ortiz, your vision, creativity, commitment, and insights have been a critical component in this path. You have been amazing proposing, coordinating, and providing the inputs to move the vision forward. We built this research path together, all four of us, and I am humbled by your trust and unwavering mentorship.

In profound appreciation

MIT's School of Architecture and Planning and its Department of Urban Studies and Planning foster a tremendously creative and interdisciplinary environment, full of souls with generous hearts and a deep passion to make our world a better place. I am forever thankful to Professor Eran Ben-Joseph and to Dean Hashim Sarkis, for resolutely believing in my work and creating the opportunities for negotiation teaching, research, and practice to spread from our department and thrive across the entire MIT community.

Elena Alschuler, thank you so much for that wonderful conversation, where you said I should look into attending 11.601 and 11.255. Those numbers represent two tremendously significant, fun, and meaningful MIT classes taught by Professor Susskind, in which I was fortunate to learn from and collaborate with Carri Hulet, Danya Rumore, Todd Schenk, Ellen Czaika, Parrish Berquist, and Tijs Van Maasakkers, among many others. The way each of you shared your expertise and generous words of wisdom will always remain a sweet memory and an absolute joy in this journey. The same goes for the caring thoughts and inspiring conversations along the way with Layla Shaikley, Leah Stokes, Yasmin Zaerpoor, Kelly Heber-Dunning, Andrea Beck, Ali Kazerani, Shiree Rafaeli, and Jessica Gordon, among many others.

To navigate the corridors of MIT, I've had the pleasure of counting on Sandy Wellford, Karen Yegian, Janine Marchese, Ellen Rushman, Sossi Arroyan, and Duncan Kincaid, who have been always brilliant and gracious. I thank you for your guidance and support, as it has made a big difference every step of the way. I am also deeply inspired by the generous and transformative friendship of Takeo Kuwabara. I am forever thankful to Dwayne Daughtry, Aurora Brule, and Sylvia Hiestand, for your outstanding commitment, creativity, and trust. You made this happen!

There are so many faculty and experts whose gestures of kindness have meant so much to me. Among so many, I am grateful to Shafik Islam, James Wescoat, William Moomaw, Michael Wheeler, James Sebenius, Sheila Heen, John Richardson, Bob Mnookin, Jared Curhan, Bob Bordone, Brian Mandell, Joel Schindall, David Niño, and Leo McGonagle, for sharing your wisdom with hope, humor, and generosity.

Viva!

I am extremely thankful to a wide array of experts and leaders at CONACYT, SENER, PEMEX, and BANOBRAS, who are responsible for believing in my research and making it come true. To each and every single one of you, I owe the opportunity to continue to learn and work hard every day. I cherish this responsibility deeply. Thank you for your resolute and critical support Néstor Díaz, Enrique Puchet, Rosa María Turriza, Jesús Antonio Zavala, Pablo Rojo, Rafael Ramos, Samuel Manterola, Genaro Vilchis, Jaime Jiménez, Soledad Ramos, Alejandro Castillo, Daniel Sosa, José Ramón Montiel, and Olinka García, as well as many, many others!

As faculty and practitioners, there are a number of inspiring mentors who paved the way for me to have this opportunity too. I embrace with deep gratitude all that you have generously taught me from day one. Aldo Flores Quiroga, Antonio Ortiz Mena, Lorena Ruano, Allyson Benton, and Jorge Schiavon, you have opened so many doors with your strong advice, memorable generosity, and luminous wisdom. Your friendship and advice always stays with me.

With a big smile, to my beautiful family

My sister, who is an angel, and quite unique in her uncanny ability to bring strength and hope to my life, used to say when we were much younger, that one day I would find myself doing research in this part of the world. I believe, as happens with many beautiful dreams, that they come true to a great extent because these dreams also beat in the hearts of the people who love us. Through their hard work and prayers, they put in a good word for us up above. So, I begin with you, my dear sister, because the road of my life is always paved with your devotion, talent, and tenderness.

And as I think of every step in which you have been there to support me, I see our very luminous mom, whose strength and love has protected a path for my soul to find happiness. Mom, your warm embrace has been there for me at every crossroads in my life. Your sensibility and the language that your heart speaks, ever since you brought me to life, is a beacon of sweet light.

My dear father, as we all know at home, is a very passionate man with an incredibly keen eye for what moves me. Dad, I admire how, through your words of wisdom and ceaseless hard work, you have shaped a family where laughter blossoms and where a simple life, a life of freedom to pursue what burns in our hearts and to serve the people around us, is what is valued.

You three are a beautiful reflection of my grandparents, Fernand, Madeleine, Celes, and Viví, who have lived lives with absolute devotion to goodness, from fighting in World War II to saving hundreds of lives in the operating room, and who have nurtured and protected my path with their wisdom and love.

Encore

This book would not be possible without Alexandria Miskho and Kathleen Schwind, the best peers and friends one could ever dream to have. With unparalleled brilliance, courage, and kindness, you bring tremendous light, hope, and joy to the personal and professional life of everyone around you. The very same applies to the amazing MIT students who, through their immense creativity, unstoppable drive, and superlative talent, render the Art and Science of Negotiation the highlight of my every week. I learn so much from each of you and admire your generosity, vision, and commitment to shape our societies into fairer and happier places. You know how much you mean to me. I am forever thankful!

Index